SUPPLEMENT

TO THE

CATALOGUE

OF THE

LIBRARY

OF THE

U. S. MILITARY ACADEMY,

WEST POINT, N. Y.

CONTAINING THE ADDITIONS FROM THE FIRST OF JANUARY, 1853, TO THE FIRST OF OCTOBER, 1859.

PREPARED UNDER THE DIRECTION OF

COLONEL DELAFIELD,

SUPERINTENDENT OF THE MILITARY ACADEMY,

BY

LIEUT. O. O. HOWARD LIBRARIAN,
ANDRÉ FREIS, ASSISTANT LIBRARIAN.

New York:
PRINTED BY G. W. WOOD, No. 2 DUTCH STREET.
1860.

SUPPLEMENT

TO THE

CATALOGUE

OF THE

LIBRARY

OF THE

U. S. MILITARY ACADEMY,

WEST POINT, N. Y.

CONTAINING THE ADDITIONS FROM THE FIRST OF JANUARY, 1853, TO THE FIRST OF OCTOBER, 1859.

PREPARED, UNDER THE DIRECTION OF

COLONEL DELAFIELD,

SUPERINTENDENT OF THE MILITARY ACADEMY,

BY

LIEUT. O. O. HOWARD, Librarian,

ANDRÉ FREIS, Assistant Librarian.

New York:

PRINTED BY G. W. WOOD, No. 2 DUTCH STREET.

1860.

CLASSIFIED TABLE OF CONTENTS,

(ACCORDING TO SUBJECTS, WITH REFERENCE TO PAGE.)

1. Military Engineering, Fortifications, Attack, Defence, and Mines . . . 5
2. Artillery and Pyrotechny 11
3. Strategy, Grand Tactics, and Military Miscellanies . . . 19
4. Cavalry Tactics 23
5. Infantry and Infantry Tactics 26
6. Fencing and the use of the Sword 28
7. Equitation and Veterinary Art, &c. 29
8. Military Administration and Organization 32
9. Military Laws, Regulations, and Orders 34
10. General Military and Naval History 37
11. Battles, Sieges, and Campaigns 39
12. Military Biography and Memoirs 42
13. Military Antiquities 43
14. Military and Naval Periodicals 44
15. Military and Naval Dictionaries 44
16. Army and Navy Registers 45
17. Civil and Naval Architecture and Landscape Gardening . . . 46
18. Machinery, Instruments, Applied Mechanics, and Carpentry . . . 49
19. Hydraulic Constructions, Canals, Bridges, &c. 52
20. Civil Engineering 54
21. Works on Materials 57
22. Works on Warming and Ventilating 57
23. Law of Nature and Nations, Treaties, &c. 58
24. Government and Politics 58
25. Political Economy, Metrology, Finance, Commerce, &c. . . 61
26. Laws, Law Treatises, Commentaries, and Reports 61
27. Mathematics in General 63
28. Arithmetic 64
29. Algebra 64
30. Geometry 65
31. Perspective and Descriptive Geometry 65
32. Trigonometry 66
33. Analytical Geometry 67
34. Method of Fluxions, Differential and Integral Calculus . . . 67
35. Mensuration, Surveying, and Practical Geometry 68

36. Logarithms and Mathematical Tables 69
37. Mechanics, including Statics, Dynamics, Hydrostatics, and Hydrodynamics 70
38. Natural and Experimental Philosophy in General 71
39. Optics 72
40. Navigation 73
41. Astronomy 73
42. Astronomical Observations 75
43. Astronomical Tables 75
44. General Works on Arts and Sciences 76
45. Chemistry 78
46. Electricity, Magnetism, Galvanism, and Meteorology 80
47. Natural History 82
48. Botany and Agriculture 84
49. Mineralogy 85
50. Geology 86
51. Medical and Surgical Works 88
52. Geography, Topography, and Statistics 90
53. Geography—Loose Sheets of Maps 93
54. Voyages and Travels 96
55. Universal History and Chronology 99
56. Ancient History, Antiquities, and Mythology 99
57. Modern History of Continental Europe 101
58. English, Scotch, and Irish History 102
59. French History and Civil Memoirs 104
60. Asiatic and African History 104
61. American History 105
62. Biographical, Historical, and Classical Dictionaries 107
63. Biography and Personal Memoirs 108
64. Literary History 111
65. Metaphysical Philosophy 112
66. Logic and Intellectual Philosophy 113
67. Moral Philosophy 114
68. Poetry and Fictions 115
69. Grammar and Philology 118
70. Rhetoric and Criticism 120
71. Addresses 120
72. Journals and Treatises upon Education 122
73. Works on Painting, Sculpture, Music, and Illustrated Works of Engravings 124
74. Gymnastics and Swimming 125
75. Literary and Political Periodicals, Reports and Registers . . 126
76. Bibliography 128
77. Dictionaries and Encyclopædias 129
78. Theology and Ecclesiastical History 131
79. Miscellanies 136
Alphabetical Index, referring to the Authors or Titles, etc. . . 139

CATALOGUE.

Subj. 1. MILITARY ENGINEERING.

FORTIFICATION, ATTACK, DEFENCE, AND MINES.

6258 **Ahrenberg** (le prince Ernest d'). See Ernest Nos. 52 & 6280.

6259 **Andréossy** (Comte). Opérations des Pontonniers Français en Italie, pendant les compagnes de 1795 à 1797, et reconnaissance des Fleuves et Rivières de ce Pays, (avec Planches). 1 vol. 8vo. Paris, 1843.

6260 **Audé** (Lieut.-Col.). Nouvelles expériences sur la poussée des terres, mémoire revu par M. le général Poncelet, avec des additions par M. Domergue, capitaine du génie et une notice sur l'auteur. 1 vol. 8vo. Paris, 1849.

6261 **Barnard** (Major J. G.). The Dangers and Defences of New York. 1 8vo. Pamphlet, (2 *copies.*) New York, 1859.

6262 **Bélidor.** La Science des Ingénièurs dans la conduite des Travaux de Fortification et d'Architecture civile. 1 vol. 4to. Paris, 1739.

6263 **Bélidor.** The same. 2 vols. 4to. Paris, 1729.

6264 **Bellavéne** (le Général). Cours Elémentaire de Fortification, ou Elémens de l'art de construire, attaquer et défendre les retranchemens et les places, à l'usage des Éléves de l'École Spéciale Impériale Militaire. 1 vol. 8vo. Paris, 1806.

6265 **Biddulph** (M. A. S. Capt. & Bvt. Maj.). A series of Topographical sketches of the Ground before Sevastopol, accompanied by explanatory descriptions. 1 vol. fol. London, 1855.

6266 **Birago's** Military Bridges. 15 sheets in folio.

6267 **Birago** (le Chev. de). Nouveau Système de Ponts de chevalets. See Maurice de Sellon, No. 6312.

6268 **Blesson** (Louis). Esquisse Historique de l'art de la Fortification Permanente. Traduite de l'allemand par Ed. de la Barre Duparcq capitaine du Génie. 1 vol. 8vo. Paris, 1849.

6269 **Born.** Notice Historique sur les Ponts Militaires depuis les temps les plus reculés jusqu' à nos jours. 1 vol. 8vo. Paris, 1838.

6270 **Boutault.** Cours de Mines, fait à MM. les officiers. (Lithog.) 1840. 1 vol. folio.

6271 **Carnot.** De la Défense des Places Fortes. See vol. V. No. 7495.

6272 **Cavalli** (J.). Mémoire sur les Équipages de Ponts Militaires avec dix Planches. 1 vol. 8vo. Paris, 1843.

6273 **Chasseloup de Laubat.** System of Fortification, as executed at Alessandria, See Macaulay, No. 6305.

6274 **Cours** de Fortification permanente. Projet de Fortification permanente en terrain Varié. Programmes et Modèles, (Lithog.) Avril, 1854. 1 vol. 4to.

6275 **Documents** relatifs à l'emploi de l'Électricité, pour mettre le feu aux Fourneaux des Mines et à la démolition des Navires sous l'eau. Avec Planche. 1 vol. 8vo. Paris, 1841.

6276 **Douglas** (Sir Howard). An Essay on the Principles and Construction of Military Bridges and the Passage of Rivers in Military Operations. 3d edition, containing much additional matter. 1 vol. 8vo. London, 1853.

6277 **Dziobek** (Ernst). Taschenbuch für den Preussischen Ingenieur. 2te Verbesserte auflage. | A Hand-book for the Prussian Engineers. 2d edition, revised. 1 vol. 16mo. Coblenz, 1853.

6278 **Ecole de Sapes.** See No. 108.

6279 **Erlam** (J. S.). Outlines of Military Fortification: with a Plan of the Citadel of Antwerp and the Forts, and a notice of the Siege by the French in 1832. 1 vol. 12mo. London, 1855.

6280 **Ernest d'Arenberg** (le Prince). L'Art de la Fortification appliqué à la Défense des grandes et moyennes Places de Guerre, par lequel on donne les moyens d'augmenter considérablement la force de résistance et de diminuer les frais de construction des Forteresses. 2e edition augmentée de plusieurs nouveaux systèmes et suivi d'un Appendice avec vingt trois Planches. 1 vol. 4to. Venise, 1848.

6281 **Expérience de Bapaume.** Rapport fait à M. le Ministre de la Guerre par la commission mixte d'officiers d'artillerie et du Gènie, instituée la 12 juin, 1847, pour étudier, sur les fortifications de Bapaume les principes de l'exécution des bréches par la Canon et par la mine. Avec 28 Planches. 1 vol. 8vo. (2 *copies.*) Paris, 1852.

6282 **Fergusson** (James). An Essay on a proposed new system of Fortification: with hints for its application to our National Defences. 1 vol. roy. 8vo. London, 1849.

6283 **Fesca** (F. A.). Handbuch der Befestigungskunst für die jüngeren officiere der Infanterie und Cavallerie und die Officier-Aspiranten beider Waffen. Zweiter Theil: permanente Befestigung und Angriff und Vertheidigung der Festungen. | Hand-Book of Fortification for the younger officers of Infantry and Cavalry and the "Officer Aspirants" of both Arms. Second Part: Permanent Fortification and the attack and defence of Fortresses. 1 vol. 8vo. Berlin, 1853.

6284 **Fielding** (Newton). Lessons on Fortification: Part first: with Plates. 1 vol. 8vo. London, 1853.

6285 **Forrest** (R.). Illustrated Handbook of Military Engineering and of the Implements of War. 1 vol. 8vo. London, 1856.

6286 **Fortification.** General principles of. See No. 6345.

6287 **Garcia** (Don José Herrera). Théorie analytique de la Fortification permanente; traduit d'Espagnol par Ed. de la Barre Duparcq.
1 vol. 8vo. & Atlas. Paris, 1847.

6288 **General** Instructions for the Teaching and Work of Sapper and Pioneer Battalions.
Part 1st. Garrison and Field duty. (2 copies of Part 1st.)
Part 2d. One volume of text and an Atlas of Plates.
(In the Russian Language.)
2 vols. 8vo. & Atlas in 4to. St. Petersburg, 1824.

6289 **Goulier** (Prof.). Cours de Topographie. Instruction Spéciale sur le Lever de Fortification à la Planchette, approuvée par décision du Conseil d'Instruction, du 13 Juin, 1848. 1 vol. 4to. Metz, 1848.

6290 **Goulier** (Prof.). Instruction pratique sur le 1er Lever de Reconnaissance Militaire. Approuvée par décision du Conseil d'Instruction le 1er Juin, 1847, Réimprimée en Juillet, 1851. (Lithog.) 1 vol. 4to.

6291 **Grivel** (M. Richild). La Marine dans l'Attaque des Fortifications et le Bombardement des Villes du Littoral. Sébastopol. Bomarsund. Odessa. Sweaborg. Kinburn. 1 vol. 8vo. Paris, 1856.

6292 **Grivel** (M. Richild). Attaques et Bombardements Maritimes avant et pendant la Guerre d'Orient. Sébastopol. Bomarsund. Odessa. Sweaborg. Kinburn. 2me édition. 1 vol. 8vo. Paris, 1857.

6293 **Hand-Book** for Engineers and Sappers. (In the Russian Language.)
1 vol. 12mo. St. Petersburg, 1848.

6294 **Hand-Book.** Handbuch des Ingenieur-Dienstes. Erster Theil. Permanente Befestigung. Mit 23 Steindrucktafeln.	Hand-Book of Engineer Service. First Part. Permanent Fortification. With 23 Lithographed Plates.

1 vol. 8vo. & Atlas fol. (2 *copies.*) Berlin, 1854.

6295 **Hand-Book** for Field Service. See Hand-Book, No. 6489.

6296 **Hauser** (Georg Freyherrn V.). Abhandlung über die Befestigungskunst. Zum Gebrauche der k. k. Ingenieurs-Academie. (Erster Theil.)	Treatise on the Art of constructing Military Works. For the use of the Imperial Academy of Engineers. (First Part.)

1 vol. 4to. & Atlas 4to. Vienna, 1826.

6297 **Hoburg** (K.). Geschichte der Festungswerke Danzigs.	History of the Fortifications of Dantzic.

1 vol. 8vo. & Atlas in folio. Danzig, 1852.

6298 **Instruction** sur le mode d'exécution des Dessins de Fortification. See Instruction, No. 6842.

6299 **Jourjon** (C. L.). Cours d'art Militaire. 4me Partie. Fortification passagère, (Lithog.), Juillet, 1853. 1 vol. 4to. —— ——.

6300 **Kimber** (Thomas). Field Works, as executed at Sandhurst and Addiscombe; with observations on their construction and uses.
1 vol. 8vo. London, 1858.

6301 **Landmann** (Isaac). The Principles of Fortification, reduced into questions and answers for the use of the Royal Military Academy at Woolwich. 6th edition corrected and revised by George Landmann.
1 vol. 8vo. London, 1831.

6302 **Lebas** (Lucien). Aide-Mémoire portatif d'art Militaire et de Fortification. 2e edition revue et augmentée, entre beaucoup d'autres choses, d'une Théorie pratique sur les Levèes et le Nivellement.
1 vol. 18mo. Paris, 1843.

6303 **Lectures** on Fortification. Outlines of a course of Lectures on Fortification, Military Tactics, and Perspective; with the Attack and Defence of Fortresses. 2d edition. 1 vol. 8vo. London, 1848.

6304 **Macaulay** (J. S.). Treatise on Field Fortification, and other subjects connected with the Duties of the Field Engineer. Illustrated with 12 Plates. 3d edition. 1 vol. 12mo. & Atlas. London, 1850.

6305 **Macaulay** (J. S.). Description of Chasseloup de Laubat's System of Fortification, as executed at Alessandria.
1 vol. 12mo. & Atlas. London, 1851.

6306 **Maurice de Sellon** (le baron). Études sur la Fortification permanente. (I.) Plan et Description de la Citadelle Fédéral de Rastadt. Avec un Atlas de 3 Planches.
1 8vo. Pamphlet & Atlas fol. (2 *copies.*) Paris, 1850.

6307 **Maurice de Sellon** (le baron). Études de Fortification permanente. (II.) Examen du Tracé. Enseigné aux troupes du génie qui font partie du huitième corps d'armée de la Confédération Germanique et appréciation de sa Capacité de résistance. Avec un Atlas de 2 Planches.
1 8vo. Pamphlet & Atlas fol. Paris, 1850.

6308 **Maurice** (le Baron). Fortification Permanente. Études sur les Places de Mayence et d'Ulm, accompagnées de Plans exacts et détaillés.
1 vol. 8vo. & Atlas fol. Paris, 1852.

6309 **Maurice de Sellon** (P. E.). Mémoires sur la Fortification Tenaillée et Polygonale et sur la Fortification Bastionnée, contenant une analyse critique de l'Histoire de la Fortification permanente, par A. de Zastrow.
1 vol. 8vo. & Atlas fol. (2 *copies*). Paris, 1850.

6310 **Maurice** (le Baron P. E.). De la Défense Nationale en Angleterre. (Avec une Carte.) 1 vol. 8vo. Paris, 1851.

6311 **Maurice de Sellon** (P. E.). Mémorial de l'Ingénieur Militaire, ou Analyse abrégée des Tracés de Fortification permanente des principaux Ingénieurs, depuis Vauban jusqu' à nos jours. Ouvrage accompagné d'un Atlas de 17 Planches gravées sur cuivre.
1 vol. 8vo. & Atlas fol. Paris, 1849.

6312 **Maurice de Sellon** (le Baron P. E.). Examen du Nouveau Systéme de Ponts de Chevalets, proposé par le Chevalier de Birago. Suivi de l'exposé d'un nouveau Systéme de Ponts Militaires à supports flottants.
1 8vo. Pamphlet. Paris, 1847.

6313 **Memorial de Ingenieros.** Memorias, articulos y noticias interesantes al arte de la Guerra en general y a la Profesion del Ingeniero en Particular, 1846–56. 11 vols. 8vo. Madrid, 1846–56.

6314 **Mémorial** de l'officier du génie ou Recueil de mémoires, expériences, observations et procédes généraux, propres à perfectionner la fortification et les constructions militaires; rédigé par les soins du comité de fortifications.
Nos. 1 à 15 (Première Série.) 15 vols. 8vo. Paris, 1821–48.
No. 16 (Deuxiéme Série.) 1 vol. 8vo. Paris, 1854.

6315 **Mentz.** Festung Mainz. | Fortress of Mentz.
In case. No date.

6316 **Mines.** Abhandlung über die Kriegs-Minen. Zum gebrauche der k. k. Osterr. Mineur-Schulen. 3 Theile, mit einem Atlas. | Treatise on Military Mines. For the use of the Imperial Austrian Schools of Miners. 3 Parts, with an Atlas.
1 vol. 4to. & Atlas fol. obl. Vienna, 1852.

6317 **Murray** (John). On the Stability of retaining Walls. See Murray, No. 6938.

6318 **Neuchéze** (Ernest de). Traité théorique et pratique de Fortification Passagère et de la défense des Postes de Guerre, avec un Résumé des Petites Opérations de la guerre. 1 vol. 8vo. Paris, 1850.

6319 **Niel** (le Général). Siége de Sebastopol. Journal des opérations du Génie. 1 vol. 4to. & Atlas fol. Paris, 1858.

6320 **Noizet.** Cours de Fortification permanente. Leçons sur de dessin de la Fortification. (Lithog.). Réimprimées en Avril, 1850. 1 vol. 4to.

6321 **Noizet** (le Général). Principes de Fortification.
2 vols. 8vo. Paris, 1859.

6322 **Notice** Historique sur les Ponts Militaires. See Born, No. 6269.

6323 **Parmentier** (Théodore). Exposition et Description d'un Systéme de Fortification Polygonale et à Caponnières. Par un officier du génie prussien, traduit de l'allemand par Théodore Parmentier. See Schwinck, No. 6329.

6324 **Programmes** pour l'Enseignement de la Fortification permanente, de l'attaque et de la Défense des Places. (Lithog.) Juin, 1841.
1 vol. 4to. Metz.

6325 **Programme** du Journal d'attaque. (Lithog.). Janvier, 1852.
1 vol. 4to.

6326 **Programmes** du Cours de Fortification permanente d'attaque et de Défense des Places. (Lithog.). September, 1854. 1 vol. 4to.

6327 **Programme** du Simulacre de Siége. (Lithog.) Octobre, 1854.
1 vol. 4to.

6328 **Rabusson** (A.). De la défense général du Royaume dans ses rapports avec les moyens de défense de Paris. 1 vol. 8vo. Paris, 1843.

6329 **Schwinck** (G.). Exposition et Description d'un Systéme de Fortification Polygonale et à Caponniéres. Essai sur la science de la Fortification, arrivée à son état actuel de perfectionnement, traduit de l'allemand par Théodore Parmentier. Avec 2 Planches.
1 vol. 8vo. & Atlas fol. Paris, 1850.

6330 **Sevastopol.** 13 Photographs of the Forts of Sevastopol. In folio.

6331 **Specification** for the erection of a Fort at Cliff's End, near Yarmouth, in the Parish of Freshwater, in the Isle of Wight, County of Hants.
1 folio pamphlet. Portsea, 1854.

6332 **Straight** (Hector). Treatise on Fortification and Artillery. 6th edition.
2 vols. 8vo. & Atlas folio. London, 1852.

6333 **Teliakoffsky** (A.). Manuel de Fortification permanente. Traduit du Russe par A. Goureau.
1 vol. 8vo. & Atlas fol. obl. (2 *copies.*) Saint-Pétersbourg, 1849.

6334 **Teliakoffsky** (A.). Elementary Treatise on Field Fortification. Part I. For the use of the Military Schools. (In the Russian language.)
1 vol. roy. 8vo. St. Petersburg, 1852.

6335 **Teliakoffsky** (A.). Elementary Treatise on Fortification. Part II. Permanent Fortification. (In the Russian language.)
1 vol. 8vo. & Atlas 4to. obl. St. Petersburg, 1846.

6336 **Thierry** (Capitaine). Extrait d'un mémoire sur le chevalet belge, adressé en Janvier, 1849, à Monsieur le Lt. Général Baron Chazal, Ministre de la Guerre. (Lithog.) 1 vol. folio. —— ——.

6337 **Verdu** (Don Gregorio). Nouvelles Mines de Guerre appliquées à la Défense, suivant un nouveau procédé pour mettre le feu aux fourneaux de poudre à l'aide de l'électricité. Traduit de l'Espagnol. 1 vol. 8vo. Paris, 1855.

6338 **Wasserthal** (Konstantin). Technischer Pionier-Dienst im Felde. 2te verbesserte und vermehrte auflage. | Pioneer Service in the Field. 2d edition, revised and enlarged.
1 vol. 8vo. Vienna, 1852.

6339 **Wurmb** (Julius von). Lehrbuch der Kriegs-Baukunst, zum gebrauche der kais. kon. Génie-Academie. | An Elementary Treatise on Military Architecture, for the use of the Imperial Engineer Academy.
1 vol. 8vo. & Atlas folio. Olmütz, 1852.

6340 **Zaccone** (J.). Résumé de Fortification, à l'usage des officiers d'Infanterie.
1 vol. 8vo. & Atlas 4to. Paris, 1849.

6341 **Zastrow** (A. de). Histoire de la Fortification permanente, ou Manuel des meilleurs systèmes et manières de Fortification. 3me édition traduite de l'Allemand. Par Ed. de la Barre Duparcq.
2 vols. 8vo. & Atlas folio, (2 *copies*). Paris, 1856.

Subj. 2. ARTILLERY AND PYROTECHNY.

6342 **Aide-Mémoire,** à l'usage des officiers d'Artillerie de France, attachés au Service de Terre. 3me édition, revue et augmentée.
2 vols. 12mo. Paris, 1801.

6343 **Aide-Mémoire** à l'usage des officiers d'Artillerie. 3me édition.
1 vol. 8vo. Paris, 1856.

6344 **Allin** (E. S.). Rules for the Management and Cleaning of the Rifle Musket, Model 1855. For the use of Soldiers. With Descriptive Plates drawn by A. D. Allin. 1 vol. 12mo. (4 *copies.*) Philadelphia, 1858.

6345 **Arms.** On the Arms in use. General principles of Fortification.
1 vol. 4to. —— ——.

6346 **Artillerie** Nouvelle (1850) ou considérations sur les progrés récents faits dans l'art de Lancer les Projectiles. Par M**** Capitaine d'Artillerie.
1 8vo. Pamphlet. Paris, 1850.

6347 **Artillery** drill. Evolutions of the line for Foot Batteries. (In the Russian language.) 1 vol. 24mo. St. Petersburg, 1846.

6348 **Artillery.** Notes on Artillery. On the Construction of Gun Carriages. Part 1st with Plates. (In the Russian language.) "Plates Wanting."
1 vol. 12mo. St. Petersburg, 1844.

6349 **Artillery** Signals. See Collection No. 6537.

6350 **Bonaparte** (Louis-Napoléon). Études sur le Passé et l'Avenir de l'Artillerie. 2 vols. 4to. Paris, 1846–51.

6351 **Bonaparte** (Louis-Napoléon). Nouveau Systéme d'Artillerie de Campagne. Résultats des Expériences faites en 1850. Énoncé et examen de toutes les objections. Par le Capitaine Favé. Publié avec l'autorisation du Ministre de la guerre. 1 vol. 8vo. Paris, 1851.

6352 **Bormann** (Major-General). The Shrapnel Shell in England and in Belgium with some reflections on the use of this Projectile in the late Crimean War. A Historico-Technical Sketch.
1 vol. 8vo. Brussels, 1859.

6353 **Boxer** (Capt. E. M.). Treatise on Artillery, prepared for the use of the practical class, Royal Military Academy, in the course of Instruction prescribed by the Regulations of the Master General of the 10th August, 1848. Sect. I. Part I. 1 vol. 8vo. London, 1853.

6354 **Boxer** (Capt. E. M.). Chapter on Congreve Rockets. Forming part of part 2. Sec. 1, of Treatise on Artillery.

6355 **Boxer** (Capt. E. M.). Diagrams to illustrate the Service and Management of Heavy Ordnance, referred to in Treatise on Artillery, prepared for the use of the Royal Military Academy. Section II. Part I. (*Plates.*)
1 vol. fol. London, 1853.

6356 **Boxer** (Capt. E. M.). Diagrams of Guns referred to in Treatise on Artillery, prepared for the use of the Royal Military Academy. Section II. Part II. (*Plates.*) 1 vol. fol. London, 1853.

6357 **Brettes** (Martin de). Des Artifices Éclairants en usage à la guerre et de la Lumiére Électrique. (Avec Planches.). 1 vol. 8vo. Paris, 1851.

6358 **Brettes** (Martin de.) Études sur les appareils Électro-Magnétiques destinés aux Expériences de l'Artillerie en Angleterre, en Russie, en France, en Prusse, en Belgique, en Suede, &c. 1 vol. 8vo. Paris, 1854.

6359 **Bunsen** (R.) & **Schischkoff** (L.). Théorie chimique de la Combustion de la Poudre. Traduit par M. A. Terquem. Avec une Planche. 1 8vo. Pamphlet. Paris, 1859.

6360 **Burn** (Lieut. Col.). Questions and answers on Artillery. 2d edition, revised and enlarged, specially for the use of the Militia Artillery. 1 vol. 12mo. Woolwich, 1854.

6361 **Busch** (W.) & **Hoffmann** (C.). Die Kriegsfeuerwerkerei der Königlich Preuszischen Artillerie. | Military Pyrotechny of the Royal Prussian Artillery. 1 vol. 8vo. Berlin, 1854.

6362 **Cavalli** (J.). Mémoire sur divers perfectionnements Militaires, comprenant: quelques essais sur les Canons se chargeant par la Culasse et sur les Canons Rayés pour l'Artillerie de Place, de Siége, de Campagne et de la Marine; quelques Propositions sur les moyens d'accroitre la mobilité de l'Artillerie, &c., &c. Mémoire lu dans la séance de l'Académie des sciences de Turin, du 25 Mars, 1855. Traduit de l'Italien. 1 vol. 8vo. Paris, 1856.

6363 **Charpentier** (F. E. A.). Essai sur le Matériel de l'Artillerie de nos Navires de guerre. 1 vol. 8vo. Paris, 1845.

6364 **Cibrario** (Chev. Louis). Lettre; sur l'Artillerie du XIIIe au XVIIIe siècle (Turin, 1847.) Traduite de l'Italien et annotée par Terquem. 1 8vo. pamphlet. Paris, 1847.

6365 **Corréard** (J.). Recueil des bouches á feu. See Recueil No. 6424.

6366 **Cours** d'Artillerie. See Virlet No. 6459.

6367 **Dahlgren** (J. A.). Shells and Shell-Guns. 1 vol. 8vo. Philadelphia, 1856.

6368 **Dahlgren** (J. A.). Boat Armament of the U. S. Navy. Designed by and executed under the direction of J. A. Dahlgren. 2d edition. 1 vol. 8vo. Philadelphia, 1856.

6369 **Deanes'** Manual of the History and Science of Fire-Arms. 1 vol. 8vo. London, 1858.

6370 **Decker** (E.). Traité de l'art de combattre de l'Artillerie à cheval, réunie à la Cavalerie. Traduit de l'allemand avec des notes relatives à l'armée Française, par Ravichio de Peretsdorf. 1 vol. 8vo. Paris, 1831.

6371 **Delobel** (L.). Revue de Technologie Militaire, ou Recueil de Mémoires, Expériences, observations et Procédés relatifs à cette science, choisis dans les meilleurs écrits Périodiques et non Périodiques, qui se publient en langues étrangères, ou empruntés à des documents officiels de dates régentes et provenant de tout autre pays que la France et la Belgique; traduits, analysés et annotés par L. Delobel. In 8vo. Liége, 1854. vols. 1, 2.

6372 **De Massas.** See Massas No. 6408.

6373 **Didion** (Capitaine). Résumé des Tables de Construction des Bouches à feu et des Projectiles. (Lithog.) Février, 1841. 1 folio Pamphlet.

6374 **Didion** (Is.). Calcul des Probabilités appliqué au tir des Projectiles. 1 vol. 8vo. Paris, 1858.

6375 **Douglas** (Gen. Sir Howard). Treatise on Naval Gunnery, 4th edition. 1 vol. 8vo. London, 1855.

6376 **Dusaert** (Édouard). Essai sur les Obusiers. 1 vol. 8vo. Paris, 1842.

6377 **Examen** du Système d'artillerie de Campagne de M. le Lieutenant Général Allix. (Janvier, 1826.) 1 8vo. Pamphlet. Paris, 1841.

6378 **Exercices** des Bouches à feu en usage dans la Marine. 2d édition. 1 vol. 18mo. Paris, 1850.

6379 **Expériences** d'Artillerie exécutées à Gavre, par ordre du Ministre de la Marine pendant les années 1830, 1831, 1832, 1834, 1835, 1836, 1837, 1838, et 1840. 1 vol. 4to. Paris, 1841.

6380 **Favé** (Capitaine). Des nouvelles Carabines et de leur emploi. Notice historique sur les progrés effectués, en France, depuis quelques années dans l'accroissement des portées et dans la justesse de tir des armes à feu portatives. 1 8vo. Pamphlet. Paris, 1847.

6381 **Favé** (Capitaine). Nouveau Systéme d'Artillerie de Campagne. See Bonaparte, No. 6351.

6382 **Fevre** (E., Capitaine d'Artillerie). Programme et Sommaire des Leçons du Cours de tir et de mécanisme des armes à feu portatives professé à l'École Normale de Tir de Vincenne. Année 1856. (Lithog.) 1 fol. Pamphlet. Vincenne, 1856.

6383 **Field** Battery Exercise and Movements, for the Royal Regiment of Artillery. See No. 351.

6384 **Fitz Clarence** (Frederick). On the three Arms. 1 sheet, folio. — 1853.

6385 **Gräfe** (Carl). Das Reitzeug und die Geschirre der Batterieen und Kolonnen der Preussichen Artillerie. | The Riding Equipage and Harness of Batteries and Columns of the Prussian Artilery. 1 vol. 18mo. Berlin, 1855.

6386 **Greener** (William). Gunnery in 1858: being a Treatise on Rifles, Cannon, and Sporting Arms; explaining the Principles of the Science of Gunnery, and describing the newest improvements in Fire-Arms. With numerous illustrations. 1 vol. 8vo. London, 1858.

6387 **Guzman** (Sebastian). Lecciones de Artilleria, traducidas y estractadas de varios para el estudio de los Alumnos del Colegio Militar de la Republica Mexicana. 2 vols. 8vo. Mexico, 1846.

6388 **Hand Book** for Field Service. See Hand Book, No. 6489.

6389 **Heth** (Capt. Henry). System of Target Practice. For the use of Troops when armed with the Musket, Rifle Musket, Rifle, or Carbine. Prepared principally from the French, "Instruction provisoire sur le Tir, à l'usage des bataillons de Chasseurs à Pied." See Nos. 354 and 355. 1 vol. 8vo. Philadelphia, 1858.

6390 **Hoffmann** (W.). Die Waffenlehre. Ein Leitfaden zur Vorbereitung für das Offizier Examen. | A Treatise on Weapons. Being a Guide to preparation for the Officer's Examination. 1 vol. 8vo. Berlin, 1855.

6391 **Instruction** of Musketry. (Adjutant-General's Office, Horse Guards, 1st January, 1856.) 1 vol. 8vo. London, 1858.

6392 **Instruction** for Foot Artillery, Schools of the Piece, Division, (half Battery,) and Battery. (In the Russian Language). 1 vol. 8vo. St. Petersburg, 1840.

6393 **Instruction** sur le Tir, à l'usage des Troupes d'Artillerie approuvé par le Ministre de la guerre le 13 février 1848. 1 vol. 32mo. Strasbourg, 1854.

6394 **Instruction** provisoire sur le tir. See Heth, No. 6389.

6395 **Jacobi** (G. A.). État actuel de l'Artillerie de Campagne en Europe. Artillerie autrichienne. 2 livraisons réunies en un seul volume (avec 9 Planches). 1 vol. 8vo. Paris, 1854.

6396 **Jeffers** (William N.). Concise Treatise on the Theory and Practice of Naval Gunnery. 1 vol. 8vo. New York, 1850.

6397 **Jervis** (Capt. Jervis-White). Our Engines of War and how we got to make them. 1 vol. 8vo. London, 1859.

6398 **Kameke** (H. F.). Die Einrichtung und der Gebrauch des Perkussions-Gewehrs. Nebst einem Anhange über das Exerzieren, den Wachtdienst, &c. | The arrangement and use of Percussion-Arms. With an Appendix concerning the Drill, Guard duty, &c. 1 8vo. Pamphlet. Berlin 1848.

6399 **Kameke** (H. F.). Die Einrichtung der materiellen Gegenstände der Preussischen Artillerie. In sieben Hefte. | The Prussian System of Artillery. In seven Parts. 1 vol. 8vo. & Atlas 4to. obl. Berlin, 1843.

6400 **Kameke** (H. F.). Die Preussische Feld-Artillerie, nach der Construction vom Jahre 1842. | Prussian Field-Artillery, from the year 1842. 1 vol. 8vo. & Atlas 4to. obl. Berlin, 1847.

6401 **Kamptz** (W. de). Influence des Progrés du Fusil d'Infanterie sur la Construction des Batteries de Siége. Traduite de l'allemand à l'École d'application de l'Artillerie et du Génie par Henry Benoit. 1 8vo. Pamphlet. Paris, 1853.

6402 **Lafay** (J.). Aide-Mémoire d'Artillerie Navale. 1 vol. 8vo. Paris, 1850.

6403 **Liege.** Forerie de Liège—Plan. 1 sheet.
Forerie de Liège—Élévation vue en coupe. 2 sheets.
Outils de Forage d'après l'ancien et le nouveau système en usage à la Fonderie de Canons à Liège. 1 sheet.
Relevé de quelques bouches à feu en fonte coulées à Liège qui ont été soumises à des tirs ordinaires de polygone, &c. 1 sheet.

6404 **Mallet** (Robert). On the Physical Conditions involved in the Construction of Artillery: with an investigation of the relative and absolute Values of the Materials principally employed, and of some hitherto unexplained causes of the Destruction of cannon in service. 1 vol. 4to. London, 1856.

6405 **Mangeot** (H.). Des Armes Rayées. Aperçu pratique et théorique de ces armes au point de vue de la guerre, l'art d'en régler le tir, la portée, &c., suivi d'une Notice sur le Revolver Mangeot-Comblain considéré comme arme défensive. 1 vol. 16mo. Paris, 1857.

6406 **Marion.** Journal des Opérations de l'Artillerie au Siège de Schweidnitz en 1807. 1 8vo. Pamphlet. Paris, 1842.

6407 **Marion** (le Général). Recueil des Bouches à feu. See Recueil, No. 6424.

6408 **Massas** (de). Mémoire sur les cuivres, Etains et Bronzes employés pour la fabrication des Bouches à feu. 1 vol. 8vo. Paris, 1850.

6409 **Mémorial** de l'Artillerie, ou recueil de Mémoires, expériences, observations et procédés relatifs au service de l'Artillerie, rédigé par les soins du comité. Nos. 1 à 7. 7 vols. 8vo. Paris, 1826–52.

6410 **Musketry.** Instruction of, See Instruction, No. 6391.

6411 **Navez.** Application de l'Électricité à la mesure de la vitesse des Projectiles. Avec deux Planches. 1 vol. 8vo. Paris, 1853.

6412 **Navez.** Expériences de Balistique exécutées en Russie dans le courant de l'année, 1858. 1 8vo. Pamphlet. Paris, 1859.

6413 **Observations** sur l'ouvrage de M. le Capitaine Thiéry, ayant pour titre Applications du fer aux constructions de l'artillerie. 1 8vo. Pamphlet. Paris, 1835.

6414 **Organisation** (de l'). De l'Artillerie en France, par M. M.***** 2 vols. 8vo. Paris, 1845.

6415 **Page** (C. E.). Théorie du Pointage, à l'usage des sous-officiers d'Artillerie, publiée avec autorisation du Comité de l'artillerie. 1 vol. 12mo. Strasbourg, 1848.

6416 **Panot** (L.). Cours sur les Armes à feu portatives. 4me édition revue et considérablement augmentée. 1 vol. 8vo. Paris, 1851.

6417 **Piobert** (G.) Mémoires sur les Poudres de Guerre de différents procédés de fabrication; avec résumés des épreuves comparatives faites sur ces Poudres à Esquerdes en 1831 et 1832, et à Metz en 1836 et 1837. 1 vol. 8vo. Paris, 1844.

6418 **Piobert** (G.). Traité d'Artillerie théorique et pratique. Partie théorique et expérimentale. Propriétés et effets de la Poudre. 2e édition, revue et augmentée. 1 vol. 8vo. Paris, 1859.

6419 **Programme** du Cours de sciences Physiques et chimiques appliquées aux arts militaires et Instruction sur la Rédaction des Procés verbaux d'analyses chimiques. (Lithog.) Decembre, 1848. 1 vol. 4to.

6420 **Programme** du cours de sciences appliquées aux arts Militaires. (Lithog.) Septembre, 1854. 1 vol. 4to.

6421 **Programme** du Cours d'Artillerie. (Lithog.) Septembre, 1854. 1 vol. 4to.

6422 **Projet** d'instruction sur le Tir des Carabines d'Infanterie avec les balles à culot. Par un officier de l'École Normale de tir de Vincennes. 1 vol. 24mo. Paris, 1850.

6423 **Rapports** pour l'Établissement des Principes du Tir. Premier et second Rapports, 1834. (Commission formée par ordre du Ministre de la Guerre, en date du 29 Mai 1833.) (Lithog.) Juillet 1835. 1 vol. folio.

6424 **Recueil** des Bouches à feu le plus remarquables depuis l'origine de la Poudre à Canon jusqu' à ce jour commencé par le Général d'artillerie Marion et continué sur les documents fournis par MM. les officiers des armées Françaises et Étrangéres, par J. Corréard. (En 3 parties.) 1 vol. 4to. & Atlas fol. Paris, 1853.

6425 **Réglement** sur les Exercices et les Évolutions de l'artillerie Belge. 1 vol. 18mo. Bruxelles, 1853.

6426 **Reports** of Experiments with small Arms for the Military Service, by officers of the Ordnance Department U. S. Army. (Published by authority of the Secretary of War. 1 vol. 8vo. (4 *copies.*) Washington, 1856.

6427 **Restorff** (C. Von). Die Theorie des Schieszens mit besonderer Beziehung auf die gezogenen Handfeuerwaffen. Mit 2 Figurentafeln und 1 Tabelle. | The Theory of Firing with particular reference to Rifled Small Arms. With 2 Plates and 1 Table. 1 vol. 8vo. Berlin, 1855.

6428 **Resvoy** (Col.). Notes on Artillery. Part I. Technical Part. Part. II. Additional Notes on Art of Artillery. (In the Russian Language). 2 vols. 8vo. & Atlas fol. obl. St. Petersburg, 1849–53.

6429 **Richardot** (Ch.). De l'Organisation des principales parties du service de l'Artillerie. 1 8vo. Pamphlet. Paris, 1842.

6430 **Rifle Musket.** A companion to the New Rifle Musket: comprising practical Information on the cleaning and management of Arms, and on the making of Cartridges. Illustrated by tinted Plates. 1 vol. 12mo. London, 1855.

6431 **Rifled Ordnance.** A Practical Treatise on the application of the principle of the Rifle to Guns and Mortars of every calibre. 2d edition, revised and corrected, with Addenda. 1 vol. 8vo. London, 1857.

6432 **Roche** (A.). Traité de Balistique appliquée à l'artillerie Navale. Première partie. Notions préliminaires et applications. 1st part in 8vo. Paris, 1841.

6433 **Rüstow** (Cæsar). Die Kriegshandfeuerwaffen. Eine genaue Darstellung ihrer Einrichtung in den europäischen Armeen, ihrer Anfertigung, ihres Gebrauchs und ihrer allmäligen Entwicklung. | Small Arms. A Plain Treatise on the organization, manufactures, and use of Small Arms in the European Armies. 1 vol. 8vo. Berlin, 1857.

6434 **Saint-Robert** (Paul de). Des effets de la Rotation de la Terre sur le mouvement des Projectiles, avec planche. 1 8vo. Pamphlet. Paris, 1858.

6435 **Sar** (P. C.). Cours d'Études Militaires, ou Matériaux pouvant contribuer à la netteté et à l'étendue des connaissances Militaires de ceux qui n'ont vu que les élémens des sciences Mathématiques. 1 vol. 8vo. Brest, 1836.

6436 **Schimmel** (F.). Die percussionirten Schusz-Waffen der preussischen Kavallerie. | Percussion Arms of the Prussian Cavalry. 1 18mo. Pamphlet. Düsseldorf, 1851.

6437 **Schön** (Julius). Das gezogene Infanterie-Gewehr, Kurze darstellung der Neuzeit und ihrer Anwendung in den Armeen Europa's. | The Infantry Rifle Musket. A short explanation of the system and use of Arms of modern times by the European Armies. 1 vol. 8vo. Dresden, 1854

6438 **Schön** (J.) Geschichte der Handfeuerwaffen. Eine darstellung des Entwickelungsganges der Handfeuerwaffen von ihrem entstehen bis auf die Neuzeit. | History of Small Arms. An explanation of the various modes of manufacturing them from their origin to the present time. 1 vol. 4to. Dresden, 1858.

6439 **Scoffern** (J.). Projectile Weapons of War and explosive Compounds. 3rd edition, revised. 1 vol. 8vo. London, 1858.

6440 **Simmons** (Capt. T. F.). Ideas as to the effect of Heavy Ordnance directed against and applied by Ships of War particularly with reference to the use of Hollow Shot and loaded Shells. 1 vol. 8vo. London, 1837.

6441 **Simons** (Capt. F. C.). The leading Principles of Gunnery, those parts of it relating to rotatory motion, in particular the Minié, Jacobian, and other practical facts examined. 1 vol. 8vo. Calcutta, 1858.

6442 **Small-Arms.** Reports of Experiments with. See Reports, No. 6426.

6443 **Smola** (Carl & Joseph Freiherren von) Taschenbuch für Österreichische Artillerie-Officiere. In zwei Theile. A Hand-Book for the use of Austrian Artillery Officers. In two Parts. 1 vol. 18mo. Vienna, 1831.

6444 **Spearman** (Capt. J. Morton). The British Gunner. 4th edition, revised and enlarged. 1 vol. 18mo. London, 1850.

6445 **Steinle** (Uepomuck). Die Spitzgeschosse und ihr Einflusz auf das Kriegswesen, mit besonderer Beziehung auf Schweizer-Waffen. Conical Balls and their influence upon Warfare, with particular reference to the Swiss Arms. 1 vol. 8vo. Landau, 1858.

6446 **Streffleur** (V.). Die Dienst-Vorschriften Sämmtlicher Waffengattungen, &c., der Östreichischen Armee. 9te abtheilung. The Regulations and Orders relating to Arms, &c., of the Austrian Army. 9th division. 1 vol. 8vo. Vienna, 1846.

6447 **Streubel** (Woldemar). Die 12pfündige Granatkanone und ihr Verhältnisz zur Taktik der Neuzeit. Artilleristisch-taktische untersuchung. The 12 pdr. Howitzer and its effect upon Tactics of the present time. Experiment on Artillery-Tactics. 1 vol. 8vo. Kaiserslautern & Leipzig, 1857.

6448 **Taubert** (Capt.). On the use of Field Artillery on service: with especial reference to that of an Army-corps. For officers of all Arms. Translated from the German by Henry Hamilton Maxwell. 1 vol. 18mo. London, 1856.

6449 **Thackeray** (Thomas James). The Soldier's Manual of Rifle Firing at various distances. 2d edition, carefully revised, and considerably enlarged. 1 vol. 16mo. London, 1858.

6450 **Thiroux.** Réflexions et études sur les Bouches à feu de Siège, de Place et de Côte, (avec planches.) 1 vol. 8vo. Paris, 1849.

6451 **Thiroux.** Essai sur les Projectiles allongés. 1 vol. 8vo. Paris, 1857.

6452 **Thiroux.** Essai sur le mouvement des Projectiles dans les milieux résistants. Deuxième Cahier. Partie pratique. 1 vol. 8vo. Paris, 1857.

6453 **Thiroux.** Mémoire sur le Tir à Mitraille. 1 8vo. Pamphlet. Paris, 1859.

6454 **Timmerhans** (C.). Expériences faites à Liége en 1839 sur les Carabines à double rayure, et celles à Canons lisses. 1 vol. 8vo. Paris, 1840.

6355 **Treadwell** (Daniel). On the practicability of constructing cannon of great caliber, capable of enduring long continued use under full charges. (From the Memoirs of the American Academy.) 1 8vo. Pamphlet. Cambridge, 1856.

6456 **Vessell** (General). Artillery. 1st Part. (In the Russian language.) 1 vol. 8vo. St. Petersburg, 1851.

6457 **Vignau** (A. du). Ueber die Veränderungen welche dem Artillerie-Wesen durch das verbesserte Infanterie-Gewehr auferlegt werden. | On the modifications which will be made necessary in Artillery by the improvements in Infantry Arms. 1 vol. 8vo. Schweidnitz, 1855.

6458 **Virlet** (Capitaine). Extrait des Tables de Construction des Bouches à feu et des Projectiles de l'artillerie de terre et de l'artillerie de Marine. (Lithog.) Mars, 1849. 1 vol. 4to.

6459 **Virlet** (Capitaine). Cours d'Artillerie. Instruction Sommaire sur le Projet de Bouche à feu. (Lithog.) Fevrier, 1850. 1 vol. 4to. Metz, 1850.

Subj. 3. STRATEGY, GRAND TACTICS, AND MILITARY MISCELLANIES.

6460 **Aksenovime** (Lieut.). Skirmish Drill. Published with the Imperial consent. (In the Russian language.) 1 vol. 24mo. St. Petersburg, 1848.

6461 **Algarotti** (Count). Letters Military and Political. Translated from the Italian. 1 vol. 8vo. London, 1782.

6462 **Barre Duparcq** (Éd. de la). Considérations sur l'art Militaire Antique et sur l'utilité de son étude. 1 vol. 8vo. Paris, 1849.

6463 **Barre Duparcq** (Éd. de la). Commentaires sur le Traité de la Guerre de Clausewitz. 1 vol. 8vo. Paris, 1853.

6464 **Barre Duparcq** (Éd de la). Éléments d'art et d'histoire Militaires, comprenant le Précis des Institutions Militaires de la France, l'histoire et la Tactique des armes isolées, la combinaison des armes et les Petites opérations de la guerre. 1 vol. 8vo. Paris, 1858.

6465 **Baumann** (Bernhard von). Der Sicherheitsdienst im Marsche.—Bearbeitet und durch kriegsgeschichtliche Beispiele erläutert. | Precautions for security on the March. Prepared and Illustrated by examples from Military History. 1 vol. 12mo. Dresden, 1857.

6466 **Buschbeck** (F.). Preussisches Feld-Taschenbuch, für offiziere aller Waffen zum Kriegs und Friedens Gebrauch. | Hand-Book of Prussian Field Service, for the use of officers of all arms in time of War and Peace. 1 vol. 18mo. Berlin, 1853.

6467 **Cessac** (Comte de). Des connaisances nécessaires à un Général en chef d'armée. See vol. V., No. 7495.

6468 **Cessac-Lacuée** (Comte de). Guide de l'officier particulier en campagne. Nouvelle édition, revue et augmentée, avec l'agrément de l'auteur, par M. Mellinet. 2 vols. 8vo. Paris, 1805.

6469 **Clausewitz** (le Gén. Charles de). De la Guerre. Publication Posthume. Traduite de l'allemand, par le Major d'artillerie Neuens. 3 vols. 8vo. Paris, 1849–51.

6470 **Clausewitz** (le Gén. Charles de). Commentaires sur le Traité de la guerre de Clausewitz. See Barre Duparcq, No. 6463.

6471 **Decker** (Colonel). Rasssemblement, campement et grandes manœuvres des troupes Russes et Prussiennes réunies à Kalisch pendant l'été de 1835, (avec plans), suivi de deux notes supplémentaires sur le camp de Krasnoïe Selo et l'autre sur la nouvelle organisation de l'armée Russe. Traduit de l'allemand par M. C. A. Haillot. 1 vol. 8vo. Paris, 1836.

6472 **Douglas** (General Sir Howard). On Naval Warfare with Steam. 1 vol. 8vo. London, 1858.

6473 **Dress** of General, Staff and Regimental Officers of the Army. Regulations for the 1st April, 1846. 1 vol. 8vo. London, 1846.

6474 **Dwyer** (F.). Feld-Taschenbuch für offiziere. | Hand-Book of Field Service for Officers. 1 vol. 18mo. Vienna, 1853.

6475 **Ecole** Impériale Polytechnique, 1re Division. Portefeuille des Éléves, dessins croquis et tableaux relatifs au cours d'art Militaire. 2e édition, 1er Tirage, 1853–54. 1 vol. folio. —— ——.

6476 **Essai** Général de Tactique, précédé d'un discours sur l'état actuel de la Politique et de la science Militaire en Europe ; avec le Plan d'un ouvrage intitulé la France Politique et Militaire. 2 vols. 8vo. Liège, 1775.

6477 **Etudes** sur l'art de la guerre, par un officier Général Russe. 1 vol. 24mo. Paris, 1852.

6478 **Etudes** Politiques et Militaire. Revue du Monde Militaire actuel. 1 vol. 8vo. Paris, 1848.

6479 **Fantaisies** Militaires. See Préjugés, No. 6507.

6480 **Feuquiere.** Extraits de. See vol. IV., No. 7495.

6481 **Folard.** Extraits de. See vol. IV., No. 7495.

6482 **Fonscolombe** (Ph. de). Résumé historique des progrés de l'art Militaire depuis les temps les plus anciens jusqu' à nos jours, avec des applications aux différents cas de la guerre tirées des faits d'armes et des campagnes les plus célébres, servant de base à un cours pratique de Tactique, avec 14 planches explicatives. 1 vol. 8vo. Paris, 1854.

6483 **Frédéric II.,** Roi de Prusse. Instruction Militaire pour ses Généraux. See Instruction, Nos. 6491, 6492.

6484 **General** Instructions for the Teaching and Work of Sapper and Pioneer Battalions. In two parts. (2 copies of part 1st). (In the Russian language.) 2 vols. 8vo. & Atlas 4to. St. Petersburg, 1824.

6485 **Giustiniani** (Henri de). Commentaires sur les opérations Militaires en Crimée, (extrait du Spectateur Militaire.) 1 vol. 8vo. Paris, 1857.

6486 **Gleig** (Capt.). The Crimean Enterprise, what should have been done and what might be done. Predictions and Plans. 1 vol. 18mo. Edinburgh & London, 1855.

6487 **Graham** (Lieut.-Col. J. J.). Elementary History of the Progress of the Art of War. 1 vol. 8vo. London, 1858.

6488 **Guibert.** De l'état actuel de la Politique et de la Science Militaire en Europe. See vol. V., No. 7495.

6489 **Hand-Book** for Field Service ; or, Field Pocket-Book. 2d edition revised, and Edited by Captain C. W. Younghusband, F. R. S. Royal Artillery. 1 vol. 18mo. Woolwich, 1857.

6490 **Hoyt** (E.). Practical Instructions for Military officers : comprehending a concise system of Military Geometry, Field Fortification and Tactics of Riflemen and Light Infantry, &c., &c. To which is annexed a new Military Dictionary. Illustrated with Plates. 1 vol. 8vo. Greenfield, 1811.

6491 **Instruction** Militaire du Roi de Prusse, pour ses Généraux. See vol .V., No. 7495.

6492 **Instruction** Secrette, dérobée à Frédéric II., Roi de Prusse, contenant les orders secrets expédiés aux officiers de son armée, particuliérement à ceux de la Cavalerie, pour se conduire dans la guerre. Traduit de l'original allemand, par le Prince de Ligne. Nouvelle édition. 1 vol. 18mo. Strasbourg, 1791.

6493 **Jervis** (Lieut. Jervis White). Manual of Field Operations adapted for the use of Officers of the Army. 1 vol. 12mo. London, 1852.

6494 **Joly de Maizeroi.** Théorie de la Guerre. 1 vol. 8vo. Paris, 1777.

6495 **Jomini** (le Baron de). Précis de l'art de la guerre. See vol. V., No. 7495.

6496 **Jomini** (Baron de). Summary of the Art of War, or a new analytical compend of the Principal Combinations of Strategy, of Grand Tactics, and of Military Policy. Translated from the French by Major O. F. Winship and Lieut. E. E. McLean. 1 vol. 8vo. New York, 1854.

6497 **Koch** (Fréd.). Ternay's Traité de Tactique. See Ternay, No. 6515.

6498 **Lacuée** (Comte de Cessac.) See Cessac, Nos. 500, 6467, 6468.

6499 **Lebas** (Lucien). Aide-Mémoire portatif d'art Militaire et de Fortification, 2e édition, revue et augmentée, entre beaucoup d'autres choses, d'une Théorie pratique sur les levées et le Nivellement. 1 vol. 18mo. Paris, 1843.

6500 **Le Vasseur.** Commentaires de Napoléon suivis d'un résumé des Principes de Stratégie du Prince Charles. 2 vols. 8vo. Paris, 1851–52.

6501 **Lloyd** (Général). Mémoires Militaires et Politiques servant d'introduction à l'histoire de la guerre en Allemangne, en 1756, entre le Roi de Prusse et l'Impératrice Reine et ses Alliés. See vol. V., No. 7495.

6502 **Lord de Ros** (Colonel). The Young Officer's Companion; or, Essays on Military Duties and Qualities; with examples and illustrations from history. A new edition. Edited with numerous corrections and additions. 1 vol. 18mo. London, 1851.

6503 **Macdougall** (Lieut.-Col. P. L.). The Theory of War. Illustrated by numerous examples from Military History. 2d edition. 1 vol. 16mo. London, 1856.

6504 **Montecuculli.** Extraits de. See vol. IV., No. 7495.

6505 **Moorsom** (Capt. W.). The Organization and Manœuvres of Steam Fleets. 2d edition. 1 4to. Pamphlet. Portsea, 1856.

6506 **Napoléon.** Commentaires de. See Le Vasseur, No. 6500.

6507 **Préjugés** et Fantaisies Militaires. Par un officier Autrichien. See No. 561. 2 vols. 12mo. Kralovelhota, 1780.

6508 **Programmes** du cours d'art Militaire et de Fortification passagère. (Lithog.) Septembre, 1854. 1 vol. 4to. —— ——.

6509 **Puységur.** Extraits de. See vol. IV., No. 7495.

6510 **Rüstow** (W.). Allgemeine Taktik nach dem gegenwärtigen standpunkt der Kriegskunst bearbeitet. Mit erläuternden Beispielen. | General Tactics, according to the present state of the Art of War. Illustrated with examples. 1 vol. 12mo. Zürich, 1858.

6511 **Rüstow** (W.). Die Feldherrnkunst des neunzehnten Jahrhunderts. Zum selbstudium und für den unterricht an höhern Militärschulen. | Generalship of the 19th Century. For Self-Instruction and for use in higher Military Schools.
1 vol. 8vo. Zürich, 1857.

6512 **Saxe** (Maréchal de). Extraits du. See vol. IV., No. 7495.

6513 **Schimmel** (Friedrich). Compendium des kleinen Krieges für Infanterie und Cavallerie offiziere. 2te auflage. | Manual of Petite-guerre for the use of Infantry and Cavalry officers. 2d edition.
1 vol. 16mo. Düsseldorf, 1854.

6514 **Streffleur** (V.). Die Dienst-Vorschriftender Östreichisc hen Armee, für alle Kommanden, &c., sechste abtheilung. | The Regulations and Orders for the Austrian Army, for all commands, &c., sixth division.
1 vol. 8vo. Vienna, 1844.

6515 **Ternay** (Marquis de). Traité de Tactique, revu, corrigé, augmenté, par Fréd. Koch. (Avec un atlas.) 2 vols. 8vo. & Atlas fol. Paris, 1832.

6516 **Tevis** (Lieut.-Col.). Du Service des Avant-Postes et des petites opérations de la guerre. 1 vol. 8vo. Paris, 1858.

6517 **Végece.** Traité de l'art Militaire, traduction nouvelle par Victor Develay.
1 vol. 8vo. Paris, 1859.

6518 **Végece.** Institutions Militaires. See vol. III., No. 7495.

6519 **Ward** (James H.). Manual of Naval Tactics; together with a brief critical analysis of the Principal Modern Naval Battles. With an appendix, being an extract from Sir Howard Douglas' Naval Warfare with Steam.
1 vol. 8vo. New York, 1859.

6520 **Wellington.** The Wisdom of. Or Maxims of the Iron Duke.
1 vol. 18mo. London, 1852.

6521 **Wittich.** Zur Taktik des leichten Percussions-Gwehres nebst darauf bezüglichen Exercirübungen. | A supplement to the Tactics on the light percussion musket, together with the relative drill.
1 vol. 8vo. Düsseldorf, 1853.

6522 **Wittich.** Militairisches Vade Mecum. 3te stark, vermehrte auflage. | Military Vade Mecum. 3d edition, greatly enlarged.
1 vol. 18mo. Düsseldorf, 1854.

6523 **Wittich.** Rathgeber beim ausmarsch für unteroffiziere und soldaten. | Instruction for the Departure, for use of non-commissioned officers and privates.
1 vol. 18mo. Düsseldorf, 1854.

6524 **Younghusband** (Capt. C. W.). Hand-Book for Field Service. See Hand-Book, No. 6489.

Subj. 4. CAVALRY TACTICS.

6525 **Aldéguier** (Flavien d'). Des Principes qui servent de Base à l'instruction et à la tactique de la Cavalerie précédés d'une revue historique de divers systèmes d'instruction et des ordonnances de cette arme; suivis d'un Mémoire sur les remontes actuelles de la Cavalerie, relativement à l'éléve des chevaux et à l'agriculture; avec lettres ornées et illustrations. 1 vol. roy. 8vo. Toulouse, 1843.

6526 **Arentschildt** (Lt.-Col. Von). Instructions for officers and non-commissioned officers of Cavalry, on outpost duty; with an abridgement of them, by Lt.-Col. the Hon. F. Ponsonby. 1 12mo. Pamphlet. London, 1854.

6527 **Baker** (Capt. Valentine). The British Cavalry. With Remarks on its practical organization. 1 vol. 8vo. London, 1858.

6528 **Beamish** (North Ludlow). On the uses and application of Cavalry in War, from the text of Bismark, with practical examples selected from ancient and modern History. 1 vol. 8vo. London, 1855.

6529 **Bismark.** On the uses of Cavalry in War. See Nos. 642, 6528.

6530 **Brack** (F. de). Avant-Postes de Cavalerie Légére. Souvenirs. 2e édition. 1 vol. 18mo. Paris, 1844.

6531 **Carbine** Exercise for the Royal Regiment of Artillery. 1 8vo. Pamphlet. Woolwich, 1856.

6532 **Carbine,** Pistol and Lance Exercise. See Instructions, Nos. 6547, 6548.

6533 **Cavalry** Tactics. Kommando-Tabelle aus dem Exerzir-Reglement für die Kavallerie der Königlich Preussischen Armee. | Table of Commands from the Cavalry Tactics of the Royal Prussian Army. 1 vol. 16mo. Berlin, 1855.

6534 **Cavalry** Tactics. (In the Russian Language.) 5 vols. 24mo. St. Petersburg, 1853.

6535 **Cavalry.** Regulations for the Instruction, Formations, and Movements of the Cavalry. See Regulations, Nos. 667, 6554.

6536 **Cavalry** Signals. See Collection, No 6537.

6537 **Collection** of Cavalry and Horse Artillery Signals and Dragoon Drum beats. (In the Russian language.) 1 vol. 24mo. St. Petersburg, 1854.

6538 **D'Aldéguier.** See Aldéguier, No. 6525.

6539 **Guerin** (A.). École du Cavalier au Manége Basée sur les Principes de l'ordonnance de Cavalerie, à l'usage des Instructeurs. 1 vol. 8vo. Paris, 1852.

6540 **Hand-Book.** Handbuch des Felddienstes für Cavallerie offiziere. | Hand-Book of Field service for Cavalry officers.
1 vol. 18mo. Lemberg, 1855.

6541 **Herstatt** (C.). Anweisung zum Satteln und Packen bei der Preussischen Kavallerie. | Instructions for Saddling and Packing of the Prussian Cavalry.
1 18mo. Pamphlet. Düsseldorf, 1850.

6542 **Herstatt** (C.). Reit-Instruction für die leichte Kavallerie. | Riding Instruction for the light Cavalry.
1 vol. 18mo. Düsseldorf, 1850.

6543 **Herstatt** (C.). Das Eskadrons-Exerziren bei der Preussischen Kavallerie. Ein Handbuch für Kavalleristen. | The Squadron Drill of the Prussian Cavalry. A Hand-Book for mounted troops.
1 vol. 18mo. Düsseldorf, 1850.

6544 **Herstatt** (C.). Kavallerie-Katechismus. Fragen und antworten über Reiterei. | Cavalry Catechism. Questions and answers on Cavalry.
1 24mo. Pamphlet. Düsseldorf, 1851.

6545 **Herstatt** (C.). Das Exerzieren mit dem Pistol und Karabiner. | The Pistol and Carbine Drill.
1 24mo. Pamphlet. Düsseldorf, 1852.

6546 **Hofzinser** (Franz Xav.). Ueber den innern Dienst der schweren und leichten Cavallerie. Ein ausführliches Hülfsbuch für offiziere. | On the Interior Service of heavy and light Cavalry. A complete vade mecum for officers.
3 vols. 8vo. Vienna, 1852.

6547 **Instructions** for the Carbine Exercise; the Pistol Exercise; and the Lance Exercise. Revised and corrected. (Horse Guards, 1st January, 1850.) 1 vol. 16mo. London, 1850.

6548 **Instructions** for the Sword, Carbine, Pistol, and Lance Exercise. Together with Standing Gun drill, for the use of the Cavalry. Revised edition. (Adjutant-General's Office, Horse Guards, 1st July, 1858.)
1 vol. 16mo. London, 1858.

6549 **Maury** (Lt. D. H.). Skirmish Drill for mounted troops. An addendum to the Cavalry Tactics for the Regiment of Mounted Riflemen.
1 18mo. Pamphlet. Washington, 1859.

6550 **Mémorial** des Officiers de Cavalerie. See No. 6576.

6551 **Nolan** (Capt. L. E.). Cavalry; its History and Tactics.
1 vol. 8vo. London, 1853.

6552 **Ordonnance** Provisoire sur l'Exercice et les Manœuvres de la Cavalerie, rédigée par ordre du Ministre de la guerre. Du 1er Vendémiaire an XIII.
2 vols. 18mo. Paris, 1804.

6553 **Ordonnance** du Roi Sur le Service intérieur des Troupes à cheval du 2 Novembre 1833, annotée de toutes les dispositions qui l'ont modifiée jusqu' au 1er janvier 1854; par Al. Garrel 1 vol. 18mo. Paris, 1854.

6554 **Regulations** for the Instruction, Formations, and Movements of the Cavalry. Revised and corrected. Horse Guards, 20th May, 1851.
1 vol. 12mo. (2 *copies.*) London, 1851.

6555 **Regulations.** Abrichtung-Reglement für die kaiserl. königl. Cavallerie, 1854. | Regulations for the Instructions of the Imperial Cavalry, 1854.
1 vol. 8vo. Vienna, 1854.

6556 **Regulations** Exercir-Reglement für die kaiserl. königl. Cavallerie, 1854. | Regulations for the Exercise of the Imperial Cavalry, 1854. 1 vol. 8vo. Vienna, 1854.

6557 **Regulations.** Manövrier - Reglement für die kaiserl. königl. Cavallerie, 1854. | Regulations for Manœuvring the Imperial Cavalry, 1854. 1 vol. 8vo. Vienna, 1854.

6558 **Regulations.** Exerzir-Reglement für die Kavallerie der Königlich Preussischen Armee. | Regulations for the Cavalry Exercise of the Royal Prussian Army. 1 vol. 16mo. Berlin, 1855.

6559 **Robbins** (Lieut.). The Cavalry Catechism; or, Instructions on Cavalry Exercise and Field Movements, Brigade Movements, Out-post Duty, Cavalry supporting Artillery, Artillery attached to Cavalry, and on various other subjects connected with cavalry. 1 vol. 12mo. London, 1851.

6560 **Schauenburg** (le Baron de). De l'emploi de la Cavalerie à la guerre. 1 vol. 8vo. & Atlas 4to. Paris, 1838.

6561 **Siegmann** (W.). Die Elementartaktik der Reiterei. Nebst 29 Tafeln mit abbildungen. | Elementary Cavalry Tactics. With 29 Plates. 1 vol. 8vo. & Atlas fol. obl. Leipsic, 1854.

6562 **Skirmish** Drill of Mounted Troops. By Lt. D. H. Maury. See Maury, No. 6549.

6563 **Unger** (L. A.). Histoire critique des exploits et vicissitudes de la Cavalerie pendant les guerres de la Revolution et de l'Empire jusqu' à l'armistice du 4 Juin 1813. 2 vols. 8vo. Paris, 1848.

Subj. 5. INFANTRY AND INFANTRY TACTICS.

6564 **Barre Duparcq** (Éd de la). Histoire sommaire de l'Infanterie. 1 8vo. Pamphlet. Paris, 1853.

6565 **Förster** (S. von). Der Felddienst der leichten Infanterie nach ihrer neuen Bewaffnung. | Field Service of Light Infantry in accordance with the new arming. 1 vol. 8vo. Berlin, 1854.

6566 **French** Field Service. See Macdonald, No. 698.

6567 **Guide** (le). Des sous-officiers de l'Infanterie Française, en Campagne, en Marche, en Cantonnement et en Garnison; 3e édition, revue, corrigée, augmentée de plusieurs Tarifs, &c. 1 vol. 18mo. Paris, 1807.

6568 **Guide.** Anleitung für die Ausbildung der Linien-Infanterie in der Vertheidigung und im Angriffe einzelner Gegenstände und Oertlichkeiten. 1845. | A Guide for the improvement of Infantry of the Line in the defence and attack of single objects and localities. 1845. 1 vol. 8vo. Vienna, 1845.

6569 **Hardee** (Brevet Lieut.-Col. W. J.). Rifle and Light Infantry Tactics; for the exercise and manœuvres of Troops when acting as Light Infantry or Riflemen. Prepared under the direction of the War Department.
Vol. 1st. Schools of the Soldier and Company; Instruction for Skirmishers.
Vol. 2d. School of the Batallion. 2 vols. 18mo. Philadelphia, 1855.

6570 **Infantry** Manual: Containing directions for the Drill and Instruction of Recruits; the Manual and Platoon Exercises; an abstract of the Field Exercises and Evolutions of the Army, &c., &c. Revised 1st June, 1850. 1 vol. 18mo. London, 1850.

6571 **Infantry Drill.** See Regulations, Nos. 6582 to 6594.

6572 **Instructions** for the conduct of Infantry on actual service. See Macdonald, No. 698.

6573 **Intruction** for Markers. (In the Russian language.) 1 vol. 24mo. St. Petersburg, 1852.

6574 **Lavelaine de Maubeuge** (le Colonel). Les Evolutions de ligne par Battaillons en Masse comme complément de l'ordonnance du 4 Mars, 1831, en considerant, dans l'exécution des mouvements, chaque Bataillon comme un Peloton, suivies de documents necessaires à la guerre; présentées à sa Majesté Impériale Napoléon III. 1 vol. 4to. Paris, 1852.

6575 **Marguery.** Théorie pour apprendre à battre aux Tambours; suivie des signaux du Tambours-Major pour les différentes Batteries, d'après l'ordonnance du 4 Mars, 1831. 1 vol. 32mo. Paris, 1833.

6576 **Mémorial** des officiers d'Infanterie et de Cavalerie. Rédigè d'après les Documents officiels et les cours professés dans l'École Militaires. 1 vol. 12mo. Paris, 1846.

6577 **Military** Regulations concerning Infantry Service. (In the Russian language.) 2 vols. 24mo. St. Petersburg, 1852.

6578 **Ordonnance** sur l'Exercice et les Manœuvres de l'Infanterie. Du 4 Mars, 1831. 3 vols. 32mo. Paris, 1831.

6579 **Platoon Exercise** (The), and different firings for the ordinary or Rifle Musket. (Horse Guards, 13th June, 1854.) 1 12mo. Pamphlet. London, 1854.

6580 **Réglement** concernant l'Exercice et les Manœuvres de l'Infanterie. Du 1er Août, 1791. 2 vols. 18mo. Paris, 1793.

6581 **Réglement** concernant l'Exercice et les Manœuvres de l'Infanterie. Du 1er Août, 1791. 2 vols. 8vo., one of text & one of plates. Paris, 1792.

6582 **Regulations.** Exerzir-Reglement für die Infanterie der Königlich Preussischen Armee.
Regulations for the Infantry Exercise of the Royal Prussian Army. 1 vol. 16mo. Berlin, 1847.

6583 **Regulations.** Abrichtungs-Reglement für die Linien-Infanterie, 1843.
Regulations for the Instructions of Infantry of the line, 1843.
2 vols. 8vo. one vol. of text & one of plates. Vienna, 1843.

6584 **Regulations.** Exercir-Reglement für die Linien-Infanterie, 1844.
Regulations for the Exercise of Infantry of the line, 1844. 1 vol. 8vo. Vienna, 1844.

6585 **Regulations.** Exercir-Reglement für die k. k. Linien und Grenz-Infanterie, 1851.
Regulations for the Exercise of the Imperial Infantry of the line, 1851. 1 vol. 8vo. Vienna, 1854.

6586 **Regulations.** Abrichtungs-Reglement für die k. k. Linien und Grenz-Infanterie, 1851.
Regulations for the Instructions of the Imperial Infantry of the line, 1851. 1 vol. 8vo. Vienna, 1854.

6587 **Regulations.** Manövrir - Reglement für die kaiserl. königl. Infanterie.
Regulations for Manœuvring the Imperial Infantry. 1 vol. 8vo. Vienna, 1853.

6588 **Regulations.** Abrichtungs-Reglement für die kaiserl. königl. Pionniere, 1853.
Regulations for the Instructions of the Imperial Pioneers, 1853. 1 vol. 8vo. Vienna, 1853.

6589 **Regulations.** Exercir-Reglement für die kaiserl. königl. Pionniere, 1853.
Regulations for the Exercise of the Imperial Pioneers, 1853. 1 vol. 8vo. Vienna, 1853.

6590 **Regulations.** Abrichtungs-Reglement für die k. k. Jäger, 1851.
Regulations for the Instructions of the Imperial Riflemen, 1851. 1 vol. 8vo. Vienna, 1851.

6591 **Regulations.** Exerzir-Reglement für die k. k. Jäger, 1851.
Regulations for the Exercise of the Imperial Riflemen, 1851. 1 vol. 8vo. Vienna, 1851.

6592 **Regulations.** Abrichtungs-Reglement für die kais. kön. Genie-Truppen, 1853.
Regulations for the Instructions of the Imperial Engineer Troops, 1853. 1 vol. 8vo. Vienna, 1853.

6593 **Regulations.** Exercir-Reglement für die kais. kön. Genie-Truppen, 1853.
Regulations for the Exercise of the Imperial Engineer Troops, 1853. 1 vol. 8vo Vienna, 1853.

6594 **Regulations** for Infantry Tactics. (In the Russian language.) 4 vols. 24mo. St. Petersburg, 1848.

6595 **Scott** (Major Gen.). On percussion locks and bayonets with claps. A supplement to the Manual of Arms, Infantry Tactics. 1 18mo. Pamphlet. Washington, 1844.

6596 **Traité** sur la Constitution des troupes Légéres et sur leur emploi à la guerre, &c. See No. 6702.

6597 **Witzleben** (A. Von). Heerwesen und Infanteriedienst der Königlich Preuszischen Armee. 4te vermehrte und verbesserte auflage. | Army affairs, together with the Infantry Service of the Royal Prussian Army. 4th edition, revised and enlarged. 1 vol. 8vo. Berlin, 1854.

Subj. 6. FENCING AND THE USE OF THE SWORD.

6598 **Angelo's** Bayonet Exercise. New edition. (Adjutant-General's office, Horse Guards July, 1857.) 1 vol. 16mo. London, 1857.

6599 **Gomard** (A. J.-J. Possellier dit). La Théorie de l'Escrime enseignée par une méthode simple, basée sur l'observation de la Nature. Illustrée de vingt dessins faits d'aprés nature, par Th. Guerin. 1 vol. 8vo. Paris, 1845.

6600 **Infantry** Sword Exercise. Revised edition. January, 1845. 1 vol. 18mo. London, 1845.

6601 **Instructions** for the Sword and Lance. See Instructions, Nos. 6547, 6548.

Subj. 7. EQUITATION AND VETERINARY ART, &c.

6602 **Baucher** (F.). Oeuvres completes. Méthode d'Équitation Basée sur de nouveaux Principes, 2e édition suivie des Passe-Temps Équestres, Dialogue sur l'Équitation, Dictionnaire raisonné d'Équitation, Réponse à la critique. 1 vol. royal 8vo. Paris, 1854.

6603 **Baumeister** (Wilh.). Anleitung zur Kenntnisz, des aeuszern des Pferdes für Thierärzte, Pferdeliebhaber und Pferdebesitzer. Zweite vermehrte auflage.
A Guide for judging of a Horse by his external appearance, for the use of Veterinary Surgeons, Horse-fanciers and Horse-possessors. 2d edition enlarged.
1 vol. 8vo. Stuttgart, 1845.

6604 **Bouley et Reynal.** Nouveau Dictionnaire pratique de Médecine, de Chirurgie et d'Hygiène Vétérinaires. (Vol. 2d, &c., wanting). 1st vol. large 8vo. Paris, 1856.

6605 **Cardini** (F.). Dictionnaire d' Hippiatrique et d'Équitation, ouvrage ou se trouvent réunies toutes les connaissances Hippiques. 2e édition. Ornée de 70 figures. 2 large 8vo. vols. Paris, 1848.

6606 **Curnieu** (le Bon de). Leçons de Science Hippique générale, ou Traité complet de l'art de connaitre, de gouverner et d'élever le cheval. (2e partie, &c., wanting). 1st vol. 8vo. Paris, 1855.

6607 **Delwart** (L. V.). Traité de Médecine Vétérinaire pratique. 3 vols. 8vo. Bruxelles, 1850–53.

6608 **Günther** (Dr. Friedrich August). Der homöopathische Thierarzt. Ein Hülfsbuch für Cavallerie offiziere, Gutsbesitzer, &c. &c. Dritter Theil: Die homöopathische Hausapotheke.
The homœopathic Veterinary Surgeon. A vade mecum for Cavalry officers, Farmers, &c., &c. Third Part: The homœopathic domestic medicines.
1 vol. 8vo. Sondershausen, 1840.

609 **Haycock** (William). Treatise on the Principles and Practice of Veterinary Medicine and Surgery. (2d part wanting). 1st part in 8vo. London, 1858.

6610 **Hertwig** (Dr. Carl Heinrich). Praktische Arzneimittellehre für Thieraerzte. 3te sehr vermehrte und verbesserte auflage.
Practical pharmacology for Veterinary Surgeons. 3rd edition, revised and enlarged.
1 vol. 8vo. Berlin, 1847.

66 11 **Hertwig** (Dr. C. H.). Taschenbuch der gesammten Pferdekunde. Für jeden Besitzer und Liebhaber von Pferden. Mit neun Tafeln.
A complete Hand Book of information concerning the Horse. For possessors and amateurs of Horses. With nine Plates.
1 vol. 16mo. Berlin, 1851.

6612 **Hertwig** (Dr. H. C.). Praktisches Handbuch der chirurgie für Thierärzte. | Practical Hand Book of Surgery for Veterinary Surgeons. 1 vol. 8vo. Berlin, 1850.

6613 **Hunersdorf** (Ludwig). Anleitung zu der natürlichsten und leichtesten Art, Pferde abzurichten. 6te auflage. | Directions as to the best and easiest mode of breaking Horses. 6th edition. 1 vol. 18mo. Cassel, 1840.

6614 **Hurtrel d'Arboval.** Dictionnaire de Médecine, de Chirurgie et d'Hygiéne Vétérinaires. 2e edition. 6 vols. 8vo. Paris, 1838–39.
See Leblanc & Trousseau, No 6615.

6615 **Leblanc et Trousseau.** Anatomie chirurgicale des principaux Animaux Domestiques, ou Recueil de trente Planches représentant 1° l'anatomie des Régions du Cheval, du Boeuf, du Mouton, du Cochon, sur lesquelles on pratique les opérations les plus Graves; 2° les divers états des Dents du Cheval, du Boeuf, du Mouton, du Chien, indiquant l'âge de ces Animaux; 3° les Instrumens de chirurgie Vétérinaire avec un Texte explicatif: Atlas pour servir de suite au Dictionnaire de Médecine et de chirurgie Vétérinaires de M. Hurtrel d'Arboval. 1 vol. folio. Paris, 1828.

6616 **Manuel** de Maréchalerie. Rédigé par le conseil d'instruction de l'École de cavalerie, et approuvé par décision de M. le Ministre de la guerre, en date 31 Octobre, 1849, pour l'usage des éléves Maréchaux de l'École de cavalerie. 1 vol. 18mo. Saumur, 1856.

6617 **Miles** (William). A Plain Treatise on Horse-Shoeing, with illustrations. 2d edition. 1 vol. square 16mo. London, 1858.

6618 **Mussot** (P.). Commentaires Historiques et élémentaires sur l'Équitation et la Cavalerie, (avec 20 Planches). 1 vol. 8vo. Paris, 1854.

6619 **Nadosy** (Alexander von). Equitations-Studien. Mit besonderer Rücksichtsnahme auf den unterricht in den Artillerie-Equitationen. 2te vermehrte und verbesserte auflage. | Studies upon Equitation, particularly relating to Artillery instruction. 2d edition, revised and enlarged. 2 vols. 16mo. Vienna, 1855.

6620 **Oeynhausen** (B. von). Leitfaden zur Abrichtung von Reiter und Pferd, nebst der Zäumungslehre und einem anhange über Schulreiterei. 3te auflage. | Guide for training both Rider and Horse, together with the mode of bitting, and an appendix upon School of Cavalry. 3d edition. 1 vol. 8vo. Vienna, 1852.

6621 **Pembroke** (Henry, Earl of). A Method of breaking Horses, and teaching Soldiers to Ride, designed for the use of the Army. 1 vol. 18mo. London, 1761.

6622 **Percival** (Veterinary Surgeon). A series of Elementary Lectures on the Veterinary Art: wherein the Anatomy, Physiology, and Pathology of the Horse are essayed on the general Principles of Medical Science. 3 vols. 8vo. London, 1823–26.

6623 **Percival** (William). Twelve Lectures on the Form and Action of the Horse. With eight Engravings on Steel, by Joseph Lawrence. 1 vol. 8vo. London, 1850.

6624 **Percival** (William). The Anatomy of the Horse, embracing the Structure of the Foot. 1 vol. 8vo. London, 1858.

6625 **Petite** notice sur la possibilité de faire manger les Chevaux sans les débrider. (Lithog.) 1 folio Pamphlet. No date.

6626 **Programme** du Cours d'hippiatrique. (Lithog.) Septembre, 1854. 1 vol. 4to. —— ——.

6627 **Rarey** (J. S.). The Art of Taming Horses, a new edition, revised, with important additions and illustrations, including chapters on Riding and Hunting, for the Invalid and Timid. By the Secretary. 1 vol. 18mo. London, 1858.

6628 **Recueil** de Mémoires et Observations sur l'Hygiène et la Médecine Vétérinaires Militaires, Rédigè sous la surveillance de la Commission d'Hygiène Hippique. 6 vols. 8vo. Paris, 1847–55.

6629 **Reynal.** Nouveau Dictionnaire pratique de Médecine de Chirurgie et d'Hygiène Vétérinaires. See No. 6604.

6630 **Röll** (Dr. M. F.). Lehrbuch der Arzneimittellehre für Thierärzte. | Elementary Treatise on the Study of Medicine for Veterinary Surgeons. 1 vol. 8vo. Vienna, 1853.

6631 **Rul** (Louis). Le Bauchérisme réduit à sa plus simple expression ou l'art de dresser les Chevaux d'Attelage, de Dame, de Promenade, de Chasse, de Course, d'Escadron, de Cirque, de Tournoi, de Carrousel, Programme des Cours d'Équitation Civile et Militaire professées à Bruxelles, Malines, Coblentz, Prague, Vienne, Breslau, Naples, &c., suivi de notes Militaires, (organisation, instruction de l'armée, Académie Militaire.) 1 vol. 8vo. Paris, 1857.

6632 **Saint-Ange** (M. B. de). Abrégé du Cours d'Hippologie, à l'usage des sous-officiers de Cavalerie. 4e édition, revue et corrigée. 1 vol. 32mo, Paris, 1855.

6633 **Seidler** (E. F.). Die Dressur difficiler Pferde, die Korrektion Verdorbener und böser Pferde. | The breaking of difficult Horses, the correction of spoiled and bad Horses. 1 vol. 8vo. Berlin, 1846.

6634 **Seidler** (E. F.). Leitfaden zur Systematischen Bearbeitung des Campagne und Gebrauchs-Pferdes. 2te unveränderte auflage. | Guide for the systematic training of Horses for Military and other uses. 2d edition, unchanged. 1 vol. 8vo. Berlin, 1843.

6635 **Seifert** (Joseph). Bildliche Darstellung zur übersicht aller, von aussen am Pferde möglichst ersichtlich gemachten Fehler und Krankheiten. | Graphical representations of all possible faults and diseases, visible and representable on the exterior of a Horse. 1 4to. Pamphlet, and 3 Plates in folio. Vienna, 1842.

6636 **Sind's** Pferdearzt. | Veterinary-Surgeon. 1 vol. 8vo. No title-page.

Subj. 8. MILITARY ADMINISTRATION AND ORGANIZATION.

6637 **Administration** et Comptabilité des Escadrons de Cavalerie et des Batteries d'Artillerie, en ce qui concerne les sous-officiers, brigadiers et soldats. 1 vol. 24mo. Paris, 1849.

6638 **Administration** (Manuel d') et de Comptabilité des sous-officiers, caporaux et soldats d'Infanterie. 1 vol. 24mo. Paris, 1849.

6639 **Compte** Rendu sur le Recrutement de l'armée pendant l'années 1841, 1842, 1844, et 1850. 4 vols. 4to. Paris, 1843–52.

6640 **Compte** général du Matériel de la Guerre pour l'année 1852. 1 vol. 4to. Paris, 1853.

6641 **Comptes** généraux présentés par le Ministre de la Guerre pour l'exercice 1851, 1852. 2 vols. 4to. Paris, 1853–54.

6642 **De Peyster** (J. Watts). Report to his excellency Washington Hunt, Governor of the State of New York, &c., &c., on the subject of the organizations of the National Guards, and Municipal Military Systems of Europe, and the Artillery and Arms best adapted to the State Service. 1 vol. 8vo. Albany, 1853.

6643 **Fonblanque** (Edward Barrington de). Treatise on the Administration and Organization of the British Army, with especial reference to Finance and Supply. 1 vol. 8vo. London, 1858.

6644 **Guillot** (Léon). Administration Militaire. See Guillot, No. 6671.

6645 **Hirtenfeld** (J.). Allgemeines Militärisches Handbuch. Organisation der europäischen Heere. | General Military Hand Book. Organization of European Armies. 1 vol. 16mo. Vienna, 1854.

6646 **Kalkstein** (R. V.). Die Preuszische Armee nach ihren reglementarischen Formen und Einrichtungen, zusammengefaszt in Form einer "Dienst-Instruktion" für Offizier Aspiranten. | Regulations for the Formation and Organization of the Army of Prussia, for Officer Aspirants, selected from the "Service Instructions." 1 vol. 8vo. Berlin, 1855.

6647 **Le Noble** (Le Citoyen). Essai sur l'administration Militaire. 1 vol. 4to. Paris, 1800.

6648 **Manuel** d'Administration, &c. See Administration, No. 6638.

6649 **McClellan** (Capt. George B.). Report in relation to the Armies in Europe, and the Campaign in the Crimea. 1 vol. 4to. Washington, 1857. See Special Session, Ex. Doc. No. 1, 34th Congress.

6650 **Napier.** Comments, by Lieut.-General Sir William Napier, K. C. B., upon a memorandum of the Duke of Wellington, and other documents, censuring Lieut.-General Charles James Napier, G. C. B., with a defence of Sir C. Napier's government of Scinde, by Captain Rathborne, late Collector in Scinde. 2d edition. 1 vol. 8vo. London, 1854.

6651 **Preval** (le Général). Mémoires sur l'Avancement Militaire et sur les Matières qui s'y rapportent. 1 vol. 8vo. Paris, 1842.

6652 **Réponse** à l'article sur l'État Major Général de l'Armée par un officier supérieur en Retraite ayant fait les guerres de l'Empire. 1 8vo. Pamphlet. Paris, 1846.

6653 **Robert** (Ch.). Administration Militaire. See Robert, Nos. 6699 and 6700.

6654 **Roguet** (le Général). De l'Approvisionnement des Armées au XIXme Siècle. 1 vol. 8vo. Paris, 1848.

6655 **Shirley** (Lt.-Col. Arthur). Remarks on the Transport of Cavalry and Artillery: with hints for the management of Horses, before, during, and after a long sea voyage. 1 12mo. Pamphlet. London, 1854.

6656 **Streffleur** (V.). Die Dienst-Vorschriften der Östreichischen Armee. Die Organisation im Frieden, &c., erste bis vierte abtheilung. | The Regulations and Orders for the Austrian Army. The Organization in time of Peace, &c., first to fourth divisions. 1 vol. 8vo. Vienna, 1843.

6657 **Streffleur** (V.). Die Dienst-Vorschriften der Östreichischen Armee. Das Militär-Justizwesen. 8te abtheilung. | The Regulations and Orders for the Austrian Army. Military administration. 8th division. 1 vol. 8vo. Vienna, 1844.

6658 **Streffleur** (V.). Die Organisation und der Geschäftsbetrieb bei einer Armee im Felde. | Organization and Service of an Army in the Field. 1 vol. 8vo. Vienna, 1854.

6659 **Thackeray** (Thomas James). The Military Organization and Administration of France. Drawn from official and other authentic sources of information. 2 vols. 8vo. London, 1856.

6660 **Thomson** (H. Byerley). Military Forces and Institutions of Great Britain and Ireland: their Constitution, Administration, and Government, Military and Civil. 1 vol. 8vo. London, 1855.

6661 **Vauchelle.** Cours d'Administration Militaire. 3e édition. 3 vols. 8vo. Paris, 1854.

6662 **Witzleben** (A. von). Heerwesen und Infanteriedienst der Königlich Preuszischen Armee. 4te vermehrte und verbesserte auflage. | Army affairs, together with the Infantry Service of the Royal Prussian Army. 4th edition, revised and enlarged. 1 vol. 8vo. Berlin, 1854.

Subj. 9. MILITARY LAWS, REGULATIONS, AND ORDERS.

6663 **Army Acts.** An act for limiting the time of service in the Army, (passed 21st June, 1847,) and an Act for Punishing Mutiny and Desertion, and for the better payment of the Army and their Quarters, (passed 22d April, 1848,) together with Rules and Articles of War.
1 vol. 12mo. London, 1848.

6664 **Army Regulations.** See Regulations, No. 6694.

6665 **Articles** de Guerre pour l'Armée Prussienne. Édition Officielle.
1 8vo. Pamphlet. Berlin, 1854.

6666 **Callan** (John F.). Military Laws of the United States, relating to the Army, Marine Corps, Volunteers, Militia, and to Bounty Lands and Pensions, from the Foundation of the Government to the year 1858.
1 vol. 8vo. (3 *copies.*) Baltimore, 1858.

6667 **Collection** of Warrants and Regulations issued to the Army on Matters of Finance. To which are added Regulations and Allowances applicable to Corps of Yeomanry Cavalry; also information for the use of Military and Naval Officers proposing to settle in the British Colonies. With an index. 1 vol. 12mo. London, 1846.

6668 **Craufurd** (Major-General Robert). Standing orders during the years 1809, 1810, and 1811, then serving under his command in the Army of the Duke of Wellington. Edited by Brevet-Major Campbell and Captain Shaw. 1 vol. 32mo. London, 1852.

6669 **Garrel** (Al.). Ordonnance du Roi sur le Service intérieur des troupes à cheval. See Ordonnance, No. 6681.

6670 **General** Regulations for the Military Forces of the State of New York, 1858. 1 vol. 12mo. Albany, 1858.

6671 **Guillot** (Léon). Législation et administration Militaires ou Programme detaillé des matiéres enseignées à l'École Impériale d'État-Major. Publié par ordre du général Foltz, Commandant l'École, sur la proposition du Comitié Consultatif d'État-Major et avec l'autorisation de S. Exc. le Maréchal Ministre de la guerre. 1 vol. roy. 8vo. Paris, 1855.

6672 **Hetzel** (Capt. A. R.). Military Laws of the United States; including those relating to the Army, Marine Corps, Volunteers, Militia, and to Bounty Lands and Pensions, to which is prefixed the Rules and Articles of War, and the Constitution of the United States. 3d edition.
1 vol. 8vo. (5 *copies.*) Washington, 1846.

6673 **Hough** (W.). Precedents in Military Law, including the Practice of Courts Martial; the mode of conducting Trials; the duties of Officers at Military Courts of Inquests, Courts of Inquiry, Courts of Requests, &c.
1 vol. 8vo. London, 1855.

6674 **Manuel** d'Administration et de Comptabilité. See Administration, Nos. 6637 and 6638.

6675 **Manuel** portatif des Pensions de l'armée du Terre. Contenant la loi du 11 Avril, 1831, le Réglement d'Administration du 2 juillet de la dite année, &c., &c. 1 vol. 32mo. Paris, 1833.

6676 **Manuel** Réglementaire à l'usage des Officiers Éléves de l'École d'application du corps impérial d'État-Major. 1 vol. 24mo. Paris, 1855.

6677 **Marlborough** (John Churchill, first Duke of). The Letters and Dispatches of, from 1702 to 1712. Edited by General the Right Hon. Sir George Murray. 5 vols. 8vo. London, 1845.

6678 **Military** Regulations concerning Infantry Service. (In the Russian language.) 2 vols. 24mo. St. Petersburg, 1852.

6679 **Ordnance** Regulations, 1852. See Regulations, No. 6695.

6680 **Ordonnance** du Roi sur le Service des Armées en Campagne, du 3 Mai, 1832, Modifiée par celles des 8 Avril, 1837, et 9 Decembre, 1840. 1 vol. 32mo. Paris, ——.

6681 **Ordonnance** du Roi sur le service intérieur des Troupes à cheval du 2 Novembre, 1833, annotée de toutes les dispositions qui l'ont modifièe jusqu' au 1er janvier, 1854 ; par Al. Garrel. 1 vol. 18mo. Paris, 1854.

6682 **Paixhans** (H. J.). Constitution Militaire de la France, étude sur les modifications à apporter au Systéme de nos Forces de Terre et de Mer ; tant pour opérer les progrés devenus nécessaires, que pour diminuer les dépenses, sans que la Puissance National en soit altérée. 1 vol. 8vo. Paris, 1849.

6683 **Prendergast** (Harris). The Law relating to officers in the Army. Revised edition. 1 vol. 16mo. London, 1855.

6684 **Queen's** Regulations and Orders for the Army, 1st July, 1844. 3d edition. 1 vol. 8vo. London, 1844.

6685 ——— Addenda to the Queen's Regulations and Orders for the Army, from the first of July, 1844, to the twelfth of July, 1847. 1 vol. 8vo. London, ——.

Continuation of the Addenda to the Queen's Regulations and Orders for the Army, from July, 1847, to December 31st, 1849. 1 vol. 8vo. London, 1850.

6686 **Quillet** (P. N.). État actuel de la Législation sur l'administration des troupes. Nouvelle édition. 2 vols. 8vo. Paris, 1805.

6687 **Quillet** (P. N.) The same. 3e édition. 3 vols. 8vo. Paris, 1808.

6688 **Reglamento** de nueva constitucion en el Colegio Militar de Caballeros Cadetes del real cuerpo de artilleria establecido en Segovia. 1 vol. 8vo. Madrid, 1804.

6689 **Réglement** Provisoire sur le service de l'Infanterie en Campagne. Du 5 Avril 1792. 1 vol. 18mo. Paris ——.

6690 **Réglement** Provisoire sur le service des troupes à cheval en Campagne. Du 12 Août 1788. 1 vol. 18mo. Paris, 1793.

6691 **Réglement** pour l'exécution des travaux des Éléves de l'École Impériale d'application de l'artillerie et du Génie. See Réglement, No. 7854.

6692 **Regulations** for the admission of Gentlemen Cadets into the Royal Military Academy at Woolwich, January, 1851. 1 sheet.

6693 **Regulations** for admission into the Ordnance School at Carshalton, January, 1851. 1 sheet.

6694 **Regulations** for the Army of the United States, 1857. 1 vol. 12mo. (2 *copies.*) New York, 1857.

6695 **Regulations** for the Government of the Ordnance Department. 1 vol. 12mo. Washington, 1852.

6696 **Regulations** of the United States Military Academy at West Point, New York. 1 vol. 12mo. New York, 1853.

6697 **Regulations.** The Same. 1 vol. 8vo. New York, 1857.

6698 **Ringgold** (Commander Cadwalader). Defence before Court of Inquiry, No. 2, convened at Washington city. Read by Hon. Charles M. Conrad, November 27, 1857. 1 8vo. Pamphlet. Washington, 1857.

6699 **Robert** (Ch.). Sommaire des Leçons de Législation et d'administration militaires. (Lithog.) Juillet 1852. 1 4to Pamphlet. —— ——.

6700 **Robert** (Ch.). Cours de Législation et d'administration militaires, professé à l'École Impériale d'application de l'artillerie et du Génie. (1re partie.) (Lithog.) Octobre 1853. 1 vol. 4to.

6701 **Simmons** (Thomas Frederick). Remarks on the constitution and practice of Courts Martial; with a summary of the Law of Evidence, as connected with such courts; also some notice of the criminal Law of England, &c. 4th revised edition. 1 vol. 8vo. London, 1852.

6702 **Traité** sur la Constitution des troupes Légéres, et sur leur emploi à la guerre; auquel on à joint un supplément contenant la Fortification de Campagne. Avec un grand nombre de figures. 1 vol. 8vo. Paris, 1782.

6703 **War** office Regulations. Royal Warrant and Regulations regarding army service and Explanatory directions for the information and guidance of Paymasters and others; with an index. 1 vol. 8vo. London, 1848.

Subj. 10. GENERAL MILITARY AND NAVAL HISTORY.

6704 **Cathcart** (Colonel the Hon. George). Commentaries on the War in Russia and Germany in 1812 and 1813. With Plans and Diagrams. 1 vol. 8vo. London, 1850.

6705 **Cooper** (J. Fenimore). History of the Navy of the United States of America. Continued to 1853. From the Author's Manuscripts and other authentic sources. Three volumes in one. 1 vol. 8vo. New York, 1854.

6706 **Headley** (J. T.). The second War with England. 2 vols. 12mo. New York, 1853.

6707 **Ingersoll** (Charles J.). History of the second War between the United States of America and Great Britain, declared by act of Congress, the 18th of June, 1812, and concluded by Peace, the 15th of February, 1815. Second series. Embracing the events of 1814 and 1815. 2 vols. 8vo. Philadelphia, 1852.

6708 **Klapka** (General George). War in the East. From the year 1853 till July, 1855. An historico-critical sketch of the campaigns on the Danube, in Asia, and in the Crimea; with a glance at the probable contingencies of the next campaign. Translated from the original manuscript by Lt.-Col. A. Mednyánszky. 1 vol. 12mo. London, 1855.

6709 **Koch** (le Général). Mémoires de Massena. See Massena, No. 6710.

6710 **Massena.** Mémoires de Massena, rédigés d'aprés les documents qu' il laissés et sur ceux du Dépot de la guerre et du Dépot des Fortifications par le général Koch. Avec un Atlas. 7 vols. 8vo. and Atlas fol. Paris, 1848–50.

6711 **Maxwell** (W. H.). The Victories of Wellington and the British Armies. New edition completed to the present time. 1 vol. 12mo. London, 1852.

6712 **Mémoires** sur la dernière guerre entre la France et l'Espagne dans les Pyrenées Occidentales. Par le Citoyen B. * * *. (Bound with Thiébault's Journal des Opérations Militaires.) 1 vol. 8vo. Paris, 1801.

6713 **Mexican History.** The Other Side; or, Notes for the History of the War between Mexico and the United States. Written in Mexico. Translated from the Spanish, and edited, with notes, by Albert C. Ramsey. 1 vol. 12mo. New York, 1850.

6714 **Read & Co.** Panoramic Views of the Seat of War, East and North. See War, No. 6723.

6715 **Russian War.** See War, Nos. 6722 to 6724.

6716 **Simcoe's** Military Journal. A History of the Operations of a Partisan Corps called the Queen's Rangers, commanded by Lieut.-Col. J. G. Simcoe, during the War of the American Revolution; illustrated by ten Engraved Plans of Actions, &c. Now first published, with a Memoir of the Author and other additions. 1 vol. 8vo. New York, 1844.

6717 **Soult.** Mémoires du Maréchal-Général Soult, Duc de Dalmatie. Publiés par son fils. Premiére partie. Histoire des guerres de la Revolution. 3 vols. 8vo. & Atlas fol. Paris, 1854.

6718 **Sprague** (John T.). The Origin, Progress, and Conclusion of the Florida War. 1 vol. 8vo. New York, 1848.

6710 **Stanford's** Panoramic View of Helsingfors and Svéaborg. See War, No. 6723.

6720 **Tableau** Historique de la Guerre de la Revolution de France. See No. 916.

6721 **Vigneron** (Hippolyte). Précis Critique et Militaire de la guerre d'orient rédigé sur des documents inédits suivi d'un aperçu sur les opérations des Flottes Alliées dans la Mer Noire et la Baltique. Ouvrage orné du Portrait sur acier de S. M. Napoléon III. et de quatre Plans pour servir aux batailles de l'Alma, d'Inkermann, de Tracktir et de Sébastopol. 1 vol. 8vo. Paris, 1858.

6722 **War** in the East. On the Conduct of the War in the East. The Crimean Expedition. Memoir addressed to the Government of H. M. the Emperor Napoleon III. By a General Officer. 1 8vo. Pamphlet. London, 1855.

6723 **War** in the East and North. Views, &c., of—

1. Panoramic View of Helsingfors and Svéaborg. Published by Edward Stanford. 1 Sheet.
2. Tête d'Armée, or how the British General Stormed the Redan. 1 Sheet.
3. Panoramic Views of the Seat of War, East and North. 24 Sheets, Colored. Published by Read & Co.
4. Views of Nicholaief, Genitchi, Baktchiserai, Simpheropol, Perekop, Kherson. Published by Read & Co. (Bound in paper.)
5. Views of Kars, Bombardment of Kinburn, Retreat of the Russians across the Harbor of Sebastopol. Published by Read & Co. 3 Sheets, Colored.

6724 **War** in the East. The Sardinian Expedition to the Crimea. See Ricordo, No. 6749.

Subj. 11. BATTLES, SIEGES, AND CAMPAIGNS.

6725 **Amherst** (Maj.-Gen. Jeffrey). Expedition against Ticonderoga and Crown Point. See Expedition, No. 6739.

6726 **Arnoul** (H.). Sièges mémorables des Français. See Robert, No. 6750.

6727 **Battle** of Tchernaya or Traktir, (Map of the,) fought by the Russians against the French and Sardinians, 16th August, 1855. Published by Stanford. In case.

6728 **Bertrand** (le Général). Napoléon's Campagnes d'Égypte et de Syrie 1798, 1799. See Napoléon, No. 6743.

6729 **Bouet-Willaumez** (Comte E.). Bataille de Terre et de Mer jusques et y compris la Bataille de l'Alma. Ouvrage orné de 70 planches ou gravures de batailles, vaisseaux, costumes, &c., &c. 1 vol. 8vo. Paris, 1855.

6730 **Brackenbury & Simpson.** Campaign in the Crimea: an Historical Sketch, by George Brackenbury, illustrated by forty Plates, from drawings taken on the spot by William Simpson. 1 vol. 4to. London, 1855.

6731 **Braddock** (Maj.-Gen. Edward). History of an Expedition against Fort Du Quesne, in 1755. See Sargent, No. 6753.

6732 **Campagne** sur le Mein et la Rednitz de l'armée de Gallo-Batave aux ordres du Général Augereau, 1800 et 1801. Avec une Carte des opérations, comprenant depuis Coblentz jusqu' à Égra, et depuis la ligne de neutralité jusqu' au Danube. (Bound with "Bulow's Campagne de 1800.") See Augereau, No. 1000. 1 vol. 8vo. Paris, 1802.

6733 **Casse** (Albert du). Mémoires pour servir à l'histoire de la Campagne de 1812 en Russie, suivis des Lettres de Napoléon au Roi de Westphalie pendant la Campagne de 1813. 1 vol. 8vo. Paris, 1852.

6734 **Chesney** (Col.). The Russo-Turkish Campaigns of 1828 and 1829: with a view of the Present state of affairs in the East. With Maps. 3d edition. 1 vol. 12mo. London, 1854.

6735 **Creasy** (E. S.). The fifteen decisive Battles of the World; from Marathon to Waterloo. 1 vol. 12mo. New York, 1852.

6736 **Damitz** (le Major de). Histoire de la Campagne de 1815, pour faite suite à l'histoire des guerres des temps modernes, d'aprés les Documents du général Grolman. Traduite de l'allemand, par Léon Griffon, revue et accompagnée d'observations par un officier général Français, temoin oculaire. (Avec Plans.) 2 vols. 8vo. Paris, 1840–41.

6737 **De Peyster** (J. Watts). The Battle of the Sound or Baltic; fought October 30th, (O. S.), (November 9th, N. S.) 1658, between the Victorious Hollanders, under Jacob Baron Wassenoer, Lord of Opdam, &c., &c., and the Swedes, commanded by Charles Gustavus Wrangel, Lord High Admiral of the Swedish Realm, Field Marshal, &c., &c. 1 8vo. Pamphlet. Poughkeepsie, 1858.

6738 **Documents** relatifs aux Campagnes en France et sur le Rhin. Pendant les années 1792 et 1793. Tirés des papiers militaires de S. M. le feu Roi de Prusse Frédéric Guillaume III. Traduits de l'allemand, par Paul Mérat. 1 vol. 8vo. Paris, 1848.

6739 **Expedition** of the British and Provincial Army under Maj.-Gen. Jeffrey Amherst, against Ticonderoga and Crown Point, 1759. (Commissary Wilson's orderly Book.) 1 vol. 8vo. Albany, 1857.

6740 **Fonton** (Félix). La Russie dans l'Asie-Mineure, ou Campagnes du Maréchal Paskévitch en 1828 et 1829; et Tableau du caucase. 1 vol. roy. 8vo. & Atlas fol. Paris, 1840.

6741 **Jomini** (General Baron de). Political and Military History of the Campaign of Waterloo. Translated from the French. By S. V. Benet, U. S. Ordnance. 1 vol. 12mo. New York, 1853.

6742 **Kellermann** (Duc de Valmy). Histoire de la Campagne de 1800 écrite d'aprés des documents nouveaux et inédits. 1 vol. 8vo. Paris, 1854.

6743 **Napoléon.** Campagnes d'Égypte et de Syrie 1798–1799. Mémoires pour servir à l'Histoire de Napoléon dictés par lui-même à Saint-Héléne, et Publiés par le Général Bertrand. 2 vols. 8vo. & Atlas folio. Paris, 1847.

6744 **Niel** (le Général). Siége de Sebastopol. Journal des Opérations du Génie. 1 vol. 4to. & Atlas folio. Paris, 1858.

6745 **Paskévitch** (Maréchal). Campagnes en 1828 en 1829. See Fonton, No. 6740.

6746 **Paskévitch** (Maréchal). Rapport adressé à sa Majesté l'Empereur Nicolas Premier. Relatif de l'attaque et la prise de Varsovie. 1 vol. 8vo. Varsovie, 1840.

6747 **Plotho.** Capitulation de Danzig, traduite de l'allemand par P. Himly; avec observations critiques par le général baron de Richemont. 1 8vo. Pamphlet. Paris, 1841.

6748 **Plotho** (Col. Charles de). Relation de la Bataille de Leipzig (16, 17, 18, et 19 Octobre, 1813). Traduite de l'allemand par M. Philippe Himly. Suivie de la relation Autrichienne de l'affaire de Lindenau, &c. 1 vol. 8vo. Paris, 1840.

6749 **Ricordo** Pittorico Militare della Spedizione Sarda in Oriente negli anni 1855–56. Pubblicato d'ordine del Ministre di Guerra per Cura del Corpo Reale di Stato Maggiore. 1 vol. folio obl. Torino, 1857.

6750 **Robert** (L.) **et Arnoul** (H.). Siéges Mémorables des Français depuis le XVe Siécle jusqu' à nos jours. 1 vol. 18mo. Paris, 1855.

6751 **Rohan** (Duc de). Campagne dans la Valteline en 1635, précédée d'un discours sur la guerre des Montagnes. 1 vol. 18mo. Amsterdam, 1788.

6752 **Russell** (W. H.). The British Expedition to the Crimea. A revised edition, with numerous emendations and additions. Illustrated with Plans, Wood Cuts, &c. 1 vol. 8vo. London, 1858.

6753 **Sargent** (Winthrop). The History of an Expedition against Fort Du Quesne, in 1755, under Major-General Edward Braddock, edited from the Original Manuscripts, by Winthrop Sargent. 1 vol. 8vo. Philadelphia, 1855.

6754 **Schweinitz.** Die Expedition gegen die Alands-Inseln im Jahre 1854. | The Expedition against the Aland Islands in the year 1854. 1 8vo. Pamphlet. Berlin, 1855.

6755 **Ségur** (P. Philippe). Lettre sur la Campagne du Gal Macdonald dans les Grisons, (bound with Thiébault's Journal des Opération Militaires.) 1 vol. 8vo. Paris, 1802.

6756 **Siége** de Rome en 1849 par l'armée Française. Journal des Opérations de l'Artillerie et du Génie. 1 vol. 4to. Paris, 1851.

6757 **Siege** of Bomarsund, 1854. Journal of Operations of the Artillery and Engineers. Published by permission of the Minister of War. Illustrated by Maps and Plans. Translated from the French by an Army Officer, (Lieut. F. Prime, U. S. Corps of Engineers). 1 vol. 12mo. New York, 1856.

6758 **Stanford's** Map of the Battle of Tchernaya. See Battle, No. 6727.

6759 **Tchernaya** or Traktir. Battle of. See Battle, No. 6727.

6760 **Thiébault** (Général). Journal des Opérations Militaires du Siége et du Blocus de Gênes. 1 vol. 8vo. Paris, 1801.

6761 **Thiébault** (Paul). Journal des Opérations Militaires du Siége et du Blocus de Gênes, précédé d'un Coup-d'œil sur la Situation de l'armée d'Italie. See vol. V., No. 7495.

6762 **Turenne** (Vicomte de). Mémoires du. See vol. IV., No. 7495.

6763 **Valmy** (Duc de). See Kellerman, No. 6742.

6764 **Vaudoncourt** (Guillaume de). Histoire des Campagnes d'Italie en 1813 et 1814, avec un Atlas Militaire. (Bound with the Programmes d'Artillerie et du Génie, No. 185). In 4to. Londres, 1817.

Subj. 12. MILITARY BIOGRAPHY AND MEMOIRS.

6765 **Abbott** (John S. C.). History of Napoleon Bonaparte. See Napoleon, No. 6778.

6766 **Barre Duparcq** (Éd. de la). Biographie et Maximes de Maurice de Saxe. 1 vol. 8vo. Paris, 1851.

6767 **Barre Duparcq** (Éd. de la). Le plus grand Homme de guerre dissertation historique. 1 vol. 8vo. Paris, 1848.

6768 **Barre Duparcq** (Éd. de la). Biographie et Maximes de Blaise de Montluc. 1 8vo. Pamphlet. Paris, 1848.

6769 **Barre Duparcq** (Éd. de la). Capitaines Anciens et Modernes. See San-Miguel, No. 6782.

6770 **Bernadotte** (John-Baptiste-Julius). King of Sweden and Norway by the name of Charles John. Memoirs and Campaigns. See Philippart, No. 6779.

6771 **Charles John,** Prince Royal of Sweden. Memoirs and Campaigns. See Phillippart, No. 6779.

6772 **De Peyster** (J. Watts). History of the Life of Leonard Torstenson, Senator of Sweden, Count of Ortola, Chief of the Swedish Artillery, under, and Generalissimo of the Swedish Armies, subsequent to the death of Gustavus Adolphus. 1 vol. 8vo. Poughkeepsie, 1855.

6773 **Froment-Coste** (Auguste-Laurent-Adolphe). Notice Nécrologique sur. See Labretonnière, No. 6775.

6774 **Jomini** (General Baron de). Political and Military History of the Campaign of Waterloo. Translated from the French. By S. V. Benet, U. S. Ordnance. 1 vol. 12mo. New York, 1853.

6775 **Labretonniére** (Em.). Notice Nécrologique sur M. Auguste-Laurent-Adolphe Froment-Coste, Commandant du 8ᵉ Bataillon des Chasseurs d'Orléans, Officier de la Légion-d'Honneur. 2ᵉ édition. 1 8vo. Pamphlet. Paris, 1846.

6776 **Lowe** (Lieut. General Sir Hudson). History of the Captivity of Napoleon at St. Helena; and Official Documents not before made Public. 2 vols. 12mo. New York, 1853.

6777 **McRee** (Major Griffith J.). Memoir of. 1 8vo. Pamphlet. ——, 1853.

6778 **Napoleon Bonaparte.** History of. With Maps and Illustrations. By John S. C. Abbott. 2 vols. roy. 8vo. New York, 1855.

6779 **Philippart** (John). Memoirs and Campaigns of Charles John, Prince Royal of Sweden. 1 vol. 8vo. London, 1814.

6780 **Réveil.** L'Empereur Napoléon Tableaux et Récits des Batailles, Combats, actions et faits Militaires des armées sous leur immortel Général, 90 gravures par Réveil d'aprés les peintures du Musée de Versailles et autres Monumens. 1 vol. 16mo. Paris, 1837.

6781 **Ricraft** (Josiah). A Survey of Englands Champions and Truths faithfull Patriots, or a chronologicall Recitement of the Principall proceedings of the most worthy commanders of the prosperous Armies raised for the preservation of Religion, the Kings Majesties Person, the Priviledges of Parliament, and the Liberty of the Subject, &c.
1 vol. 8vo. London, 1647.

6782 **San-Miguel** (Don Evaristo). Capitaines anciens et modernes. Traduit de l'Espagnol, par Éd. de la Barre Duparcq.
1 8vo. Pamphlet. Paris, 1848.

6783 **Stobo.** Memoirs of Major Robert Stobo, of the Virginia Regiment.
1 vol. 18mo. Pittsburgh, 1854.

6784 **Torstenson** (General Leonard). The History of the Life of. By J. Watts de Peyster. 1 vol. 8vo. Poughkeepsie, 1855.

Subj. 13. MILITARY ANTIQUITIES.

6785 **Annibal.** Campaigns of. See Macdougall, No. 6793.

6786 **Ciriacy** (Maj. F. de). Histoire de l'art Militaire chez les anciens, ouvrage traduit de l'allemand par Éd. de la Barre Duparcq.
1 vol. 8vo. Paris, 1854.

6787 **Essai** sur la Tactique des Grecs. See vol. I., No. 7495.

6788 **Essai** sur les Milices Romaines. See vol. II., No. 7495.

6789 **Frontin** (S. Jul). Stratagêmes. See vol. III., No. 7495.

6790 **Hannibal.** See Annibal, No. 6785.

6791 **Hewitt** (John). Ancient Armour and Weapons in Europe: From the Iron period of the Northern Nations to the end of the thirteenth century: with Illustrations from Cotemporary Monuments.
1 vol. 8vo. Oxford & London, 1855.

6792 **Léon** (l'Empereur). Institutions Militaires. Traduction de Joly de Maizeroy. See No. 1238, and vol. III., No. 7495.

6793 **Macdougall** (Lieut.-Col. P. L.). The Campaigns of Hannibal arranged and critically considered expressly for the use of Students of Military History. 1 vol. 16mo. London, 1858.

6794 **Onosander.** Le Général en chef. See vol. III., No. 7495.

6795 **Polyen.** Ruses de guerre. See vol. III., No. 7495.

6796 **Roy** (William). The Military Antiquities of the Romans in Britain.
1 vol. fol. London, 1793.

Subj. 14. MILITARY AND NAVAL PERIODICALS.

6797 **Eclaireur** (The). A Military Journal, devoted to the interests of the Military Forces of the State of New York, and the Official Military Circular of the 9th Brigade, M. F. S. N. Y. In fol. & 8vo. vols. 1, 2, 3.

6798 **Journal** des Sciences Militaires des Armées de Terre et de Mer. Publié sur les Documents fournis par les Officiers des Armées Françaises et Étrangéres, par J. Corréard. 3e Série. 28 vols. 8vo. Paris, 1840–46.

6799 **Journal.** The same. 4e Série. 28 vols. 8vo. Paris, 1847–53.

6800 **Journal.** The same. 5e Série. 8 vols. 8vo. Paris, 1854–55.

6801 **Journal** des Armes Spéciales et de l'État-Major. Publié sur les Documents fournis par les Officiers des Armées Françaises et Étrangéres. Par J. Corréard. 3e Série. 14 vols. 8vo. Paris, 1847–53.

6802 **Journal.** The same. 4e Série. 12 vols. 8vo. Paris, 1854–59.

6803 **Journal** of Engineering. Published by authority of the Chief Engineer. (In the Russian language). (Part 1st of vol. 25 wanting.) 40 vols. & part 1st of vol. 41 in 8vo. St. Petersburg, 1826–54.

6804 **Spectateur** Militaire, recueil de science, d'art et d'histoire militaires. vols. 1 to 18 incl. and vols. 48, 49, & 50, in 8vo. Paris, 1826–51.

6805 **Spectateur** Militaire. The same. 2e Série. 28 vols. 8vo. Paris, 1851–59.

Subj. 15. MILITARY AND NAVAL DICTIONARIES.

6806 **Bardin** (le Général). Dictionnaire de l'armée de Terre, ou Recherches historique sur l'art et les usages Militaires des anciens et des modernes, ouvrage terminé sous la Direction du général Oudinot de Reggio. 4 vols. 8vo. Paris, 1851.

6807 **Burn** (Lieut. Colonel). Naval and Military Technical Dictionary of the French Language. In two parts: French-English, and English-French; with explanations of the various Terms. 1 vol. 12mo. London, 1852.

6808 **Dupain de Montesson.** Vocabulaire de Guerre, ou Recueil des principeaux terms de Guerre, de Marine, d'Artillerie, de Fortification, d'Attaque et de Défense des Places, et de Géographie. 2 vols. 18mo. Paris, 1783.

6809 **Enrile** (D. Joaquin-Maria). Vocabulario Militar. Francés é Inglés Español. 1 vol. 8vo. Paris, 1853.

Subj. 16. ARMY AND NAVY REGISTERS.

6810 **Annuaire** Militaire, Historique, Topographique, Statistique et Anecdotique, par une Société de Militaires et de Gens de lettres, sous la direction de M. le Capitaine Sicard, pour les années, 1839 & 1840. 2 vols. 8vo. Paris, 1839–40.

6811 **Annuaire** des Armées de Terre et de Mer pour l'année 1836. Publié sur les documents fournis par les officiers des Armées Françaises et Étrangères. Par J. Corréard jeune. 1 vol. 8vo. Paris, 1836.

6812 **Army** Registers for the years, (1853, 3 *copies*,) 1854, 1855, 1856, (1857, 2 *copies*,) 1858, 1859. In 8vo. Washington, 1853–59.

6813 **Blue Book** for 1855. Register of officers and Agents, civil, Military, and Naval, in the service of the United States, on the Thirtieth September, 1855; with the Names, Force, and condition of all ships and vessels belonging to the United States, and when and where built; together with the Names and compensation of all Printers in any way employed by Con gres, or any Department or officer of the Government. 1 vol. 8vo. Washington, 1855.

6814 **British** Army List of the officers of the Army and of the Corps of Royal Marines, on full, retired, and half-pay; with an index. Corrected throughout to the 31st March, 1853. 1853–54. 1 vol. 8vo. London, 1853.

6815 **British** Army List for May, 1855. 1 vol. 12mo. London, 1855.

6816 **Congressional** Directory for the years, 1840, 1841–2, 1850, 1858. In 12mo. & 8vo. Washington, 1840–58.

6817 **Corréard jeune** (J.). Annuaire des Armées de Terre et de Mer, 1836. See Annuaire, No. 6811.

6818 **Gardner** (Charles K.). Dictionary of all officers, who have been commissioned, or have been appointed and served, in the Army of the United States, from 1789, to the first January, 1853, with every commission of each; including the distinguished officers of Volunteers and Militia of the States, Navy, and Marine Corps, who have served with the land forces, &c., &c. 1 vol. 12mo. New York, 1853.

6819 **Navy** Registers of the United States for the years, 1853, 1854, 1855, 1856, 1857, 1859. 6 vols. in 12mo. & 8vo. Washington, 1853–59.

6820 **Register** of officers and agents, civil, Military, and Naval, in the service of the United States. See Blue Book, No. 6813.

Subj. 17. CIVIL AND NAVAL ARCHITECTURE AND LANDSCAPE GARDENING.

6821 **Barrack** Accommodation. See Report, No. 6848.

6822 **Barracks.** Pläne von Casernen bei Moabit in Preussen. | Plans of Barracks near Moabit Prussia. 9 sheets. No date.

6823 **Barracks.** See Bâtiments Militaires, No. 6824 to 6830.

6824 **Batiments Militaires.**
Bâtiment double pour loger 180 hommes et 100 chevaux.
Détails relatifs aux écuries.
Manége Couvert.
Magasin aux fourrages.
Caserne d'Infanterie Voûtée à l'épreuve de la bombe.
Circulaire Ministérielle du 8 Novembre, 1843.
5 large Sheets folded, and 6 pages of Text.

6825 **Batiments Militaires.**
Manège couvert avec fermes en bois droits, sans tirans.
Bâtiment voûté à l'épreuve de la bombe. Dispositions des chapes. Citerne simple.
Citerne double.
Circulaire Ministérielle du 20 Septembre, 1845.
3 large Sheets folded, and 4 pages of Text. (Lithog.)

6826 **Batiments Militaires.**
Études d'un nouveau type de Magasin à fourrages.
Circulaire Ministérielle du 28 Juillet, 1846.
1 large Sheet folded, and 2 pages of Text. (Lithog.)

6827 **Batiments Militaires.**
Manége couvert. Modèle d'une ferme en bois et fer, pour la charpente des Manèges couverts.
Circulaire Ministérielle du 10 Juin, 1849.
1 large Sheet folded, and 2 pages of Text. (Lithog.)

6828 **Batiments Militaires.**
Ameublement des chambres de la troupe.
Circulaire Ministérielle du 30 Septembre, 1853.
2 large Sheets folded, and 6 pages of Text.

6829 **Batiments Militaires.**
Casernement de la Cavalerie—Manèges couverts.
Détails des fermes en bois et fer.
Circulaire Ministérielle du 21 Septembre, 1854.
1 large Sheet folded, and 7 pages of Text.

6830 **Batiments Militaires.**
Circulaires Ministérielles des 23 Septembre, 1840, et 6 janvier, 1842.
2 fol. Pamphlet Paris, 1840–42.
Mécanismes divers pour mouvoir les chassis de croisées dans les Ecuries.
1 large sheet folded.

Barre d'Ecurie et systéme d'attache les chevaux à la mangeoire. 1 large sheet folded.

Plan d'Ensemble d'un Quartier pour un Régiment de Cavalerie. Composé de 5 Escadrons présentant un effectif total de 960 hommes et 814 chevaux. 1 large sheet folded.

6831 **Becker** (M.).

Allgemeine Baukunde des Ingenieurs. Mit Atlas enthaltend 25 gravirte Tafeln.	Compendium of Architecture in general for the use of Engineers. With an Atlas containing 25 engraved Plates.

1 vol. 8vo. & Atlas fol. Stuttgart, 1853.

6832 **Brandon** (Raphael and J. Arthur). An Analysis of Gothick Architecture: illustrated by a series of upwards of seven hundred examples of Doorways, Windows, &c. New edition. 2 vols. 4to. London, 1849.

6833 **Brooks** (S. H.). Modern Architecture: being a series of Designs for Street Elevations, Shop Fronts, Buildings adapted for Towns, and the Embellishment of Gentlemen's Demesnes, for Labourers' Cottages, &c. With specifications, estimates, quantities, prices, and other practical remarks. 1 vol. fol. London, 1852.

6834 **Bullock** (John). American Cottage Builder: a series of designs, plans, and specifications from $200 to $20,000 for homes for the people. 1 vol. 12mo. New York, 1854.

6835 **Carrillo** (D. Mariano). Prontuario Elemental de Construcciones de Arquitectura por el General Director Subinspector de Ingenieros del Egercito en la Isla de Cuba. Edicion Estereotipica. 1 vol. 8vo. & Atlas 4to. (2 *copies.*) Nueva York, 1854.

6836 **Casernes.** See Bâtiments Militaires, Nos. 6824 to 6830, & Barracks, No. 6822.

6837 **Cleaveland and Backus.** Village and Farm Cottages. The Requirements of American Village Homes Considered and Suggested; with designs for such Houses of moderate cost. By Henry Cleaveland, William Backus, and Samuel D. Backus. 1 vol. 8vo. New York, 1856.

6838 **Dempsey** (G. D.). Engineering Examples. Details of Buildings as applicable for Stations, Engine-Houses, Manufactories, Warehouses, Workshops, &c., &c. Containing Elevations, Plans, and Sections, of Buildings for General and Especially for industrial Purposes; details of Iron Columns and Girders, Flooring, Sashes, Stairs, &c., &c. 1 vol. 4to. & Atlas fol. London, 1856.

6839 **Downing** (A. J.). Rural Essays. 1 vol. 8vo. New York, 1853.

6840 **Downing** (A. J.). Cottage Residences; or a series of designs for Rural Cottages and Cottage Villas, and their Gardens and Grounds adapted to North America. Illustrated by numerous Engravings. 4th edition. 1 vol. 8vo. New York, 1853.

6841 **Gwilt** (Joseph). An Encyclopædia of Architecture, Historical, Theoretical, and Practical. 2d edition, with a supplemental View of the Symmetry and stability of Gothic Architecture. 1 vol. 8vo. London, 1851.

6842 **Instruction** du Mars 1834 sur le mode d'exécution des dessins de la Fortification et des Bâtiments Militaires, avec modifications résultant de l'instruction du 22 Mars, 1842, sur la rédaction des Projets. (Lithog.) Octobre, 1849. 1 vol. 4to.

6843 **Instruction** sur le Projet de Bâtiment Militaire. (Lithog.) Novembre, 1850. 1 vol. 4to.

6844 **Instruction** sur le Lever de Bâtiment, approuvée par le conseil d'Instruction le 1er Décembre, 1848. (Lithog.) Novembre, 1849. 1 vol. 4to.

6845 **Moniteur** des Architectes (le). Recueil des Maisons de Ville et de Campagne, architecture urbaine et rurale, édifices Publics, &c. In 4to. Nos. 1–50. Paris, 1847–50.

6846 **Public** Buildings of the U. S. Plans of Public Buildings in course of construction under the Direction of the Secretary of the Treasury, including the specifications thereof. 1 vol. 8vo. Plans in fol. Washington, 1855–58.

6847 **Pugin** (A. Welby). Detaile of antient timber houses of the 15th and 16th centuries selected from those existing at Rouen, Caen, Beauvais, Gisors, Abbeville, Strasbourg, &c., drawn on the spot and etched. 1 vol. 4to. London, 1837.

6848 Report from an official committee on Barrack accommodation for the Army; with the Minutes of Evidence, Appendix, and Index. 1 vol. fol. ———, 1855.

6849 **Revue** Général de l'architecture et des Travaux Publics, publiée sous la direction de M. César Daly architecte. 16 vols. 4to. Paris, 1840–58.

6850 **Reynaud** (Léonce). Traité d'Architecture, contenant des notions générales sur les principes de la construction et sur l'histoire de l'art, premiére partie. Elements des Édifices. 1 vol. 4to. & Atlas fol. Paris, 1850.

6851 **Robinet** aîne. Cours de lavis appliqué à l'enseignement du dessin d'Architecture et des Machines, avec un texte descriptif, Atlas de 50 planches, publié par J. Silveyra, architecte. 2e edition. 1 vol. fol. Paris, 1853.

6852 **Ruskin** (John). Lectures on Architecture and Painting, delivered at Edinburgh, in November, 1853. With Illustrations drawn by the Author. 1 vol. 8vo. New York, 1854.

6853 **Silveyra** (J.). Cours de Lavis, appliqué à l'enseignement du dessin d'architecture et des Machines. See Robinet aîne, No. 6851.

6854 **Sloan** (Samuel). The Model Architect. A series of original designs for Cottages, Villas, Suburban Residences, &c., accompanied by Explanations, Specifications, Estimates, and Elaborate details. 2 vols. 4to. Philadelphia, 1852.

6855 **Stuart** (Charles B.). Naval and Mail Steamers of the United States. Illustrated with thirty-six fine Engravings. 3d edition. 1 vol. 4to. New York, 1855.

6856 **Stuart** (James) and **Revett** (Nicholas). The Antiquities of Athens; and other Monuments of Greece; 2d edition. 1 vol. 18mo. London, 1841.

6857 **Tuileries.** Palais des, facade sur le Jardin (état actuel) offert en prime aux souscripteurs du Moniteur des architectes. One large sheet. Paris, 1856.

6858 **United** States Capitol Extensions, Washington City, D. C. Photographic Plans of the. In sheets.

6859 **Vaux** (Calvert). Villas and Cottages, a series of designs prepared for execution in the United States. Illustrated by 300 Engravings. 1 vol. 8vo. New York, 1857.

6860 **Vienna.** Arsenal at Vienna. 7 Photographs.

6861 **Weiss** (Franz). Lehrbuch der Baukunst zum Gebrauch der k. k. Ingenieurs-Akademie. | An Elementary Treatise upon Architecture for the use of the Academy of Engineers. 1 vol. 4to. & Atlas fol. Vienna, 1854.

Subj. 18. MACHINERY, INSTRUMENTS, APPLIED MECHANICS, AND CARPENTRY.

6862 **American** Engineering. Treatise on American Engineering; illustrated by large and detailed Engravings by F. Mone, Civil Engineer. In four divisions. 1 vol. 4to. & Atlas fol. New York, 1852.

6863 **American** Engineering. Collection of Drawings in detail of the most approved construction of American Machinery with descriptions, Calculations, and specifications, by the American Engineering Society of New York. 1 vol. fol. New York, 1852.

6864 **Andrew** (G. H.). Rudimentary Treatise on Agricultural Engineering; with Illustrations. Vol. I. Buildings. Vol. II. Motive powers and Machinery of the steading. Vol. III. Field Machines and Implements. 3 vols. 18mo. London, 1852–53.

6865 **Appletons'** Cyclopædia of Drawing, designed as a text-book for the Mechanic, Architect, Engineer, and Surveyor. Comprising Geometrical Projection, Mechanical, Arthitectural, and Topographical Drawing, Perspective and Isometry. Edited by W. E. Worthen. 1 vol. roy. 8vo. New York, 1857.

6866 **Ardant** (P.). Études théoriques et expérimentales sur l'établissement des charpentes à grande portée. 1 vol. 4to. Metz, 1840.

6867 **Armengaud & Amouroux.** The Practical Draughtsman's book of industrial design, and Machinist's and Engineer's drawing Companion; forming a complete course of Mechanical Engineering, and Architectural Drawing. Translated from the French of M. Armengaud, the elder, and MM. Armengaud, the younger, and Amouroux. Rewritten and arranged, with additional matter and Plates, selections from and examples of the most useful and generally employed Mechanism of the day. By William Johnson. 1 vol. 4to. New York, 1854.

6868 **Baker** (T.). Elements of Mechanism: elucidating the scientific principles of the practical construction of Machines. 1 vol. 18mo. London, 1852.

6869 **Bardin.** La Pratique des Levers, enseignée par des dessins. 1 vol. fol. obl. No date.

6870 **Bergery** (C. L.). Cours de Machines. See Migout, No. 6884.

6871 **Boileau** (P.). Instruction pratique sur les Machines à Vapeur Construites en France pour les usines. (Lithog.) Juin 1851. 1 vol. 4to.

6872 **Boileau** (P.). Instruction sur l'exécution des Levers d'usines. (Lithog.) Mars 1852. 1 vol. 4to.

6873 **Bourne** (John). Treatise on the screw Propeller, with various suggestions of improvement. 2d edition, revised. 1 vol. 4to. London, 1855.

6874 **Bourne** (John). Treatise on the Steam-Engine. See No. 1477.

6875 **Buchanan.** Practical Examples of modern Tools and Machines; being supplementary to the edition of Buchanan on Mill Work and other Machinery. Edited by George Rennie.
1 8vo. Pamphlet & Atlas fol. London, 1842.

6876 **Cole** (George). Contractor's book of working drawings of Tools and Machines, used in constructing Canals, Railroads, and other works, with Bills of Timber and Iron. Also Tables and data for calculating the cost of earth and other kinds of work.
1 vol. fol. obl. Buffalo, N. Y., 1855.

6877 **Dempsey** (G. D.). Machinery of the Nineteenth Century; illustrated from original drawings, and including the best examples shown at the Exhibition of the Works of Industry of all Nations. Parts 1, 2, 3, 4, 5, & 6. Text in 4to. Plates in fol. London, ——.

6878 **Emy** (A. R.). Description d'un nouveau systéme d'arcs pour les grandes Charpentes exécuté sur un Bâtiment de Vingt métres de largeur.
1 vol. fol. Liége, 1854.

6879 **Fairbairn** (William). Useful Information for Engineers; being a series of Lectures delivered to the Working Engineers of Yorkshire and Lancashire; together with a series of appendices, containing the results of Experimental inquiries into the strength of Materials, the causes of Boiler Explosions, &c. 1 vol. 8vo. London, 1856.

6880 **Girault** (Ch.). Élements de Géométrie appliquée à la Transformation du mouvement dans les Machines. 1 vol. 8vo. Caen, 1858.

6881 **Holtzapffel** (Charles). Turning and Mechanical Manipulation. Intended as a work of general reference and practical Instructions on the lathe, and the various Mechanical pursuits followed by amateurs.
3 vols. 8vo. London, 1846.

6882 **Jariez** (J.). Cours Elémentaire de Mécanique Industrielle, à l'usage des Éléves des Écoles Royales d'art et métiers. 2e édition.
2 vols. 8vo. Paris, 1848.

6883 **Mahan** (D. H.). Industrial Drawing: comprising the description and uses of Drawing Instruments, the construction of Plane figures, the projections and sections of Geometrical solids; architectural Elements, Mechanism, and Topographical drawing; with remarks on the methode of Teaching the subject. 1 vol. 8vo. New York, 1852.

6884 **Migout** (J.-C.) et **Bergery** (C. L.). Cours de Machines à l'usage des officiers d'artillerie, des Ingénieurs et des Praticiens.
1 vol. 8vo. Paris, 1842.

6885 **Mone** (F.). Treatise on American Engineering. See American Engineering, No. 6862.

6886 **Moseley** (Rev. Henry). The Mechanical Principles of Engineering and Architecture. With illustrations on Wood. 1 vol. 8vo. London, 1843.

6887 **Moseley** (Henry). The Mechanical Principles of Engineering and Architecture. First American from the second London edition. With additions by D. H. Mahan, LL. D. With illustrations on Wood.
1 vol. 8vo. New York, 1856.

6888 **Muirhead** (James Patrick). The Origin and Progress of the Mechanical Inventions of James Watt, illustrated by his correspondence with his Friends and the specifications of his Patents.
3 vols. 8vo. London, 1854.

6889 **Practical** Draughtsman's book of industrial design, and Machinist's and Engineer's drawing companion. See No. 6867.

6890 **Programme** du Cours de Mécanique appliquée. (Lithog.) Septembre, 1854. 1 vol. 4to.

6891 **Rankine** (William John Macquorn). Manual of applied Mechanics. With numerous Diagrams. 1 vol. 12mo. London & Glasgow, 1858.

6892 **Regnault** (M. V.). Relation des Expériences entreprises par ordre de Monsieur le Ministre de Travaux Publics et sur la proposition de la Commission Centrale des Machines à Vapeur, pour déterminer les Principales lois et les données numériques qui entrent dans le Calcul des Machines à Vapeur. See Mémoires de l'Academie, vol. 21.

6893 **Report** of the committee on the Machinery of the United States of America. Presented to the House of Commons, in Pursuance of their Address of the 10th July, 1855. 1 vol. fol. London, ——.

6894 **Sewell** (John). Elementary Treatise on Steam and Locomotion; based on the principle of connecting science with practice in a popular form. With Illustrations. (2 vols. in one.) 1 vol. 18mo. London, 1852.

6895 **Watt** (James). Mechanical Inventions. See Muirhead, No. 6888.

Subj. 19. HYDRAULIC CONSTRUCTIONS, CANALS, BRIDGES, &c.

6896 **Belanger** (Professor). Notes sur le cours d'hydraulique. See No. 7171.

6897 **Burnell** (G. R.). Rudiments of Hydraulic Engineering. See Law, No. 6936.

6898 **Clark** (Edwin). The Britannia and Conway Tubular Bridges. With general inquiries on Beams, and on the Properties of Materials used in construction. 2 vols. 8vo. & Atlas fol. London, 1850.

6899 **Darcy** (Henry). Les Fontaines Publiques de la Ville de Dijon, exposition et application des principes à suivre et des formules à employer dans les questions de distribution d'eau ouvrage terminé par un appendice relatif aux fournitures d'eau de plusieurs Villes au filtrage des Eaux et à la fabrication des tuyaux de fonte, de plomb, de tôle et de bitume. 1 vol. 4to. & Atlas 4to. Paris, 1856.

6900 **D'Aubuisson de Voisins** (J. F.). Treatise on Hydraulics, for the use of Engineers, translated from the French and adapted to the English units of Measure, by Joseph Bennett. 1 vol. 8vo. Boston, 1852.

6901 **Du Pont's** Artesian Well, Louisville, Kentucky. Report, analysis, and Medical Properties of its water. With remarks upon the Nature of Artesian Wells. By Prof. J. Lawrence Smith. 1 8vo. Pamphlet. Louisville, 1859.

6902 **Francis** (James B.). Hydraulic Experiments, being a selection from experiments on Hydraulic Motors, on the flow of water over weirs, and in canals of uniform rectangular section and of short length. Made at Lowell, Massachusetts. 1 vol. 4to. Boston, 1855.

6903 **King** (Charles). A Memoir of the construction, cost, and capacity of the Croton Aqueduct, compiled from official documents: together with an account of the civil Celebration of the 14th October, 1842, on occasion of the completion of the Great Work: preceded by a preliminary Essay on ancient and modern Aqueducts. 1 vol. 4to. New York, 1843.

6904 **Latham** (John Herbert). The Construction of wrought Iron Bridges: embracing the practical application of the Principles of Mechanics to wrought Iron Girder Work. With numerous detail Plates. 1 vol. 8vo. Cambridge, 1858.

6905 **Le Creulx** (le Citoyen). Recherches sur la Formation et l'existence des Ruisseaux, Riviéres et Torrens qui circulent sur le Globe Terrestre. 1 vol. 4to. Paris, 1804.

6906 **Matthews** (William). An Historical and scientific description of the mode of supplying London with water; and a particular account of the different Companies so engaged with an Exposition of the attempts to adopt other modes; &c., with 18 Plates. 1 vol. 8vo. London, 1841.

6907 **Minard** (M.). Cours de construction des ouvrages qui etablissent la Navigation des Riviéres et des canaux, professé à l'École des Ponts et chaussées de 1832 à 1841.
1 vol. 4to. & Atlas. Paris, 1841.

6908 **Neville** (John). Hydraulic Tables, Coefficients the discharge of water from orifices, notches, weirs, Pipes, and Rivers.
1 vol. 8vo. London, 1853.

6909 **New York.** Report of Commissioners relative to the Encroachment and Preservation of the Harbor of New York. See Senate Doc., No. 3, 1856.

6910 **New York.** The same.
1 vol. 8vo. Albany, 1857. Senate Doc., No. 40.

6911 **Palmer** (Henry R.). Report on the Improvement of the Rivers Mersey and Irwell, between Liverpool and Manchester, describing the means of adapting them for the Navigation of Sea-going Vessels.
1 vol. 8vo. London, 1840.

6912 **Paramelle** (M. l'Abbé). L'art de découvrir les sources.
1 vol. 8vo. Paris, 1856.

6913 **Public** Works. Papers and Practical Illustrations of Public Works of recent construction, both British and American. Supplementary to previous Publications. 1 vol. roy. 8vo. London, 1856.

6914 **Rennie** (Sir John). The Theory, Formations, and Construction of British and Foreign Harbours. With one hundred and twenty-three Engravings.
2 vols. fol. London, 1854.

6915 **Schramke** (T.). Description of the New York Croton Aqueduct, in English, German, and French. With twenty plates.
1 vol. 4to. New York, 1846.

6916 **Smith** (R. Baird). Italian Irrigation, being a Report on the Agricultural Canals of Piedmont and Lombardy, addressed to the Honourable the Court of Directors of the East India Company. 2d edition.
2 vols. 8vo. & Atlas fol. Edinburgh, 1855.

6917 **Smyth** (Prof. Piazzi). On Raising Water for the purposes of Irrigation in the Colonies. (From the Practical Mechanic's Journal of November 1st and December 1st, 1852.) 1 8vo. Pamphlet. London, 1853.

6918 **Tidal** Harbours Commission. First and second Reports of the Commissioners, with minutes of Evidence, Appendices, Supplement and Index.
5 parts fol. London, 1845–48.

6919 **Tower** (F. B.). Illustrations of the Croton Aqueduct.
1 vol. small fol. New York, 1843.

Subj. 20. CIVIL ENGINEERING.

6920 **Annales** des Ponts et chaussées. Mémoires et Documents relatifs á l'art des Constructions et au service de l'ingénieur ; Lois, ordonnances et autres Actes. 2e série. 20 vols. 8vo. Paris, 1841–50.

6921 **Annales** des Ponts et Chaussées. 3e série. 16 vols. 8vo. Paris, 1851–58.

6922 **Annales** (Nouvelles) de la Construction. Publication rapide et économique des documents les plus récents et les plus interessants relatifs à la construction Française et Étrangére, destinée aux Ingénieurs, Architectes, Conducteurs, Agents Voyers, Mécaniciens, Industriels, Artistes, Élèves des Écoles, Entrepreneurs, Ouvriers. C. A. Oppermann Ingénieur des Ponts et Chaussées, Directeur. (Nos. 5 & 10, of vol. 2d wanting.) 2 vols. fol. Paris, 1855–56.

6923 **Becker** (M.). Der Straszen und Eisenbahnbau, mit besonderer Rücksicht auf die neuesten Constructionen. | On Roads and Railways, with particular Consideration of the latest Constructions. 1 vol. 8vo. & Atlas fol. Stuttgart, 1855.

6924 **Byrne** (Oliver). The Practical Model Calculator, for the Engineer, Mechanic, Machinist, Manufacturer of Engine-Work, Naval Architect, Miner, and Millwright. 1 vol. 8vo. Philadelphia, 1852,

6925 **Byrne** (Oliver). Pocket-Book for Railroad and Civil Engineers, containing new, exact, and concise methods of laying out Railroad Curves, Switches, Frog Angles, and Crossings ; the Staking out of work, Levelling ; the calculation of Cuttings and Embankments, Earthwork, &c. 1 vol. 18mo. New York, 1856.

6926 **Clough** (A. Bryant). The Contractor's Manual and Builder's Price-Book, designed to elucidate the method of ascertaining correctly the value and quantity of every description of work and materials used in the art of building, &c. 1 vol. 18mo. New York, 1855.

6927 **Endrés** (E.). Manuel du Conducteur des Ponts et Chaussées, rédigé d'aprés le nouveau Programme Officiel, avec figures dans le texte et Planches gravées. 2 vols. 8vo. Paris, 1854.

6928 **Fairbairn** (Wm.). Useful Information for Engineers. See Fairbairn, No. 6879.

6929 **Ghega** (Ch. de). Atlas Pittoresque du chemin de fer du Semmering, précédé d'un aperçu historique et statistique sur les chemins de fer en Exploitation en Autriche. 1 vol. fol. obl. Vienne, 1854.

6930 **Ghega** (Carl Ritter Von). Uebersicht der Hauptfortschritte des Eisenbahnwesens in dem Jahrzehende 1840–1850, und die ergebnisse der Probefahren auf einer streke der Staatsbahn ueber den Semmering in Oesterreich. 3te verbesserte und vermehrte auflage. | Review of the Principal improvements that have been made in Railroad Constructions from 1840 to 1850, with the results of trial trips upon the Semmering Railroad in Austria. 3d edition revised and enlarged. 1 vol. 8vo. & Atlas fol. obl. Vienna, 1853.

6931 **Hand-Book** for Engineers and Architects, or Collection of Tabels, Principles, and Formulas, relating to Mathematics, &c. (In the Russian language.) 1st vol. 16mo. St. Petersburgh, 1854.

6932 **Haskoll** (W. Davis). Railway Construction from the Setting out of the Centre line to the Completion of the Works; containing instructions for ranging Curves and setting out lines and levels in Earthworks, permanent Way, Bridges and Viaducts on the Square, on the Skew, and on Curves. A Treatise on taking borings; with practical rules for designing works, and getting out working drawings of Masonry and Brickwork, Timber, Wrought Iron, and Cast Iron, and examples of Specifications and Tables for Earthwork. Illustrated by 250 Plates and Diagrams of executed works. 2 vols. roy. 8vo. London, 1857.

6933 **Haskoll** (W. Davis). The Practice of Engineering Field Work applied to land, Hydrographic and Hydraulic Surveying and Levelling, for Railways, Canals, Harbours, Towns' water supply, ranging curves and centre lines. Gauging streams, and Levelling Instruments, and the practical application of Trigonometrical Tables. Illustrated by numerous Plans and Diagrams. 1 vol. 8vo. London, 1858.

6934 **Journal** of Engineering. Published by authority of the Chief Engineer. (In the Russian language.) (Part 1st of vol. 25, wanting.) 40 vols. & 1st part of vol. 41, in 8vo. St. Petersburg, 1826–54.

6935 **Köszegh** (Carl Martong de). Versuche über den Seitendruck der Erde, und verbunden mit einer theoretischen abhandlung über diesen Gegenstand nach Coulomb und Français, nebst einer Nachweisung älterer Versuche dieser Art.

Experiments on the lateral pressure of earth, accompanied by the Theoretical treatise on this subject of Coulomb and Français, with reference also to older Experiments on the Subject.

1 vol. 4to. & Atlas 4to. Vienna, 1828.

6936 **Law** (Henry). The Rudiments of Civil Engineering, and the Rudiments of Hydraulic Engineering, by G. R. Burnell. Vol. III. Parts I. & II. 2 vols. 18mo. London, 1852.

6937 **Michon** (Capitaine). Stabilité des Constructions. See Michon, Nos. 6957, 6958, 6959.

6938 **Murray** (John) .Treatise on the Stability of Retaining Walls. Elucidated by Engravings and Diagrams. Part 1st, 8vo. London, 1855.

6939 **Parnell** (Sir Henry). Treatise on Roads wherein the Principles on which Roads should be made, are explained and Illustrated, by the Plans, specifications, and contracts made use of by Thomas Telford, Esq., on the Holy Head Road. 1 vol. 8vo. London, 1833.

6940 **Perdonnet** (Auguste). Traité élémentaire des chemins de fer. 2 vols. 8vo. Paris, 1855–56.

6941 **Perdonnet** (A.) **et Polonceau** (Camille). Portefeuille de l'Ingénieur des chemins de fer. 1 vol. Texte. 1 vol. Documents. 1 vol. Legendes explicatives des Planches. 1 vol. Appendices. 4 vols. 8vo. & Atlas fol. Paris, 1843–46.

6942 **Poncelet.** Examen historique et Critique des principales Théories concernant l'Équilibre des Voûtes. 1 4to. Pamphlet. Paris, 1852.

6943 **Practical** Engineering. Papers on Practical Engineering prepared by officers of the United States Corps of Engineers.
Nos. 1 to 4. Vol. 1st in 8vo. Washington, 1841–49.
Nos. 5 & 6. Vol. 2d in 8vo. Washington, 1850–57.

6944 **Programme** du Cours de Constructions. (Lithog.) Septembre 1854. 1 vol. 4to.

6945 **Public Works,** Ireland. Third Annual Report from the Board of Public Works in Ireland. With Maps and Plans. Ordered, by the House of Commons, to be printed, 27 March, 1835. 1 vol. fol. ——, ——.

6946 **Report** (9th) of the Commissioners for Roads and Bridges in the Highlands of Scotland. Ordered, by the House of Commons, to be printed, 19 April, 1821. 1 vol. fol. ——, ——.

6947 **Rondelet** (de Jean). Traité théorique et pratique de l'art de bâtir. Supplément, par G. Abel Blouet. See Rondelet, No. 1853.
2 vols. 4to. (Bound in one) & Atlas fol. Paris, 1847–48.

6948 **Royal** Engineers. Papers on Subjects connected with the duties of the Corps of Royal Engineers. Contributed by Members of the Royal and East India Company's Engineers, and Edited by a Committee of Royal Engineers. New series. 8 vols. 8vo. London, 1851–59.

6949 **Ruskin** (John). The Stones of Venice. With Illustrations drawn by the Author. 3 vols. 8vo. London, 1851–53.

6950 **Semmering** Railway. See Nos. 6929, 6930, 6952, 6954.

6951 **Stier** (Gustav). Grundlage der praktischen Baukunst. Dritter Theil. Nachträge zu den Vorlege-Blättern für Maurer und Zimmerleute, in 37 lithographirten Tafeln, mit Erläuterungen. | Practical Treatise on the art of building. Third Part. Appendix to the work for Masons and Carpenters, containing 37 lithographic Plates with Explanations.
1 vol. fol. Berlin, 1844.

6952 **Views.** Ansichten auf der Eisenbahn über den Semmering. | Views of Semmering Railway.
1 No. fol., in 8 sheets.

6953 **Vose** (George L.). Hand-Book of Railroad Construction ; for the use of American Engineers. Containing the necessary Rules, Tables, and Formulæ for the Location, Construction, Equipment, and Management of Railroads, as built in the United States. With 158 Illustrations.
1 vol. 8vo. Boston, 1857.

6954 **Vues,** Tunnels, Viaducts, &c., du chemin de fer du Semmering.
14 sheets fol. ——, ——.

Subj. 21. WORKS ON MATERIALS.

6955 **Bresse** (M.). Recherches Analytiques sur la Flexion et la Résistance des piéces courbes, accompagnées de Tables numériques pour calculer la poussée des arcs chargés de poids d'une maniére quelconque, et leur pression maximum sous une charge uniformement repartie.
1 vol. 4to. Paris, 1854.

6956 **Fairbairn** (William). On the application of Cast and Wrought Iron to building purposes. 1 vol. 8vo. New York, 1854.

6957 **Michon** (Capitaine). Stabilité des Coustructions. Instruction sur la Résistance des Matériaux, suivie d'applications aux piéces droites et aux fermes de charpente des bâtiments. (3eme partie.) (Lithog.) Janvier, 1848. 1 vol. 4to. ——, ——.

6958 **Michon** (Capitaine). Stabilité des Constructions. Instruction sur la Résistance des Matériaux. Tables relatives aux piéces droites et aux fermes de charpente. (Lithog.) Juin, 1848. 1 vol. fol. ——, ——.

6959 **Michon** (Capitaine). Stabilité des Constructions. Instruction sur la Résistance des Matériaux. Tables et Planches relatives aux piéces droites et aux fermes de charpente. (3eme partie.) (Lithog.) Novembre, 1848. 1 vol. fol. ——, ——.

Subj. 22. WORKS ON WARMING AND VENTILATING.

6960 **Audot** (L. E.). L'art de chauffer par le Thermosiphon ou Calorifére à eau chaude les serres et les Habitations suivi d'un article sur le Calorifére à aîr chaud. 2e édition. 1 vol. 4to. Paris, 1857.

6961 **Boudin** (J.-Ch.-M.). De la Ventilation et du chauffage des Hôpitaux, des Églises et des Prisons. 1 8vo. Pamphlet. Paris, 1854.

6962 **Grassi** (C.). Hygiène Publique. Chauffage et Ventilation des Hôpitaux. Étude du Systéme de chauffage et de Ventilation établi par M. le docteur Van Hecke, dans l'un des Pavillons de l'Hôpital Beaujon.
1 8vo. Pamphlet. Paris, 1857.

6963 **Papillon** (M. le D[r].). De la ventilation appliquée à l'hygiène Militaire.
1 8vo. Pamphlet. Paris, 1849.

Subj. 23. LAW OF NATURE AND NATIONS, TREATIES, &c.

6964 **Heineccii** (Joh. Gottlieb). Operum at universam juris Prudentiam, Philosophiam et Litteras Humaniores pertinentium.
8 vols. 4to. Genevæ, 1744–48.

6965 **Puffendorf** (Baron). The Law of Nature and Nations. Eight Books. Done into English by Basil Kennett, to which are added all the large Notes of Barbeyrac, translated from the best edition; together with large Tables to the whole. 4th edition, carefully corrected. To which is now prefixed Barbeyrac's prefatory discourse.
1 vol. fol. London, 1729.

Subj. 24. GOVERNMENT AND POLITICS.

6966 **Adams** (John). The works of, with a life of the Author, notes and illustrations, by his Grandson, Charles Francis Adams.
10 vols. 8vo. Boston, 1850–56.

6967 **American Archives.** See No. 6987.

6968 **Annals** of the Congress of the United States, from the first Congress to the eighteenth, comprising the period from March 3, 1789, to May 27, 1824, inclusive. 42 vols. 8vo. Washington, 1834–56.

6969 **Benton** (Thomas H.). Thirty Years View; or a History of the working of the American Government for thirty years, from 1820 to 1850, chiefly taken from the Congress Debates, the Private Papers of General Jackson, and the Speeches of Ex-Senator Benton, with his actual view of men and affairs: with Historical Notes and Illustrations, and some notices of Eminent deceased Cotemporaries. 2 vols. 8vo. New York, 1856.

6970 **Bledsoe** (Albert Taylor). An Essay on Liberty and Slavery.
1 vol. 12mo. Philadelphia, 1856.

6971 **Brougham** (Henry Lord). Political Philosophy. Part I. Principles of Government-Monarchical Government. Part II. Aristocracy-Aristocratic Governments. Part III. Democracy-Mixed Monarchy. 3d edition. 3 vols. 8vo. London, 1853.

6972 **Calhoun** (John C.). The Works of, edited by Richard K. Crallé. 6 vols. 8vo. New York, 1853–56.

6973 **Claims** between the United States and Great Britain. Report of decisions of the Commission of Claims under the Convention of February 8, 1853, between the United States and Great Britain, transmitted to the Senate by the President of the United States, August 11, 1856. 1 vol. 8vo. Washington, 1856.

6974 **Diplomatic** correspondence of the United States of America, from the signing of the definitive Treaty of Peace, 10th September, 1783, to the adoption of the Constitution, March 4, 1789. Being the letters of the Presidents of Congress, the Secretary for Foreign affairs, American Ministers at Foreign Courts, Foreign Ministers near Congress, &c., &c. 3 vols. 8vo. Washington, 1837.

6975 **Filmer** (Sir Robert). Free-holders grand inquest, touching our Sovereign Lord the King and his Parliament. To which are added observations upon Forms of Government, &c. 1 vol. 16mo. London, 1679.

6976 **Hamilton** (Alexander). The Works of, comprising his correspondence and his Political and Official Writings, exclusive of the Federalist, Civil and Military. Published from the Original Manuscripts deposited in the Department of State, by order of the Joint Library Committee of Congress. Edited by John C. Hamilton. 7 vols. 8vo. New York, 1850–51.

6977 **Indiana.** Documents of the General Assembly of Indiana at the 37th sess. commencing Thursday, Jan. 6, 1853. (Part first). 1 vol. 8vo. Indianapolis, 1853.

6978 **Jefferson** (Thomas). Writings: being his Autobiography, correspondence, Reports, Messages, Addresses, and other writings, Official and Private. Published by order of the Joint Committee of Congress on the Library, from the Original Manuscripts deposited in the Department of State. With explanatory notes, Tables of contents, and a copious index to each volume, as well as a general index to the whole, by the Editor, H. A. Washington. 9 vols. 8vo. Washington, 1853–54.

6979 **New York.** Documents of the Senate of the State of New York, 75th, 76th, 77th, 78th, 79th, 80th, and 81st sessions. 21 vols. 8vo. Albany, 1852–58.

6980 **New York.** Journals of the Senate of the State of New York at their 77th, 78th, 79th, 80th, & 81st sessions. 5 vols. 8vo. Albany, 1854–58.

6981 **New York.** Documents of the Assembly of the State of New York, 75th, 76th, 77th, 78th, 79th, 80th, & 81st sessions. 44 vols. 8vo. Albany, 1852–58.

6982 **New York.** Journals of the Assembly of the State of New York at their 77th, 78th, 79th, 80th, & 81st session. 6 vols. 8vo. Albany, 1854–58.

6983 **New York.** Reports of the Various officers of the State of New York will be found in the Documents of the State.

6984 **Seward** (William H.). The Works of, Edited by George E. Baker. 3 vols. 8vo. New York, 1853.

6985 **Sidney** (Algernon). Discourses concerning Government. Published from an original Manuscript. 2d edition carefully corrected. To which is added, the paper he delivered to the Sheriffs immediately before his death. And an alphabetical Table. 1 vol. fol. London, 1705.

6986 **Tucker** (Josiah). Treatise concerning Civil Government, in three parts. 1 vol. 8vo. London, 1781.

6987 **United States.** American Archives: fifth series, containing a Documentary History of the United States of America, from the Declaration of Independence, July 4, 1776, to the definitive Treaty of Peace with Great Britain, September 3, 1783.
3 vols. fol. (1st and 2d vols. in triplicate.) Washington, 1848–53.

6988 **United States.** Executive Documents of the House of Representatives of the, from the first session 32d Congress to the first session 35th Congress, both sessions inclusive.
102 vols. in 8vo. & 4to. Washington, 1852–58.

6989 **United States.** Miscellaneous Documents of the House of Representatives of the, from the first session 32d Congress, to the first session 35th Congress, both sessions inclusive. 10 vols. 8vo. Washington, 1852–58.

6990 **United States.** Reports of Committees of the House of Representatives of the, from the first session 32d Congress to the first session 35th Congress, both sessions inclusive. 18 vols. 8vo. Washington, 1852–58

6991 **United States.** Reports from the Court of Claims, submitted to the House of Representatives of the, from the first session 34th Congress to the first session 35th Congress, both sessions inclusive.
6 vols. 8vo. Washington, 1856–58.

6992 **United States.** Journals of the House of Representatives of the, from the first session 32d Congress to the first session 35th Congress, both sessions inclusive. 8 vols. 8vo. Washington, 1851–58.

6993 **United States.** Executive Documents of the Senate of the, from the first session 34th Congress to the first session 35th Congress, both sessions inclusive. 52 vols. in 8vo. & 4to. Washington, 1856–58.

6994 **United States.** Miscellaneous Documents of the Senate of the, from the first session 34th Congress to the first session 35th Congress, both sessions inclusive. 6 vols. 8vo. Washington, 1856–58.

6995 **United States.** Reports of the Committees of the Senate of the, from the first session 34th Congress to the first session 35th Congress, both sessions inclusive. 5 vols. 8vo. Washington, 1856–58.

6996 **United States.** Journals of the Senate of the, from the first session 34th Congress to the first session 35th Congress, both sessions inclusive.
3 vols. 8vo. Washington, 1856–58.

Subj. 25. POLITICAL ECONOMY, METROLOGY, FINANCE, COMMERCE, &c.

6997 **Gregg** (Josiah). Commerce of the Prairies: or the Journal of a Santa Fé Trader, during eight Expeditions across the great Western Prairies, and a Residence of nearly nine years in Northern Mexico. Illustrated with Maps and Engravings. 2 vols. 12mo. New York, 1844.

6998 **Van Sommer** (James). Tables exhibiting the various fluctuations in three per cent consols, in every month during each year from 1789 to 1847, inclusive, with ruled pages for their continuance to 1857. To which are annexed the amount of Navy, Victualling and Exchequer Bills funded. 1 vol. 4to. London, 1848.

Subj. 26. LAWS, LAW TREATISES, COMMENTARIES, AND REPORTS.

6999 **Brightly** (Frederick C.) An Analytical Digest of the Laws of the United States from the adoption of the Constitution to the end of the Thirty-fourth Congress, 1789–1857.
1 vol. roy. 8vo. (2 *copies.*) Philadelphia, 1858.

7000 **Comyns** (Sir John). Digest of the Laws of England.
6 vols. fol. London, 1762–76.

7001 **Constitution** of the United States of America, with the amendments thereto: to which are added Jefferson's Manual of Parliamentary practice and the standing Rules and Orders for conducting business in the House of Representatives and Senate of the United States.
1 vol. 8vo. Washington, 1854.

7002 **Cotelle** (Professeur). Cours de droit administratif. See No. 7170.

7003 **Curtis** (George Ticknor). History of the Origin, Formation, and Adoption of the Constitution of the United States; with notices of its principal Framers. 1st vol. 8vo. New York, 1854.

7004 **Dictionnaire** de l'administration Française par M. Maurice Block, avec la Collaboration de MM. Alauzet, Andral, &c., &c., &c.
1 vol. roy. 8vo. Paris, 1856.

7005 **Dunlop** (James). Digest of the general Laws of the United States, with references to the Acts repealed, supplied, or modified ; and notes of the Decisions and Dicta of the Supreme Court of the Union upon their construction. 1 vol. roy. 8vo. Philadelphia, 1856.

7006 **Hurd** (John C.). Topics of Jurisprudence connected with conditions of Freedom and Bondage. 1 vol. 8vo. New York, 1856.

7007 **Kent** (James). Commentaries on American Law. 9th edition.
4 vols. 8vo. Boston, 1858.

7008 **New York.** Code of Criminal Procedure of the State of New York. Reported complete by the Commissioners on Practice and Pleadings.
1 vol. 8vo. Albany, 1850.

7009 **New York.** The Code of Procedure of the State of New York ; as amended by the Legislature, by an act passed July 10, 1851.
1 vol. 8vo. Albany, 1851.

7010 **New York.** Laws of the State of New York passed at the 58th session, 1835, to the 81st session, 1858, inclusive.
26 vols. 8vo. Albany, 1835–58.

7011 **Opinions** (official) of the Attorneys General of the United States, advising the President and Heads of Departments in relation to their official, and Expounding the Constitution, Treaties with Foreign Governments, and with Indian Tribes, and the Public Laws of the Country.
8 vols. 8vo. Washington, 1852–58.

7012 **Selwyn** (William). An Abridgment of the Law of Nisi Prius, in two volumes. With notes and references to the Decisions of the Courts of this Country, by Henry Wheaton, Thomas J. Wharton, and Edward E. Law. 6th American edition with a supplement containing notes of recent English and American Authorities. By J. G. Marvin.
2 vols 8vo. Philadelphia, 1853.

7013 **United States** of America. Statutes at Large and Treaties of the, from the Organization of the Government in 1789, to March 3, 1859, arranged in chronological order. 11 vols. 8vo. Boston, 1845–59.

Subj. 27. MATHEMATICS IN GENERAL.

7014 **Annales** (Nouvelles) de Mathématiques. Journal des Candidats aux Écoles Polytechnique et Normale; rédigé par M. Terquem et M. Gerono. Vols. 14, 15, 16, 17 & 18 in 8vo. Paris, 1855–59.

7015 **Comte** (Auguste). Philosophy of Mathematics. Translated from the cours de Philosophie positive by W. M. Gillespie LL. D. 1 vol. 8vo. New York, 1858.

7016 **Davies** (Charles) **& Peck** (William G.). Mathematical Dictionary and Cyclopedia of Mathematical Science. 1 vol. 8vo. New York, 1855.

7017 **Duvignau** (V.-J.). Problémes de Mathématiques et de Physique pour la préparation à la composition contenant la plupart des Questions proposées aux différent concours. 1 vol. 12mo. Paris, 1854.

7018 **Elementary** Course of Mathematics, prepared for the use of the Royal Military Academy. By order of the Master-General and Board of Ordnance. 3 vols. 8vo. London, 1853.

Vol. I. containing Arithmetic and Algebra. By W. Rutherford. Application of Algebra to Geometry, plane and spherical Trigonometry, Mensuration, &c. By Stephen Fenwick. Differential and Integral Calculus. By W. Rutherford.

Vol. II. Geometry, Conic sections. By T. S. Davies & Stephen Fenwick, with an appendix, containing Algebraical demonstrations and Astronomical Problems. By Dr. Rutherford.

Vol. III. Mechanics, including Statics and Dynamics, &c. By J. F. Heather. Geodesy, including Practical Astronomy. By Capt. Yolland.

7019 **Journal** de Mathématiques pures et appliquées, ou Recueil Mensuel de Mémoires sur les diverses parties des Mathématiques; publié par Joseph Liouville. Vol. 20th in 4to. Paris, 1855.

7020 **Journal.** The same. 2ᵉ série. Vol 1st in 4to. Paris, 1856.

7021 **Lettres** sur les Mathématiques et l'Enseignement. 1 vol. 8vo. Paris, 1855.

7022 **Mathematical** Monthly. (The), Edited by J. D. Runkle, A. M. Vol. 1st in 4to. Cambridge, 1859.

7023 **Mathematical** Tracts, of Lawson, Burrow, Brinkley, Gompertz, Playfair, Woodhouse, Milner, Babbage, Horner, &c. (A collection of papers bound in two volumes.) 2 vols. 4to. ——, ——.

7024 **Mélanges** Mathématiques et Astronomiques, tirés du Bulletin Physico-Mathématique de l'Academie Impériale des Sciences de St. Petersbourg. 2 vols. 8vo. St. Petersbourg, 1850–57.

7025 **Tondeur** (Alphonse). Questionnaires et Exercices Préparatoires à la composition et à l'examen du Baccalauréat és Sciences suivis d'un recueil de Compositions. 1 vol. 12mo. Paris, 1854.

Subj. 28. ARITHMETIC.

7026 **Lionnet.** Éléments d'Arithmétique, à l'usage des Candidats au Baccalauréat és sciences et aux Écoles du Gouvernement. 3e édition, rédigée conformément au Programme Officiel des Lycées. 1 vol. 8vo. Paris, 1857.

7027 **Lionnet.** Complément des Éléments d'Arithmétique deuxième Tirage augmenté des approximations numériques. 1 vol. 8vo. Paris, 1857.

7028 **Sonnet** (H.). Problèmes et Exercices d'Arithmétique et d'Algèbre sur les principales questions usuelles relatives au commerce, à la Banque aux Fonds Publics, aux Établissement de Prévoyance à l'Industrie, aux sciences appliquées, &c. 2 vols. 8vo. Paris, 1858.

7029 **Vieille** (J.). Théorie générale des approximations numériques, suivie d'une application à la résolution des équations numériques. 2e édition, revue, corrigée et augmentée. 1 vol. 8vo. Paris, 1854.

Subj. 29. ALGEBRA.

7030 **Bertrand** (Joseph). Traité d'Algébre. 2e édition conforme aux derniers Programmes officiels de l'enseignement dans les Lycées. 1 vol. 8vo. Paris, 1855.

7031 **Serret** (J.-A.). Cours d'Algébre supérieure, professé à la Faculté des sciences de Paris. 1 vol. 8vo. Paris, 1849.

7032 **Sonnet** (H.). Problèmes et Exercices d'Arithmétique et d'Algébre. See Sonnet, No. 7028.

Subj. 30. GEOMETRY.

7033 **Legendre** (A. M.). Elements of Geometry and Trigonometry. Revised edition by Charles Davies. 1 vol. 8vo. New York, 1853.

7034 **Perkins** (George R.). Plane and Solid Geometry. To which is added plane and spherical Trigonometry and Mensuration. Accompanied with all the necessary Logarithmic and Trigonometric Tables. 1 vol. 8vo. New York, 1855.

Subj. 31. PERSPECTIVE AND DESCRIPTIVE GEOMETRY.

7035 **Alvord** (Benjamin). The Tangencies of Circles and of Spheres. (Smithsonian Contributions to Knowledge.) 1 4to. Pamphlet. (2 *copies.*) Washington, 1855.

7036 **Amiot** (A.). Leçons Nouvelles de Géométrie descriptive. 1 vol. 8vo. Paris, 1853.

7037 **Bardin.** Notes et croquis de Géométrie descriptive. 2ᵉ édition, revue, corrigée et augmentée. 1 vol. fol. Paris, 1837.

7038 **Delaistre** (Louis). Cours complet de dessin linéaire gradué et progressif. 1 vol. 4to. obl. Paris, 1855.

7039 **Engel** (Ferdinand). Axonometrical Projections of the most important Geometrical Surfaces. Drawings in descriptive Geometry. Serving at the same time as a catalogue of models executed according to the aforesaid Projections, with nine Plates. 1 fol. Pamphlet. (2 *copies.*) New York, 1855.

7040 **Gournerie** (Jules de la). Traité de Perspective linéaire contenant les tracés pour les tableaux Plans et courbes, les Bas-Reliefs et les Décorations Théatrales, avec une Théorie des effets de Perspective. 1 vol. 4to. & Atlas fol. Paris, 1859.

7041 **Heather** (J. F.). An Elementary Treatise on descriptive Geometry with a Theory of Shadows and of Perspective: extracted from the French of G. Monge. To which is added a description of the Principles and practice of Isometrical Projection. 1 vol. 18mo. & Atlas 4to. London, 1851.

7042 **Jopling** (Joseph). Practice of Isometrical Perspective. A new edition, improved. 1 vol. 8vo. London, ——.

7043 **Leroy** (C. F. A.). Traité de Stéréotomie comprenant les applications de la Géométrie descriptive à la théorie des ombres, la Perspective linéaire, la Gnomonique, la coupe des prierres et la Charpente, avec un Atlas composé de 74 planches. 1 vol. 4to. & Atlas fol. Liége, 1845.

7044 **Olivier** (Théodore). Cours de Géométrie descriptive. 2e édition, (en trois parties). 1 vol. 4to. & Atlas 4to. Paris, 1854.

7045 **Olivier** (Théodore). See Tresca, No. 2472.

7046 **Schooler** (Samuel). Elements of descriptive Geometry. Part I. the Point, the Straight line and the Plane.
1 vol. 4to. (5 *copies.*) Richmond, Va., 1853.

7047 **Sopwith** (T.). Treatise on Isometrical Drawing as applicable to Geological and Mining Plans, Picturesque delineations of ornamental Grounds. Perspective Views and working Plans of Buildings and Machinery and to general purposes of Civil Engineering. 2d edition, 35 Engravings.
1 vol. 8vo. London, 1838.

7048 **Thierry.** Méthode Graphique et Géométrique ou le dessin Linéaire appliqué aux arts en général, et en particulier à la projection des ombres, à la pratique de la coupe des Pierres, à la Perspective linéaire, et aux cinq ordres d'architecture. 2e édition, revue et corrigée par F.-C.-M. Marie. 1 vol. 8vo. Paris, 1846.

7049 **Tripon** (J.-B.). Études de Projections, d'Ombres et de Lavis à l'usage de toutes les Écoles, des Architectes et des Mécaniciens, ouvrage divisé en quatre parties :
1er partie. Études des projections orthogonales.
2e partie. Études des projections obliques.
3e partie. Études des ombres.
4e partie. Cours élémentaire de lavis appliqué à l'enseignement du dessin, des machines, de l'architecture, &c
1 vol. 8vo. & Atlas fol. Paris, 1848.

Subj. 32. TRIGONOMETRY.

7050 **Bourdon.** Trigonométrie rectiligne et sphérique.
1 vol. 8vo. Paris, 1854.

7051 **Perkins** (George R.). Plane Trigonometry, and its application to Mensuration and land Surveying, accompanied with all the necessary Logarithmic and Trigonometric Tables. 1 vol. 8vo. New York, 1853.

7052 **Serret** (J.-A.). Traité de Trigonométrie. 1 vol. 8vo. Paris, 1850.

Subj. 33. ANALYTICAL GEOMETRY.

7053 **Bourdon.** Application de l'Algébre à la Géométrie. 4e édition. 1 vol. 8vo. Paris, 1837.

7054 **Chasles.** Traité de Géométrie Supérieure. 1 vol. 8vo. Paris, 1852.

7055 **Loomis** (Elias). Elements of Analytical Geometry and of the Differential and Integral Calculus. 6th edition. 1 vol. 8vo. New York, 1854.

7056 **Mannheim** (A.). Transformation des propriétés métriques des figures à l'aide de la Théorie des polaires réciproques. 1 vol. 8vo. Paris, 1857.

Subj. 34. METHOD OF FLUXIONS, DIFFERENTIAL AND INTEGRAL CALCULUS.

7057 **Babinet et Housel.** Calculs pratiques appliqués aux sciences d'observation. 1 vol. 8vo. Paris, 1857.

7058 **Carmichael** (Rev. Robert). Treatise on the Calculus of Operations: designed to facilitate the Processes of the Differential and Integral Calculus and the Calculus of finite differences. 1 vol. 8vo London, 1855.

7059 **Courtenay** (Edward H.). Treatise on the Differential and Integral Calculus, and on the Calculus of Variations. 1 vol. 8vo. (3 *copies.*) New York, 1855.

7060 **Didion** (Is.) Calcul des Probabilités. See Didion, No. 6374.

7061 **Duhamel.** Cours d'analyse de l'École Polytechnique. 2e édition. 2 vols. 8vo. Paris, 1847.

7062 **Duhamel.** Éléments de Calcul Infinitésimal. 2 vols. 8vo. Paris, 1856.

7063 **Emerson** (W.). The Method of Increments. Wherein the Principles are demonstrated; and the Practice thereof shewn in the Solution of Problems. 1 vol. 4to. London, 1763.

7064 **Gauss** (Ch.-F.) Méthode des Moindres Carrés, Mémoires sur la Combinaison des Observations. Traduits en français et publiés avec l'autorisation de l'auteur, par J. Bertrand. 1 vol. 8vo. Paris, 1855.

7065 **Gregory** (D. F.). Examples of the processes of the Differential and Integral Calculus. 2d edition, edited by William Walton. 1 vol. 8vo. Cambridge, 1846.

7066 **Haddon** (James). Examples and Solutions in the Differential Calculus. 1 vol. 18mo. London, 1851.

7067 **Hamilton** (Sir William Rowan). Lectures on Quaternions: containing a Systematic Statement of a new Mathematical method; of which the Principles were communicated in 1843 to the Royal Irish Academy; and which has since formed the subject of successive courses of Lectures, delivered in 1848 and subsequent years, in the Halls of Trinity College, Dublin: with numerous illustrative diagrams, and with some Geometrical and Physical applications. 1 vol. 8vo. Dublin, 1853.

7068 **Laurent** (l'Abbé). Traité de calcul différentiel. 1 vol. 8vo. Paris, 1853.

7069 **Peirce** (Benjamin). An Elementary Treatise on Curves, Functions, and Forces; containing Analytical Geometry, differential Calculus, Calculus of imaginary Quantities, Residual Calculus, and Integral Calculus. New edition. 2 vols. 12mo. Boston, 1846–52.

7070 **Price** (Bartholomew). Treatise on Infinitesimal Calculus; containing differential and Integral Calculus, Calculus of Variations, applications to Algebra and Geometry, and Analytical Mechanics. 3 vols. 8vo. Oxford, 1852–56.

7071 **Reynaud** (E.). Résolution des Questions relatives à l'épreuve pratique d'aprés le Programme officiel du 20 Avril, 1853. 1 vol. 8vo. Paris, 1855.

7072 **Ritter** (Élie). Manuel théorique et pratique de l'application de la Méthode des moindres Carrés au Calcul des observations. 1 8vo. Pamphlet. Paris, 1858.

7073 **Todhunter** (I.) Treatise on the differential Calculus and the Elements of the Integral Calculus. With numerous examples. 2d edition, revised with additional examples. 1 vol 12mo. Cambridge, 1855.

Subj. 35. MENSURATION, SURVEYING, AND PRACTICAL GEOMETRY.

7074 **Francœur** (L.-B.). Géodésie ou Traité de la Figure de la Terre et de ses parties; comprenant la Topographie, l'arpentage, le Nivellement, la Géomorphie Terrestre et Astronomique, la Construction des Cartes, la Navigation; Leçons données à la Faculté des Sciences de Paris, 3e édition, revue et corrigée sur les manuscripts inédits de M. Francœur par M. Francœur fils, augmentée de notes sur la mesure des Bases, par M. Hossard. 1 vol. 8vo. Paris, 1855.

7075 **Gillespie** (W. M.). Treatise on Land-Surveying comprising the Theory developed from five elementary principles; and the Practice with the chain alone, the Compass, the Transit, the Theodolite, the Plane Table, &c. Illustrated by four hundred Engravings and a Magnetic Chart. 2d edition. 1 vol. 8vo. New York, 1855.

7076 **Goulier** (Professeur). Cours de Topographie. Instruction pratique sur le lever à la boussole nivelante. (Lithog.) Juillet, 1852.
1 vol. 4to. ——, ——.

7077 **Instruction** für die bei der Astronomisch-Trigonometrischen Landes-Vermessung und im Calcul-Bureau. | Instructions for persons employed on the Astronomical and Trigonometrical Survey and in the Bureau of Calculations.
1 vol. 4to. Vienna, 1845.

7078 **Jackson** (Lieut.-Colonel Basil). Treatise on Military Surveying; including Sketching in the Field, Plan-Drawing, Levelling, Military Reconnoissance, &c., &c., &c.; also a particular description of the Surveying Instruments commonly employed by Military Men, with instructions for using and adjusting them. 4th edition.
1 vol. 8vo. (2 *copies.*) London, 1853.

7079 **Kühne.** Handbibliothek für offiziere. 10ter Band Militairisches zeichnen und aufnehmen. | Military Library. 10th volume. Military Surveying and Sketching.
1 vol. 18mo. Berlin, 1835.

7080 **Lee** (Capt. T. J.). A collection of Tables and Formulæ useful in surveying, Geodesy, and Practical Astronomy, including Elements for the Projection of Maps. Prepared for the use of the Corps of Topographical Engineers. 2d edition with additions.
1 vol. 8vo. (2 *copies.*) Washington, 1853.

7081 **Marieni** (Johann). Trigonometrische vermessungen im Kirchenstate und in Toscana. | Trigonometrical surveys in Tuscany and the States of the Church.
1 vol. 4to. Vienna, 1846.

7082 **Programme** du Cours de Géodesie et de Gnomonique. (Lithog.) Septembre 1854.
1 vol. 4to. ——, ——.

7083 **Puissant** (L.). Mémoire sur la Projection de Cassini, pour servir de supplément à sa théorie des Projections des Cartes Geographiques.
1 4to. Pamphlet. Paris, 1812.

Subj. 36. LOGARITHMS AND MATHEMATICAL TABLES.

7084 **Bremiker** (Carolo). Logarithmorum VI. decimalium Nova Tabula Berolinensis et numerorum vulgarium ab 1 usque ad 100000 et Functionum Trigonometricarum ad decades Minutorum Secundorum.
1 vol. 8vo. Berolini, 1852.

7085 **Scheutz** (George & Edward). Specimens of Tables, Calculated, Stereomoulded, and Printed by Machinery. 1 vol. 8vo. London, 1857.

Subj. 37. MECHANICS, INCLUDING STATICS, DYNAMICS, HYDROSTATICS, AND HYDRODYNAMICS.

7086 **Airy** (George Biddell). Lecture on the Pendulum—Experiments at Harton Pit, delivered in the Central Hall, South Shields, October 24, 1854. Together with a letter containing the results of the Experiments.
1 8vo. Pamphlet. London, 1855.

7087 **Barnard** (Major J. G.). The Phenomena of the Gyroscope, analytically examined with two supplements, on the effects of initial Gyratory Velocities and of retarding forces on the motion of the Gyroscope.
1 8vo. Pamphlet. (2 *copies.*) New York, 1858.

7088 **Bartlett** (W. H. C.). Elements of Analytical Mechanics. 3d edition, revised and corrected. 1 vol. 8vo. New York, 1855.

7089 **Bonnet** (Ossian). Leçons de Mécanique élémentaire à l'usage des Candidats à l'École Polytechnique et à l'École Normale supérieure.
1st part in 8vo. Paris, 1858.

7090 **Bresson** (C.). Traité élémentaire de Mécanique appliquée aux sciences Physiques et aux arts; (Mécanique des Corps Solides.)
1 vol. 4to. & Atlas 4to. Paris, 1842.

7091 **Delaunay** (Ch.). Traité de Mécanique Rationnelle.
1 vol. 8vo. Paris, 1856.

7092 **Duhamel.** Cours de Mécanique. 2e édition.
2 vols. 8vo. Paris, 1853–54.

7093 **Guy** (Prof.). Leçons de Mécanique Industrielle avec les application numériques necessaires à l'intelligence des principes et des conditions de l'établissiment et de la bonne marche des Machines. 1 vol. 4to. Châlons, ——.

7094 **Jariez** (J.). Cours élémentaire de Mécanique Industrielle à l'usage des Éléves des Écoles Royales d'arts et métiers. 2e édition.
2 vols. 8vo. Paris, 1848.

7095 **Jullien** (P. M.). Problémes de Mécanique Rationnelle disposés pour servir d'applications aux principes enseignés dans les cours.
2 vols. 8vo. Paris, 1855.

7096 **Lagrange** (J.-L.). Mécanique analytique. 3e édition, revue, corrigée et annotée par M. J. Bertrand. 2 vols. 4to. Paris, 1853–55.

7097 **Peirce** (Benjamin). Physical and celestial Mechanics. Developed in four systems of analytical Mechanics, Celestial Mechanics, Potential Physics, and analytic Morphology. 1 vol. 4to. Boston, 1855.

7098 **Pontécoulant** (G. de). Théorie analytique du Systéme du Monde.
4 vols. 8vo. Paris, 1829–46.

7099 **Walton** (William). Collection of Problems in illustration of the Principles of Theoretical Mechanics. 2d edition. 1 vol. 8vo. Cambridge, 1855.

7100 **Williams** (Rev. S. F.). The Elements of Mechanics and Hydrostatics.
1 vol. 12mo. Cambridge, 1854.

Subj. 38. NATURAL AND EXPERIMENTAL PHILOSOPHY IN GENERAL.

7101 **Archambault** (P.-J.). Précis élémentaire de Physique rédigé conformement aux Programmes de l'enseignement dans les classes de troisième et de seconde (section des sciences). 1er partie comprenant la Pesanteur, l'Hydrostatique et la chaleur; 2e partie comprenant l'Electricité, le Magnétisme, le Galvanisme, l'Électro-dynamique, l'Acoustique et l'Optique. 2 vols. 12mo. Paris, 1855.

7102 **Babinet.** Etudes et Lectures sur sciences d'observation et leurs applications pratiques. 5 vols. 18mo. Paris, 1855–58.

7103 **Daguin** (P. A.). Traité élémentaire de Physique, Théorique et Expérimental avec les applications à la Météorologie et aux arts industriels. 2 vols. 8vo. Toulouse & Paris, 1855–56.

7104 **Durand** (F.-Aug[te]). Nouvelle théorie Physique ou études analytiques et synthétiques sur la Phys:que et sur les actions chimiques Fondamentales. 1 vol. 8vo. Paris, 1854.

7105 **Harrington** (George Fellows). Systematic Philosophy, and new theories of Light and Heat. 1 vol. 8vo. London, 1857.

7106 **Houzeau.** Physique du Globe et Météorologie. 1 vol. 16mo. Bruxelles, 1850.

7107 **Lamé** (G.). Leçons sur la Théorie Mathématique de l'Élasticité des corps solides. 1 vol. 8vo. Paris, 1852.

7108 **Loomis** (Elias). Elements of Natural Philosophy, designed for Academies and high Schools, with three hundred and sixty illustrations. 1 vol. 12mo. New York, 1858.

7109 **Peschel** (C. F.). Elements of Physics. Translated from the German, with notes, by E. West; Illustrated with Diagrams and Wood-cuts. 3 vols. 16mo. London, 1845–46.

7110 **Phillips** (Sir Richard). Twelve Essays on the Proximate Causes of the Material Phenomena of the Universe; with illustrative notes. 1 vol. 8vo. London, 1821.

7111 **Silliman** (Benjamin). First Principles of Physics, or Natural Philosophy, designed for the use of Schools and Colleges. With six hundred and seventy-seven Illustrations. 1 vol. 12mo. Philadelphia, 1859.

Subj. 39. OPTICS.

7112 **Beer** (Dr. August). Einleitung in die höhere Optik. Mit 212 in den Text eingedruckten holzschnitten und 2 Tafeln mit 50 abbildungen in Kupferstich. | An Introduction on the higher Optics. With 212 wood Engravings, printed in the Text, and 2 copper-plates of 50 figures. 1 vol. 8vo. Braunschweig, 1853.

7113 **Billet** (F.). Traité d'Optique Physique. 1st, 8vo. Paris, 1858.

7114 **Carpenter** (William B.). The Microscope: and its Revelations. Illustrated by 345 wood Engravings. 1 vol. 12mo. London, 1856.

7115 **Gœthe's** Theory of Colours; translated from the German with Notes, by Charles Lock Eastlake. 1 vol. 8vo. London, 1840.

7116 **Griffith** (J. W.) **& Henfrey** (Arthur). Micrographic Dictionary; a guide to the examination and investigation of the structure and nature of Microscopic objects. Illustrated by forty-one Plates and eight hundred and sixteen Wood-cuts. 1 vol. large 8vo. London, 1856.

7117 **Hannover** (Adolphe). On the Construction and use of the Microscope. Edited by John Goodsir. 1 vol. 8vo. Edinburgh, 1853.

7118 **Hassall** (Arthur Hill). Microscopic Examination of the Water supplied to the Inhabitants of London and the suburban Districts; illustrated by coloured Plates, &c., &c. 1 vol. 8vo. London, 1850.

7119 **Jones** (Rev. George). Observations on the Zodiacal Light. 1 vol. 4to. Washington, 1856. (See Ex. Doc. of the House of Rep., 2d sess. 33d cong. vol. 12, part 3d.)

7120 **Olmsted** (Denison). On the recent Secular Period of the Aurora Borealis. (Smithsonian Contributions to Knowledge.) 1 4to. Pamphlet. Washington, 1856.

7121 **Pereira** (Jonathan). Lectures on Polarized Light, together with a Lecture on the Microscope, illustrated by numerous wood-cuts. 2d edition, greatly enlarged from materials left by the Author. Edited by the Rev. Baden Powell. 1 vol. 16mo. London, 1854.

7122 **Quekett's** Practical Treatise on the use of the Microscope. 3d edition. 1 vol. 8vo. London, 1855.

Subj. 40. NAVIGATION.

7123 **Boitard** et Ansart-Deusy. Navigation pratique. 1 vol. 8vo. Paris, 1859.

7124 **Bowditch** (Nathaniel). New American Practical Navigator: being an Epitome of Navigation; containing all the Tables necessary to be used with the Nautical Almanac in determining the latitude and the longitude by Lunar observations and keeping a complete reckoning at sea; illustrated by proper rules and examples, &c., with an appendix. 27th new stereotype edition. 1 vol. 8vo. New York, 1857.

7125 **Maury** (M. F. Lieut. U. S. N.). Explanations and Sailing Directions to accompany the Wind and Current Charts, approved by Commodore Charles Morris, chief of the Bureau of Ordnance and Hydrography; and published by authority of Hon. J. P. Kennedy, Secretary of the Navy. 5th edition, enlarged and improved. 1 vol. 4to. & 38 charts in fol. Washington, 1853.

Subj. 41. ASTRONOMY.

7126 **Annales** de l'observatoire Impérial de Paris; Publiées par U.-J. Le Verrier. 1st vol. 4to. Paris, 1855.

7127 **Astronomical** Journal. Edited by Benj. Apthorp Gould, Jr. 5 vols. 4to. Cambridge, 1851–59.

7128 **Astronomical** Society of London. Memoirs of the, for 1821 to 1855, inclusive. 24 vols. 4to. London, 1822–56.

7129 **Astronomical** Society of London, Monthly notices of the, containing abstracts of Papers, and Reports of the Proceedings of the Society, from February, 1827, to June, 1855. 15 vols. 8vo. London, 1831–55.

7130 **Astronomische** Nachrichten, herausgegeben von H. C. Schumacher, und Professor Dr. C. A. F. Peters. 46 vols. 4to. Altona, 1823–1857.

7131 **Astronomische** Nachrichten. General Register der bände 1 bis 40. Ausgearbeitet von G. A. Jahn. 2 vols. 4to. Hamburg, 1851–56.

7132 **Bailey** (Francis). An account of the Rev. John Flamsteed. Ses Flamsteed, No. 7138.

7133 **Bartlett** (W. H. C.). Spherical Astronomy. 1 vol. 8vo. New York, 1855.

7134 **Biot** (J. B.). Traité Élémentaire d'astronomie Physique. 3e édition, corrigée et augmentée. 5 vols. 8vo. Paris, 1841–57.

7135 **Briot** (Charles). Cours de Cosmographie, ou Éléments d'Astronomie; Comprenant les Matières du nouveau Programme arrêté pour l'enseignement des Lycées et l'admission aux Écoles spéciales. 1 vol. 8vo. Paris, 1853.

7136 **Delaunay** (Ch.). Cours élémentaire d'Astronomie, concordant avec les articles du Programme officiel pour l'enseignement de la Cosmographie dans les Lycées. 1 vol. 18mo. Paris, 1853.

7137 **Dubois** (E. P.). Cours d'Astronomie, à l'usage des officiers de la Marine Impériale. 1 vol. 8vo. Paris, ——.

7138 **Flamsteed** (Rev. John). An account of the Rev. John Flamsteed, the first Astronomer Royal; compiled from his own Manuscripts, and other authentic documents, never before Published. To which is added his British Catalogue of Stars, corrected and enlarged; By Francis Bailey. 1 vol. 4to. London, 1835.

7139 **Gummere** (John). Elementary Treatise on Astronomy; 4th edition. Revised and adapted to the present state of the science, by E. Otis Kendall, A. M. 1 vol. 8vo. (3 *copies.*) Philadelphia, 1851.

7140 **Keith** (Thomas). New Treatise on the use of the Globes; or a Philosophical View of the Earth and Heavens. 1 vol. 8vo. New York, 1832.

7141 **Le Verrier** (U.-J.). Annales de l'observatoire Impérial de Paris. See Annales, No. 7126.

7142 **Loomis** (Elias). An Introduction to Practical Astronomy, with a collection of Astronomical Tables. 1 vol. 8vo. New York, 1855.

7143 **Memoirs** of the London Astronomical Society. See Nos. 7128 & 7129.

7144 **Oxley** (Thomas). The Celestial Planispheres, or Astronomical Charts. Part I. showing by inspection, or only by drawing a straight line, all the most useful problems in Astronomy, &c. Part II. a new and comprehensive system of directional Motion. Part III. containing new and improved Formulæ for Astronomical Calculations. Part IV. containing choice Astrological Aphorisms from Ptolemy; also, interesting Remarks and Calculations, on the Nativity of King William the Fourth. (Plates are wanting.) 1 vol. 8vo. London, 1830.

7145 **Smithsonian** Contributions to Knowledge. Occultations visible in the United States during the years 1848, 1849 & 1850. 3 4to. Pamphlets. Washington, 1848–49.

7146 **Wells** (Edward). The Young Gentlemen's Astronomy, containing such Elements of the Astronomical Science as are most useful and easy to be known. 4th edition. 1 vol. 8vo. London, 1736.

7147 **Woodley** (William). The Divine System of the Universe, wherein the Hypothesis of the Earth's motion is refuted, and the true basis of Astronomy laid down according to our sight, sense, and demonstration; with Diagrams, showing the daily motion of the Sun and Moon, &c., round the Earth; for illustrating their declinations; and determining the Longitude. 1 vol. 8vo. London, 1830.

Subj. 42. ASTRONOMICAL OBSERVATIONS.

7148 **Astronomical** Observations, made under the direction of M. F. Maury, Lieut. U. S. Navy, during the years 1845, 1846, 1847, 1848, 1849, and 1850, at the U. S. Naval Observatory, Washington. 5 vols. 4to. Washington, 1846–59.

7149 **Bartlett** (W. H. C.). Nineteen Photographs of Solar Eclipse, 1854, May 26th. 1 vol. 8vo. ——, ——.

7150 **Edinburgh** Astronomical Observations, made at the Royal Observatory for the years 1840, '42, '43, '44, '45, '46, '47, '49–'54. Vols. 6, 8, 9, 10, and 11 in 4to. Edinburgh, 1847–54.

7151 **Hill** (Rev. Thomas). Map of the Solar Eclipse of March 15th, 1858. 1 8vo. Pamphlet. Washington, 1858.

7152 **Johnson** (Manuel J.). Astronomical Observations made at the Radcliffe Observatory, Oxford. See No. 7153.

7153 **Radcliffe** Observatory, Oxford. Astronomical Observations made at the, in the years 1840 to 1852. By Manuel J. Johnson, M. A., Radcliffe Observer. 13 vols. 8vo. Oxford, 1842–54.

7154 **Smyth** (Prof. Piazzi). Report to the Visitors of the Royal Observatory of Edinburgh, November, 1852. 1 4to. Pamphlet. ——, ——.

7155 **Washington** Astronomical Observations. See No. 7148.

Subj. 43. ASTRONOMICAL TABLES.

7156 **British Association.** The Catalogue of Stars of the British Association for the Advancement of Science; containing the Mean Right Ascensions and North Polar distances of eight thousand three hundred and seventy-seven fixed Stars, reduced to January 1, 1850, together with their annual Precessions, Aberration, and Nutation. With a Preface Explanatory of their Construction and Application. By the late Francis Baily. 1 vol. 4to. London, 1845.

7157 **Carrington** (Richard Christopher). Catalogue of 3735 Circumpolar Stars observed at Redhill. See Redhill, No. 7161.

7158 **Greenwich.** Catalogue of the Places of 1439 Stars, referred to the 1st of January, 1840; deduced from the Observations made at the Royal Observatory, Greenwich, from 1836, January 1, to 1841, December 31. 1 vol. 4to. London, 1843.

7159 **Greenwich.** Catalogue of 2156 Stars, formed from the Observations made during twelve years from 1836 to 1847, at the Royal Observatory, Greenwich. 1 vol. 4to. London, 1849.

7160 **Nautical Almanac** for 1849, 1850, 1851, 1852, 1853, 1854, 1855, 1856, 1857, 1858, 1859. 11 vols. London, ——.

7161 **Redhill.** Catalogue of 3735 Circumpolar Stars observed at Redhill in the years 1854, 1855, and 1856, and reduced to mean Positions for 1855·0, by Richard Christopher Carrington. 1 vol. folio & Atlas folio of 10 Charts. London, 1857.

Subj. 44. GENERAL WORKS ON ARTS AND SCIENCES.

7162 **Académie** des Sciences, Comptes rendus hebdomadaires des séances de l'Académie des sciences. 47 vols. 4to. Paris, 1835–58.

7163 **American** Philosophical Society. See Nos. 7186 & 7197.

7164 **Annual** of Scientific Discovery; or Year-Book of Facts in Science and Art. Edited by David A. Wells and George Bliss. For 1850 to 1859, inclusive. 10 vols. 12mo. Boston, 1850–59.

7165 **Arago** (Francis). Oeuvres de, publiée d'aprés son ordre sous la direction de M. J.-A. Barral.
1. Astronomie populaire. 4 vols. 8vo. Paris, 1854–57.
2. Notices Scientifiques. 5 vols. 8vo. Paris, 1854–58.
3. Notices Biographiques. 3 vols. 8vo. Paris, 1854–55.
4. Voyages Scientifiques. 1 vol. 8vo. Paris, 1857.
5. Mémoires Scientifiques. 2 vols. 8vo. Paris, 1858–59.
6. Mélanges. 1 vol. 8vo. Paris, 1859.

7166 **Babinet.** Études et Lectures sur sciences d'observation et leurs applications pratiques. 5 vols. 18mo. Paris, 1855–58.

7167 **British** Association. See No. 7189.

7168 **Cambridge** Philosophical Society. See No. 7195.

7169 **Chambers'** Introduction to the Sciences. 1 vol. 18mo. Edinburgh, 1843.

7170 **Ecole** des Ponts et Chaussées. Cours de Droit administratif. M. Cotelle Professeur. Session 1847–1848. (Lithog.) 1 vol. 4to. ——, ——.

7171 **Ecole** des Ponts et chaussées. Notes sur le cours d'hydraulique. Mr. Belanger Professeur. Session 1849–1850. (Lithog.) 1 vol. 4to. ——, ——.

7172 **Ecole** des Ponts et chaussées. Légende explicative des Instruments de Géodésie, d'arpentage et de Nivellement dont il est question dans le cours de construction des Routes. (Lithog.) 1 vol. 4to. ——, ——.

7173 **Ecole** des Ponts et chaussées. Appendice au cours de Navigation, Distributions d'eau. (Lithog.) 1 vol. 4to. ——, ——.

7174 **Ecole** des Ponts et chausées. Cours de Minéralogie appliquée aux constructions. Edition de 1847. M. Dufrenoy, Professeur. (Lithog.) 1 vol. 4to. ——, ——.

7175 **Ecole** des Ponts et chaussées. Explication des planches de fossiles qui accompagnent les cours lithographié de Géologie professé à l'École des Ponts et Chaussées par M. Dufrenoy, par M. Emile Boyle. (Lithog.) 1 vol. 4to. Paris, 1847.

7176 **Ecole** des Ponts et chaussées. Recueil des Programmes des Cours professés à l'École des Ponts et chaussées, pendant les sessions 1847–1848 et 1848–1849; précédé de quelques explications sommaires sur le systéme général d'enseignement de cette École. (Lithog.) 1 vol. 4to. ——, ——.

7177 **Edinburgh** Transactions. See Transactions, No. 7194.

7178 **Herschel** (Sir J. F. W.). Essays from the Edinburgh and Quarterly Reviews, with Addresses and other Pieces. 1 vol. 8vo. London, 1857.

7179 **Hunt** (Robert). A Treatise on the progressive improvement and present state of the Manufactures in Metal. (Lardner's Cabinet Cyclopædia.) 3 vols. 16mo. London, 1853.

7180 **Irish** Academy. Transactions of the. See No. 7196.

7181 **Journal** de l'École Polytechnique, 37 Cahiers. 21 vols. 4to. Paris, 1796–1858.

7182 **London** Philosophical Transactions. See No. 7193.

7183 **Manufactures** in Metal. See Hunt, No. 7179.

7184 **Mémoires** de l'Académie Royale des Sciences de l'Institute de France. Tomes 1 à 10 et Tome 21. 11 vols. 4to. Paris, 1818–47.

7185 **Philosophical** Transactions. See Nos. 7193 to 7197.

7186 **Proceedings** of the American Philosophical Society, held at Philadelphia for Promoting Useful Knowledge. 6 vols. 8vo. Philadelphia, 1838–59.

7187 **Proceedings** of the American Association for the Advancement of Science, 1st meeting to the 11th, inclusive. 11 vols. 8vo. ——, 1849–58.

7188 **Proceedings** of the National Institute, Washington, D. C. New series. Vol. 1. No. 1. ——, 1855.

7189 **Reports** of the British Association for the Advancement of Science. 2d edition from 1831 to 1857. From the 1st meeting to the 27th, inclusive. 26 vols. 8vo. London, 1835–58.

7190 **Schœdler** (Friedrich). The Book of Nature: an Elementary Introduction to the Sciences of Physics, Astronomy, Chemistry, Mineralogy, Geology, Botany, Zoology and Physiology. Translated from the 6th German edition by Henry Medlock, illustrated by 679 engravings on wood. 1 vol. 8vo. Philadelphia, 1853.

7191 **Smithsonian** Contributions to Knowledge. 10 vols. 4to. Washington, 1848–58.

7192 **Tolhausen & Gardissal.** Technological Dictionary in the English, French, and German Languages, comprising the technical terms of Arts and Manufactures, with their different acceptations collected from the best authors in the three Languages. 3 vols. 12mo. Paris, 1854–55.

7193 **Transactions.** Philosophical Transactions of the Royal Society of London, from 1665 to 1857. 147 vols. 4to. London, 1809–58.

7194 **Transactions** of the Royal Society of Edinburgh. (Part 2d of vol. 21 wanting.) 21 vols. 4to. Edinburgh, 1788–1854.

7195 **Transactions** of the Cambridge Philosophical Society. Established November 15, 1819. 9 vols. 4to. Cambridge, 1821–56.

7196 **Transactions** of the Royal Irish Academy. 22 vols. 4to. Dublin, 1787–1855.

7197 **Transactions** of the American Philosophical Society, held at Philadelphia for promoting Useful Knowledge. New series. 10 vols. 4to. Philadelphia, 1818–53.

7198 **Ure** (Andrew). Dictionary of Arts, Manufactures, and Mines; containing a clear Exposition of their Principles and Practice. Illustrated with nearly 1600 Engravings on Wood. Re-printed from the 4th English edition, corrected and greatly enlarged. 2 vols. 8vo. New York, 1853.

Subj. 45. CHEMISTRY.

7199 **Annales** de Chimie et de Physique. Nouvelle série. Table des Tomes 1 à 75. 3 vols. 8vo. Paris, 1831–41.

7200 **Annales** de Chimie et de Physique. 3e série. 57 vols. 8vo. Paris, 1841–59.

7201 **Barreswil et Davanne.** Chimie Photographique Contenant les Éléments de Chimie expliqués par des examples empruntés à la Photographie; les Procedés de Photographie sur Glace (Collodion sec ou humide et albuminé) sur Papiers, sur Plaques; la manière de préparer soi-même, d'essayer et d'employer tous les Réactifs et d'utiliser les résidus, &c.; 2e édition entièrement refondue et ornée de figures dans le texte. 1 vol. 8vo. Paris, ——.

7202 **Belloc** (A.). Le Catéchisme de l'Opérateur Photographe. Traité complet de Photographie sur Collodion. 1 vol. 8vo. Paris, 1857.

7203 **Booth** (James) and **Morfit** (Campbell). On recent Improvements in the Chemical Arts. (Smithsonian Report). 1 vol. 8vo. Washington, 1852.

7204 **Bowman** (John E.). An Introduction to practical Chemistry, including Analysis. 1 vol. 12mo. Philadelphia, 1849.

7205 **Bunsen** (Robert). Gasometry comprising the leading Physical and Chemical Properties of Gases. Translated by Henry E. Roscoe. With sixty Illustrations. 1 vol. 8vo. London, 1858.

7206 **Clegg** (Samuel). Practical Treatise on the Manufacture and Distribution of Coal-Gas, its introduction and progressive Improvement. Illustrated by Engravings from Working Drawings, with general Estimates. 2d edition. 1 vol. 4to. London, 1853.

7207 **Fownes** (George). Elementary Chemistry, theoretical and practical. Edited, with additions by Robert Bridges, a new American from the last and revised London edition. With numerous illustrations on Wood. 1 vol. 12mo. Philadelphia, 1854.

7208 **Fresenius** (Dr. C. Remigius). System of instruction in Qualitative Chemical Analysis. 4th edition. Edited by J. Lloyd Bullock. 1 vol. 8vo. London, 1855.

7209 **Gmelin** (Leopold). Hand-Book of Chemistry. Translated by Henry Watts. 10 vols. 8vo. London, 1848–56.

7210 **Graham** (Thomas). Elements of Chemistry; including the Applications of the Science in the Arts. 2d edition, entirely revised and greatly en-enlarged. 2 vols. 8vo. London, 1850–57.

7211 **Gregory** (William). Hand-Book of Chemistry, inorganic and organic. 4th edition, corrected and enlarged. 1 vol. 8vo. London, 1857.

7212 **Hardwich** (T. Frederick). Manual of Photographic Chemistry, including the Practice of the Collodion Process. 4th edition. 1 vol. 16mo. London, 1857.

7213 **Hunt** (Robert). Manual of Photography. 4th edition, revised, illustrated by numerous Engravings. 1 vol. 12mo. London, 1854.

7214 **Johnston** (James F. W.). The Chemistry of Common Life. 2 vols. 12mo. New York, 1855.

7215 **Johnston** (James F. W.). Elements of Agricultural Chemistry and Geology. 7th edition. 1 vol. 16mo. Edinburgh & London, 1856.

7216 **Kane** (Sir Robert). Elements of Chemistry, theoretical and practical, including the most recent discoveries and applications of the science to Medicine and Pharmacy, to Agriculture and to Manufactures. Illustrated by 230 wood-cuts. 2d edition. 1 vol. 8vo. Dublin, 1849.

7217 **Lieber** (Oscar M.). Wœhler's Analytical Chemist's Assistant. See Wœhler, No. 7232.

7218 **Liebig** (J.). & **Kopp** (H.). Annual Report of the Progress of Chemistry, and the Allied Sciences, Physics, Mineralogy, and Geology, &c. Edited by A. W. Hofmann, W. de la Rue, and H. B. Jones, for 1847 to 1850, inclusive. 4 vols. 8vo. London, 1849–53.

7219 **Löwig** (Dr. Carl). Principles of Organic and Physiological Chemistry. Translated by Daniel Breed. 1 vol. 8vo. Philadelphia, 1853.

7220 **Miller** (William Allen). Elements of Chemistry: Theoretical and Practical.

Part I. Chemical Physics. 1 vol. 8vo. London, 1855.
" II. Inorganic Chemistry. 1 vol. 8vo. London, 1856.
" III. Organic Chemistry. 1 vol. 8vo. London, 1857.

7221 **Mitchell** (John). Manual of Practical Assaying, intended for the use of Metallurgists, Captains of Mines, and Assayers in general, with Copious Tables, &c. 2d edition, entirely revised and greatly enlarged with 360 illustrations. 1 vol. 8vo. London, 1854.

7222 **Morfit** (Campbell). Noad's Chemical Analysis. See Noad, No. 7224.

7223 **Napier** (James). Manual of Electro-Metallurgy: including the applications of the Art to Manufacturing Processes. 2d edition, revised and enlarged. Illustrated by Engravings. 1 vol. 8vo. London, 1852.

7224 **Noad** (Henry M.). Chemical Analysis, Qualitative and Quantitative. With numerous additions, by Campbell Morfit, with illustrations. 1 vol. 8vo. Philadelphia, 1849.

7225 **Normandy** (A.). The Dictionaries to the Chemical Atlas; being a Dictionary of Simple Substances, and of their Simple Combinations, indicating the tests by which they may be indentified; and a Dictionary of tests and reagents; indicating their preparations for the Laboratory, the means of testing their purity, and their behaviour with simple substances and their simple combinations. 1 vol. 12mo. & Atlas fol. obl. London, 1857.

7226 **Phillips** (John Arthur). Manual of Metallurgy, or, a practical Treatise on the Chemistry of the Metals. 2d edition. 1 vol. 12mo. London, 1854.

7227 **Price** (Lake). Manual of Photographic Manipulation, treating of the practice of the art; and its various application to nature. 1 vol. 12mo. London, 1858.

7228 **Regnault** (M. V.). Elements of Chemistry; Illustrated by nearly 700 wood-cuts. Translated from the French by Thomas R. Betton, and edited with notes, by James C. Booth and William L. Faber. 2 vols. 8vo. Philadelphia, 1852.

7229 **Ronalds** (Dr. E.) & **Richardson** (Dr. Thos.). Chemical Technology; or Chemistry in its applications to the Arts and Manufactures. With which is incorporated a revision of Dr. Knap's Technology. 2d edition. Parts I. & II. Vol 1, in 8vo. London, 1855.

7230 **Shaw** (George). Manual of Electro-Metallurgy. 2d edition considerably enlarged. 1 vol. 8vo. London, 1844.

7231 **Smee** (Alfred). Elements of Electro-Metallurgy. See Smee, No. 3501.

7232 **Wœhler** (Friederich). The Analytical Chemist's Assistant: a Manual of Chemical Analysis, both Qualitative and Quantitative of Natural and Artificial inorganic compounds, to which are appended the Rules for detecting arsenic in a case of Poisoning. Translated from the German, with an introduction, illustrations, and copious additions by Oscar M. Lieber. 1 vol. 12mo. Philadelphia, 1852.

Subj. 46. ELECTRICITY, MAGNETISM, GALVANISM, AND METEOROLOGY.

7233 **Allen** (Z.). Philosophy of the Mechanics of Nature, and the Source and Modes of action of Natural Motive-Power. Illustrated with numerous wood-cuts. 1 vol. roy. 8vo. New York, 1852.

7234 **Annuaire** de la Société Météorologique de France. Vol. 1st roy. 8vo. Paris, 1853.

7235 **Bakewell** (F. C.). Manual of Electricity, practical and theoretical. 2d edition, revised and enlarged. 1 vol. 12mo. London, 1857.

7236 **Becquerel** (MM.). Traité d'Électricité et Magnétisme. Leurs applications aux Sciences Physiques, aux arts et à l'industrie. 3 vols. 8vo. Paris, 1855–56.

7237 **De la Rive** (Aug.). Treatise on Electricity, in Theory and Practice. Translated for the Author by Charles V. Walker. 3 vols. 8vo. London, 1853–58.

7238 **Faraday** (Michael). Experimental Researches in Electricity. 2d edition, reprinted from the Philosophical Transactions of 1831–1852. With other Electrical Papers. 3 vols. 8vo. London, 1849–55.

7239 **Grove** (W. R.). The Correlation of Physical Forces. 3d edition. 1 vol. 8vo. London, 1855.

7240 **Grove** (W. R.). Corrélation des Forces Physiques. Traduit en Français par M. l'Abbé Moigno sur la troisième édition Anglaise avec des notes par M. Seguin aîné. 1 vol. 8vo. Paris, 1856.

7241 **Hirn** (Gustave-Adolphe). Recherches sur l'Equivalent Mécanique de la Chaleur, presentées á la Société de Physique de Berlin. 1 vol. 8vo. Colmar, 1858.

7242 **Izarn** (Joseph). Lithologie Atmosphérique, présentant la Marche et l'état actuel de la science sur le Phénoméne des Pierres de foudre, Pluies de pierres, Pierres tombées du ciel, &c. 1 vol. 8vo. Paris, 1803.

7243 **Lovett** (R.). The Electrical Philosopher. Containing a new System of Physics, founded upon the Principle of an Universal Phenum of elementary Fire, &c., &c. 2d edition. 1 vol. 8vo. Worcester, 1777.

7244 **Magnetical** and Meteorological Observations made at Toronto, in Canada, under the superintendence of Lieut. Col. Edward Sabine, vol. 1., 1840, 1841, 1842, 1843, & 1844. Vol. 2, 1843, 1844, & 1845. Vol. 3, 1846, 1847, & 1848. 3 vols. 4to. London, 1845–57.

7245 **Magnetical** and Meteorological Observations at Lake Athabasca and Fort Simpson, by Capt. J. H. Lefroy, and at Fort Confidence, in Great Bear Lake, by Sir John Richardson. 1 vol. large 8vo. London, 1855.

7246 **Matteucci** (Ch.). Cours Spécial sur l'induction, le Magnétisme de Rotation, le Diamagnétisme, et sur les relations entre la force Magnétique et les actions Moléculaires. 1 vol. 8vo. Paris, 1854.

7247 **Maury** (M. F.). Storms and Rains in North and South Atlantic. 1 sheet. (12 *copies.*) Washington, 1856.

7248 **Meteorological** Register, for twelve years, from 1843 to 1854, inclusive, compiled from observations made by the Officers of the Medical Department of the Army, at the Military Posts of the United States. 1 vol. 4to. Washington, 1855.

7249 **Meteorological** Observations, made at Sundry Academies in the State of New York, from 1826 to 1850, inclusive. See New York, No. 7251.

7250 **Napier** (James). Manual of Electro-Metallurgy including the applications of the Art to Manufacturing Processes. 2d edition, revised and enlarged. Illustrated by Engravings. 1 vol. 8vo. London, 1852.

7251 **New York.** Results of a series of Meteorological Observations, made in obedience to instructions from the Regents of the University, at Sundry Academies in the State of New York, from 1826 to 1850, inclusive. Compiled from the Original Returns, and the Annual Reports of the Regents of the University, by Franklin B. Hough. 1 vol. 4to. Albany, 1855.

7252 **Noad** (Henry M.). Manual of Electricity: including Galvanism, Magnetism, Diamagnetism, Electro Dynamics, Magneto-Electricity, and the Electric Telegraph. 4th edition, entirely re-written. 2 vols. 8vo. London, 1855.

7253 **Poisson** (S. D.). Théorie Mathématique de la Chaleur. (Avec supplement.) 1 vol. 4to. Paris, 1835–37.

7254 **Reech** (F.). Théorie générale des effets Dynamiques de la Chaleur. 1 vol. 4to. Paris, 1854.

7255 **Richardot** (Ch.). Nouveau Systéme d'Appareils Contre les Dangers de de la Foudre et le Fléau de la Grêle. 1 8vo. Pamphlet. Paris, 1825.

7256 **Rive de la** (Aug.). See de la Rive, No. 7237.

7257 **Shaw** (George). Manual of Electro-Metallurgy. 2d edition, considerably enlarged. 1 vol. 8vo. London, 1844.

7258 **Telegraph.** Book of the Telegraph. 1 vol. 12mo. Boston, 1851.

Subj. 47. NATURAL HISTORY.

7259 **Adams, Baikie, and Barton.** Manual of Natural History. See Manual, No. 7275.

7260 **Agassiz** (Louis). Lake Superior: its Physical Character, Vegetation, and Animals, compared with those of other and similar Regions. With a Narrative of the Tour, by Elliot Cabot. And Contributions by other Scientific Gentlemen. Elegantly illustrated. 1 vol. 8vo. Boston, 1850.

7261 **Agassiz** (Louis). Contributions to the Natural History of the United States of America. Vols. 1st & 2d. 4to. Boston, 1857.

7262 **Annals** and Magazine of Natural History, including Zoology, Botany and Geology. 20 vols. 8vo. London, 1838–47.

7263 **Annals.** The same. 2d series. 20 vols. 8vo. London, 1848–57.

7264 **Annals.** The same. 3d series. 4 vols. 8vo. London, 1858–59.

7265 **Cuvier** (Georges). Le Régne Animal; nouvelle édition, accompagnée de planches gravées représentant les types de tous les genres, les caractéres distinctifs des divers groupes et les modifications de structure, sur lesquelles repose cette classification, publiée par une réunion d'éléves de G. Cuvier, MM. Audouin, Blanchard, Deshayes, d'Orbigny, Duvernoy, Duges, Laurillard, Milne Edwards, Roulin et Valenciennes.
20 vols. roy. 8vo. Paris, ——.

Les Mammiféres. Avec un Atlas, par MM. Milne Edwards, Laurillard, et Roulin. 2 vols.
Les Oiseaux. Avec un Atlas, par Alcide D'Orbigny. 2 vols.
Les Reptiles. Avec un Atlas, par Duvernoy. 2 vols.
Les Poissons. Avec un Atlas, par Valenciennes. 2 vols.
Les Mollusques. Avec un Atlas, par Deshayes. 2 vols.
Les Insectes. Avec Atlases, par Audouin, Blanchard, &c. 4 vols.
Les Arachnides. Avec un Atlas, par Dugès et Milne Edwards. 2 vols.
Les Crustacés. Avec un Atlas, par Milne Edwards. 2 vols.
Les Zoophytes. Avec un Atlas, par Milne Edwards. 2 vols.
Les Annélides. Avec un Atlas, par Milne Edwards, (bound with the Arachnides)

7266 **Dalyell** (Sir John Graham). The Powers of the Creator displayed in the Creation; or observations on life amidst the various forms of the Humbler Tribes of animated Nature: with practical comments and illustrations. To which is prefixed a Memoir of the Author.
3 vols. 4to. London, 1851–58.

7267 **Dana** (James D.). On Zoophytes. With a folio Atlas of 61 Plates. (Vol. 8th of the U. S. Exploring Exp.) 1 vol. 4to. Philadelphia, 1848.

7268 **Dana** (James D.). On Crustacea. With a folio Atlas of 96 Plates. (Atlas wanting.) (Vol. 13th of the U. S. Exploring Exp.)
In 2 parts 4to. Philadelphia, 1852.

7269 **Gosse** (Philip Henry). Tenby: A Sea-Side Holiday.
1 vol. 12mo. London, 1856.

7270 **Gosse** (Philip Henry). Life in its lower, intermediate, and higher forms: or Manifestations of the Divine Wisdom in the Natural History of Animals. 1 vol. 16mo. London, 1857.

7271 **Gould** (Augustus A.). On Mollusca and Shells. With an Atlas of Plates. (Atlas wanting). (Vol. 12th of the U. S. Exploring Exp.) 1 vol. 4to. Boston, 1852.

7272 **Harvey** (W. H.). The Sea-Side Book; being an introduction to the Natural History of the British Coasts. 1 vol. 18mo. London, 1849.

7273 **Hassall** (Arthur Hill). History of the British Freshwater Algæ, including descriptions of the desmideæ and diatomaceæ. With upwards of one hundred Plates, illustrating the various species. 2 vols. 8vo. London, 1852.

7274 **Johnston** (George). An Introduction to Conchology; or, Elements of the Natural History of Molluscous animals. 1 vol. 8vo. London, 1850.

7275 **Manual** of Natural History, for the use of Travellers; being a description of the Families of the Animal and Vegetable Kingdoms: with remarks on the practical study of Geology and Meteorology. To which are appended directions for collecting and preserving. By Arthur Adams, William Balfour Baikie, and Charles Barton. 1 vol. 12mo. London, 1854.

7276 **Natural** History of New York. 19 vols. 4to. Albany, 1842–54.
Part I. Zoology, by James E. De Kay. 5 vols.
" II. Botany, by John Torrey. 2 vols.
" III. Mineralogy, by Lewis C. Beck. 1 vol.
" IV. Geology, by Mather, Vanuxen, Emmons, and Hall. 4 vols.
" V. Agriculture, by Ebenezer Emmons. 5 vols.
" VI. Palæontology, by James Hall. 2 vols.

7277 **Natural** History. The 3rd, 4th, 5th, 7th, 8th, 9th, 10th, 11th Annual Reports of the Regents of the University on the condition of the State Cabinet of Natural History, and the Historical and Antiquarian Collection annexed thereto. 8 vols. 8vo. Albany, 1850–58.

7278 **Norris** (E.). Prichard's Natural History of Man. See Prichard, No. 7282.

7279 **Nott** (J. C). **& Gliddon** (G. R). Types of Mankind: or, Ethnological Researches, based upon the ancient Monuments, Paintings, Sculptures, and Crania of Races, and upon their Natural, Geographical, Philological, and Biblical History: illustrated by Selections from the inedited papers of Samuel George Morton, and by additional contributions from Prof. L. Agassiz, W. Usher, and Prof. H. S. Patterson. 1 vol. roy. 8vo. Philadelphia, 1854.

7280 **Owen** (Charles). Essay towards a Natural History of Serpents. 1 vol. 4to. London, 1742.

7281 **Owen** (Richard). Odontography; or, a Treatise on the comparative Anatomy of the Teeth; their Physiological relations, mode of development, and Microscopic Structure, in the Vertebrate Animals. 2 vols. roy. 8vo. London, 1840–45.

7282 **Prichard** (James Cowles). The Natural History of Man; comprising inquiries into the modifying influence of Physical and Moral agencies on the different Tribes of the Human Family. 4th edition, edited and enlarged by Edwin Norris, illustrated with 62 coloured Plates engraved on Steel, and 100 engravings on Wood. 2 vols. 8vo. London, 1855.

7283 **Prichard** (J. C.). Explanatory notice of the Ethnographical Maps to the Natural History of Man. 2d edition. 1 vol. fol. London, 1851.

7284 **Say** (Thomas). The Complete writings of Say on the Conchology of the United States. Edited by W. G. Binney. 1 vol. 8vo. New York, 1858.

7285 **Swainson** (William). Treatise on the Geography and Classification of Animals. (Lardner's Cyclopædia). 1 vol. 18mo. London, 1835.

7286 **Vestiges** of the Natural History of Creation. (With a Sequel). 1 vol. 18mo. London, 1856.

7287 **Wood** (Rev. J. G.). The illustrated Natural History. With 450 original designs by William Harvey. 1 vol. 12mo. New York, 1854.

7288 **Woodward** (S. P.). Manual of the Mollusca; or, a Rudimentary Treatise of Recent and Fossil Shells. Illustrated by A. N. Waterhouse & Joseph Wilson Lowry. 2 vols. 18mo. London, 1851–54.

Subj. 48. BOTANY AND AGRICULTURE.

7289 **Morton** (John C.). A Cyclopedia of Agriculture, practical and scientific; in which the Theory, the Art, and the business of Farming are thoroughly and practical treated. By upwards of fifty of the most eminent practical and scientific men of the day. 2 vols. roy. 8vo. London, 1855.

7290 **Nuttall** (Thomas). The North American Sylva; or a description of the Forest Trees of the United States, Canada and Nova Scotia not described in the Work of F. Andrew Michaux, and containing all the Forest Trees discovered in the Rocky Mountains, the Territory of Oregon, down to the Shores of the Pacific, and into the Confines of California, as well as in various parts of the United States. Illustrated by 121 fine Plates. 3 vols. roy. 8vo. Philadelphia, 1855.

7291 **Rodet** (H. J. A.). Botanique agricole et Médicale ou étude des Plantes qui intéressent principalement les vétérinaires et les Agriculteurs. Accompagnée de 328 figures intercalées dans le texte et suivie d'une méthode dichotomique ayant pour but de conduire au nom de ces Plantes. 1 vol. 8vo. Paris, 1857.

7292 **Schleiden** (M. J.). The Plant; a Biography. In a series of Popular Lectures. Translated by Arthur Henfrey. 1 vol. 8vo. London, 1848.

7293 **Wailes** (B. L. C.). Report on the Agriculture and Geology of Mississippi. Embracing a sketch of the Social and Natural History of the State. Published by order of the Legislature. 1 vol. 8vo. ——, 1854.

Subj. 49. MINERALOGY.

7294 **Budge** (J.). Practical Miner's Guide: comprising a set of Trigonometrical Tables, adapted to all purposes of Oblique or Diagonal, Vertical, Horizontal, and Traverse Dialling, &c., &c. 3d edition, considerably enlarged. 1 vol. 8vo. London, 1854.

7295 **Chapman** (Edward J.). Practical Mineralogy; or, a Compendium of the distinguishing of Minerals. Illustrated with 13 Engravings, showing 270 specimens. 1 vol. 8vo. London, 1843.

7296 **Dana** (James D.). System of Mineralogy, comprising the most recent discoveries: illustrated by 600 wood-cuts. 4th edition, rewritten, rearranged, and enlarged. 1 vol. 8vo. New York, 1854.

7297 **Dufrenoy** (Professeur). Cours de Minéralogie appliquée aux Constructions. See No. 7174.

7298 **Greenwell** (G. C.). Practical Treatise on Mine Engineering. 1 vol. 4to. Newcastle-upon-Tyne, 1855.

7299 **Moore** (N. F.). Ancient Mineralogy; or, an Inquiry respecting Mineral Substances mentioned by the Ancients. With occasional remarks on the uses to which they were applied. 2d edition. 1 vol. 18mo. New York, 1859.

7300 **Regnault** (M. V.). Elementary Treatise on Crystallography. Illustrated with 108 wood Engravings. 1 vol. 8vo. London, 1848.

7301 **Schabus** (Jakob). Bestimmung der Krystallgestalten in Chemischen Laboratorien erzeugter producte. Mit 30 Tafeln. | Treatise on Crystallography as produced in Chemical Laboratories. With 30 Plates. 1 vol. 8vo. Vienna, 1855.

7302 **Sowerby** (Henry). Popular Mineralogy; comprising a familiar account of Minerals and their uses. 1 vol. 12mo. London, 1850.

7303 **Whitney** (J. D.). The Metallic Wealth of the United States, described and compared with that of other countries. 1 vol. 8vo. Philadelphia, 1854.

Subj. 50. GEOLOGY.

7304 **Ansted** (David T.). Elementary Course of Geology, Mineralogy, and Physical Geography. 2d edition. 1 vol. 12mo. London, 1856.

7305 **Dana** (James D.). Geology. With a folio Atlas of 21 Plates. (Vol. 10th of the U. S. Exploring Expedition.) 1 vol. 4to. & Atlas folio. Philadelphia, 1849.

7306 **D'orbigny** (Alcide). Prodrome de Paléontologie Stratigraphique universelle des Animaux Mollusques et Rayonnés faisant suite au cours élémentaire de Paléontologie et de Géologie Stratigraphiques. 2 vols. 16mo. Paris, 1850.

7307 **Dufrenoy & Bayle.** Explication des Planches de fossiles. See No. 7175.

7308 **Geological** Map of Europe, exhibiting the different Systems of Rocks according to the most recent Researches and inedited Materials by Sir Roderick I. Murchison and James Nicol. Constructed by A. Keith Johnston. 1856. In case.

7309 **Geological** Survey of Connecticut. A Report on the, by Charles Upham Shepard. 1 vol. 8vo. New Haven, 1837.

7310 **Geological** and Agricultural Survey of Rhode Island. Report on the, by Charles T. Jackson. 1 vol. 8vo. Providence, 1840.

7311 **Geological** Survey of New Jersey. Second Annual Report on the, 1 vol. 8vo. Trenton, 1856.

7312 **Geology.** Second Annual Report on the Geology of the Public Lands belonging to the two States of Maine and Massachusetts. By C. T. Jackson. 1 vol. 8vo. Augusta, 1838.

7313 **Geology.** Third Annual Report on the Geology of the State of Maine. By Charles T. Jackson. 1 vol. 8vo. Augusta, 1839.

7314 **Gray** (A.) **& Adams** (C. B.). Elements of Geology. 1 vol. 16mo. New York, 1857.

7315 **Greenwell** (G. C.). Practical Treatise on Mine Engineering. 1 vol. 4to. Newcastle-upon-Tyne, 1855.

7316 **Hawkins** (Thomas). The Book of the Great Sea-Dragons, ichthyosauri and plesiosauri, with thirty plates, copied from skeletons in the Author's collection of Fossil organic Remains, (deposited in the British Museum.) 1 vol. folio. London, 1840.

7317 **Humboldt** (Alexander de). Mélanges de Géologie et de Physique Générale. Traduits par Ch. Galusky. Vol. 1st, 8vo. Paris, 1854.

7318 **Humboldt** (Alexander de). Volcans des Cordilleres de Quito et du Mexique. 1 vol. 4to. oblong. Paris, 1854.
(The volume of "Volcans des Cordilleres," forms the Atlas to Mélanges de Géologie et de Physique Générale.)

7319 **Jackson** (Charles T.). Report on the Geological and Agricultural Survey of the State of Rhode Island. 1 vol. 8vo. Providence, 1840.

7320 **Jackson** (Charles T.). Second Annual Report on the Geology of the Public Lands belonging to the two States of Maine and Massachusetts. 1 vol. 8vo. Augusta, 1838.

7321 **Jackson** (Charles T.). Third Annual Report on the Geology of the State of Maine. 1 vol. 8vo. Augusta, 1839.

7322 **Lehon** (H.). Périodicité des grands Déluges résultant du mouvement graduel de la ligne des apsides de la terre. Théorie prouvée par les faits Géologiques. Avec une Carte des terres Européennes avant le Deluge de la Genèse. 1 vol. 8vo. Bruxelles, 1858.

7323 **Miller** (Hugh). The Old Red Sandstone; or, New Walks in an Old Field. Illustrated with numerous Engravings. From the 4th London edition. 1 vol. 12mo. Boston, 1855.

7324 **Murchison, Nicol & Johnston.** Geological Map of Europe. See No. 7308.

7325 **Murchison** (Sir Roderick Impey). Siluria. The History of the oldest known Rocks containing organic Remains, with a brief sketch of the distribution of Gold over the Earth. 1 vol. 8vo. London, 1854.

7326 **Naumann** (Dr. Carl Friedrich). Lehrbuch der Geognosie. Mit 346 figuren in holzschnitt, und einem Vollständigen Register über das ganze werk. Und mit einem Paläontologischer Atlas von 70 Tafeln enthaltend die Abbildungen von 1550 species der wichtigsten leitfossilien aus dem Thierreiche. | Elementary Treatise of Geognosy. With 346 figures of Wood-cuts, and a complete Index to the whole Work. And also with a Paleontological Atlas of 70 Plates, containing the figures of 1550 species of the most important leading Fossils of the Animal Kingdom. 2 vols. 8vo. & Atlas 4to. Leipzig, 1850–54

7327 **Owen** (David Dale). Report of a Geological Survey of Wisconsin, Iowa, and Minnesota; and incidentally of a portion of Nebraska Territory. Made under Instructions from the United States Treasury Department. 1 vol. 4to. & Atlas 4to. Philadelphia, 1852.

7328 **Rogers** (Henry Darwin). The Geology of Pennsylvania, a Government Survey, with a General View of the Geology of the United States, Essays on the Coal-formation and its Fossils, and a description of the Coal-fields of North America and Great Britain. With Maps. 2 vols. in 3 parts, 4to. Edinburgh, 1858.

7329 **Safford** (James M.). Geological Reconnoissance of the State of Tennessee; being the Author's first Biennial Report. Presented to the thirty-first General Assembly of Tennessee, December, 1855. 1 vol. 8vo. Nashville, Tenn., 1856.

7330 **Schmid** (E. E.) **& Schleiden** (M. J.). Ueber die Natur der Kieselhölzer. Mit 3 Tafeln Abbildungen. | Treatise on the nature of petrified wood. With 3 Plates of figures. 1 vol. 8vo. Jena, 1855.

7331 **Shepard** (Charles Upham). Report on the Geological Survey of Connecticut. 1 vol. 8vo. New Haven, 1837.

7332 **Tuomey** (M.). Report of the Geology of South Carolina. 1 vol. 4to. Columbia, S. C., 1848.

7333 **Vogt** (Carl). Lehrbuch der Geologie und Petrefactenkunde. Mit Kupfertafeln und illustrationen in Holzstich. Zweite vermehrte und gänzlich umgearbeitete auflage. | Elementary Treatise on Geology and Paleontology. With copper-plates and wood Engravings. 2d edition, entirely revised and enlarged. 2 vols. 8vo. Braunschweig, 1854.

Subj. 51. MEDICAL AND SURGICAL WORKS.

7334 **Auzoux** (le Docteur). Leçons élémentaires d'Anatomie et de Physiologie Humaine et Comparée, 2e édition. 1 vol. 8vo. Paris, 1858.

7335 **Bernard & Huette.** Illustrated Manual of Operative Surgery and Surgical Anatomy. Edited with notes and additions, and adapted to the use of the American medical student, by W. H. Van Buren and C. E. Isaacs, &c. 1 vol. 8vo. New York, 1855.

7336 **Bird** (Golding). Urinary deposits; their Diagnosis, Pathology, and Therapeutical indications. A new American, from the fourth revised and enlarged London edition. 1 vol. 12mo. Philadelphia, 1854.

7337 **Byrne** (Bernard M.). An Essay to prove the contagious character of Malignant Cholera; with brief Instructions for its prevention and cure; 2d edition. 1 vol. 8vo. Philadelphia, 1855.

7338 **Carpenter** (William B.). Principles of Human Physiology, with their chief applications to Psychology, Pathology, Therapeutics, &c. New American from the last London edition. With 261 illustrations. Edited with additions by Francis Gurney Smith. 1 vol. 8vo. Philadelphia, 1855.

7339 **Dunglison** (Robley). Human Physiology. With 368 Illustrations; 6th edition. 2 vols. 8vo. Philadelphia, 1846.

7340 **Erichsen** (John). The Science and Art of Surgery. Being a treatise on Surgical injuries, diseases, and operations. Edited by John H. Brinton, illustrated by 311 Engravings on wood. 1 vol. 8vo. Philadelphia, 1854.

7341 **Fergusson** (William). Notes and Recollections of a Professional life. Edited by his son, James Fergusson. 1 vol. 8vo. London, 1846.

7342 **Flagg** (J. F. B.). Ether and Chloroform: their employment in Surgery, Dentistry, Midwifery, Therapeutics, &c. 1 vol. 12mo. Philadelphia, 1851.

7343 **Gross** (S. D.). Practical Treatise on Foreign Bodies in the Air-Passages. With illustrations. 1 vol. 8vo. Philadelphia, 1854.

7344 **Guthrie** (G. J.). On the Anatomy and diseases of the Urinary and Sexual Organs. From the third London edition. 1 vol. 8vo. Philadelphia, 1845.

7345 **Headland** (Frederick). An Essay on the action of Medicines in the system; 2d edition revised and enlarged. 1 vol. 8vo. London, 1855.

7346 **Lallemand** (M.). Practical Treatise on the Causes, Symptoms, and Treatment of Spermatorrhœa. Translated and edited by Henry McDougall. 2d American edition. 1 vol. 8vo. Philadelphia, 1853.

7347 **Lawrence** (W.). A Treatise on the Diseases of the Eye. A new edition. Edited with numerous additions, and 143 illustrations, by Isaac Hays. 1 vol. 8vo. Philadelphia, 1854.

7348 **Pereira** (Jonathan). The Elements of Materia Medica and Therapeutics. 3d American edition, edited by Joseph Carson.
2 vols. 8vo. Philadelphia, 1852–54.

7349 **Reigert** (J. Franklin). Treatise on the Cause of Cholera. An interesting discovery. 1 8vo. Pamphlet. Lancaster City, Pa., 1855.

7350 **Rokitansky** (Carl). A Manual of Pathological Anatomy. Translated from the last German edition, four volumes in two.
2 vols. 8vo. Philadelphia, 1855.

7351 **Roth** (M.). The Prevention and Cure of many chronic diseases by movements. 1 vol. 8vo. London, 1851.

7352 **Thompson** (Henry). Pathology and Treatment of Stricture of the Urethra, both in male and female. Being the Treatise for which the Jacksonian Prize, for the year 1852, was awarded by the College of Surgeons of England. 1 vol. 8vo. London, 1854.

7353 **Wilson** (Erasmus). On Diseases of the Skin, 3d American from the 3d London edition. 1 vol. 8vo. Philadelphia, 1852.

Subj. 52. GEOGRAPHY, TOPOGRAPHY, AND STATISTICS.

7354 **Blackie** (W. G.). Imperial Gazetteer; a general Dictionary of Geography, Physical, Political, Statistical, and Descriptive. Compiled from the latest and best Authorities. With 700 illustrations, Views, Costumes, Maps, Plans, &c. 2 vols. imperial 8vo. London, 1855.

7355 **Carte** Topographique. Notice sur la grande Carte Topographique de la France, dite Carte de l'État-Major. 1 8vo. Pamphlet. Paris, 1853.

7356 **Carte** Topographique de la France. (190 Sheets & 16 Nos. of text.) (The whole Map will be in about 258 Sheets.)
Texte in 4to. & Atlas in folio. Paris, 1833—.

7357 **Census.** The Seventh of the United States: 1850. Embracing a Statistical View of each of the States and Territories, arranged by Counties, Towns, &c. 1 vol. imperial 4to. Washington, 1853.

7358 **Census** of the State of New York, for 1855; taken in pursuance of article third of the Constitution of the State, and of chapter sixty-four of the Laws of 1855. Prepared from the Original Returns, under the direction of Hon. Joel T. Headley, Secretary of State, by Franklin B. Hough, Superintendent of the Census. 1 vol. folio. Albany, 1857.

7359 **Coast Survey.** Reports of the Superintendent of the United States Coast Survey. See Congressional Documents, Nos. 6988 to 6995.

7360 **Colton** (George W.). Atlas of the World, illustrating Physical and Political Geography. Accompanied by descriptions, Geographical, Statistical, and Historical, by Richard Swainson Fisher.
2 vols. folio. New York, 1856.

7361 **Corréard** (J.). Guide Maritime et Stratégique dans la Mer Noire, la Mer d'Azof et sur le Théatre de la guerre en Orient. Avec Atlas de 40 Planches in-folio. 1 vol. 8vo. & Atlas folio. Paris, 1854.

7362 **Denaix** (Mme Ate.). Essais de Géographie méthodique et comparative.
1er livraison, 1er partie. Mappemonde Comparative, en 2 feuilles.
" " " " Complémentaire. Tableau orographique du Globe, 1 feuille.
" " 2e Tableau Complémentaire. Tableau Synoptique et Comparatif, 2 feuilles.
" " 3e partie Complémentaire. Tableau Synoptique et Comparatif, 1 feuille.
2e " 1er partie. Carte Physique, Politique, Statistique et Comparative de l'Europe, 4 feuilles.
" " 1er, 2e, et 3e Tableaux Complémentaire. Tableaux Géographiques-Historiques, 2 feuilles.
" " partie Complémentaire. Tableau Orographique de l'Europe, 2 feuilles.

Atlas physique, politique et historique de l'Europe, formé de 30 Cartes composant les 3e, 4e, 5e, 6e et 7e livraisons des Essais de Géographie méthodique et comparative. (Bound in one volume.)
1 vol. folio obl. Paris, 1827–29.

7363 **Findlay** (Alex. G.). Classical Atlas, to illustrate ancient Geography, comprised in 25 Maps, showing the various divisions of the world as known to the ancients; composed from the most authentic sources. With an Index to the Ancient and Modern Names. 1 vol. 4to. New York, ——.

7364 **France.** Description of the Maritime Parts of France, containing a particular account of all the fortified Towns, Forts, Harbours, Bays, and Rivers with their Tides, Currents, Soundings, Shoals, &c. Illustrated with Charts of the Sea-Coast, and Plans of all the fortified Places on it. 2d edition. 1 vol. folio obl. London, 1774.

7365 **France.** Carte Topographique de la, See Nos. 7355 & 7356.

7366 **Gazetteer.** New Complete Gazetteer of the United States. Edited by T. Baldwin and J. Thomas. With a new and superb Map of the United States. (Kept in the adjutant's office for official use). 1 vol. 8vo. Philadelphia, 1853.

7367 **Gazetteers** of the World, See Nos. 7354 & 7370.

7368 **Goulier** (Prof.). Cours de Topographie. See Goulier, Nos. 6289 & 7076.

7369 **Graham** (Col.). Report, Mexican boundary. Senate, Ex. Doc. No. 121, 32d Congress 1st session). 1 vol. 8vo. Washington, 1852.

7370 **Harper's** Statistical Gazetteer of the World. Particularly describing the United States of America, Canada, New Brunswick, and Nova Scotia, by J. Calvin Smith. Illustrated by Seven Maps. 1 vol. imperial 8vo. New York, 1855.

7371 **Hewitt** (Abram S.). On the Statistics and Geography of the Production of Iron: a paper read before the American Geographical and Statistical Society, on the 21st February, 1856, at the New York University. 1 8vo. Pamphlet. New York, 1856.

7372 **Jackson** (Col. J. R.). On Military Geography; its Nature, Object, and Importance. 1 vol. 18mo. London, 1850.

7373 **Johnston** (Alex. Keith). School Atlas of Physical Geography, illustrating, in a series of original designs, the Elementary facts of Geology, Hydrology, Meteorology, and Natural History. 4th edition. 1 vol. roy. 8vo. Edinburgh, 1853.

7374 **Lavallée** (Th.). The Military Topography of continental Europe. From the French of, edited by Col. J. R. Jackson. 1 vol. 12mo. London, 1850.

7375 **Lavallée** (Théophile). Géographie Physique, Historique et Militaire. 4e édition, revue et corrigée. 1 vol. 12mo. Paris, 1853.

7376 **Manual** of Geographical Science.
Part I. Containing Mathematical Geography, by Rev. M. O'Brien,
Physical Geography, by D. T. Ansted,
Chartography, by J. R. Jackson.
Part II. Descriptive Geography, containing Ancient Geography, by the Rev. W. L. Bevan,
Maritime discovery and modern Geography, by the Rev. C. G. Nicolay. With an Atlas of Physical and Historical Geography, to accompany the Manual of Geographical Science.
2 vols. 8vo. & Atlas fol. London, 1852–59.

7377 **Maury** (M. F.). The Physical Geography of the Sea. 3d edition, enlarged and improved. 1 vol. 8vo. New York, 1855.

7378 **Maury** (M. F.). The Physical Geography of the Sea. An entirely new edition. 1 vol. 8vo. New York, 1856.

7379 **Mitchell's** New Universal Atlas, containing Maps of the various Empires, Kingdoms, States, and Republics of the World, with a Special Map of each of the United States, Plans of Cities, &c. 1 vol. fol. Philadelphia, 1854.

7380 **Moriciere** (le Général de la). Rapport sur les travaux de la Session de 1850. See No. 7383.

7381 **Programme** du Cours de Topographie. (Lithog.) Septembre 1854. 1 vol. 4to. ——, ——.

7382 **Quin** (Edward). An Atlas of Universal History; in a series of Maps of the World as known at different periods; constructed upon an uniform scale, and coloured according to the Political changes of each Period. Engraved by Sidney Hall. New edition. 1 vol. roy. 8vo. London & Glasgow, 1856.

7383 **Rapport** sur les Travaux de la session de 1850, fait par M. le Général de la Moricière. (Conseil Supérieur des Haras.) 1 vol. 4to. Paris, 1850.

7384 **Rennell** (James). Memoir of a Map of Hindoostan; or the Mogul Empire: with an introduction, illustrative of the Geography and present division of that country: and a Map of the countries situated between the Heads of the Indian Rivers and Sea: also a Supplementary Map. 1 vol. 4to. London, 1793.

7385 **Sarrion** (O.-M. de). Manuel de Géographie à l'usage des aspirants à l'École spéciale Militaire, rédigé d'aprés le questionnaire officiel. 1 vol. 8vo. Paris, 1852.

7386 **Scotland.** Plans of Cities of, 1 vol. fol. ——, ——.

7387 **Sketching.** Collection of Models for Sketching. (In the Russian language.) 1 4to. Pamphlet obl. St. Petersburg, 1827.

7388 **Smith** (Lieut. R. S.). Manual of Topographical Drawing. 1 vol. 8vo. New York, 1854.

7389 **Taitbout de Marigny** (E.) Atlas de la Mer Noire et de la Mer d'Azov. (Text wanting) 1 vol. fol. obl. Odessa, 1850.

7390 **Usoffskime** (Capt.). Treatise on Military Topography. (In the Russian language.) 1 vol. 8vo. St. Petersburg, 1854.

7391 **Zornlin** (R. M.). Physical Geography, for Families and Schools. Revised, with additions, by William L. Gage. 1 vol. 16mo. Boston, 1855.

Subj. 53. GEOGRAPHY—LOOSE SHEETS OF MAPS.

7392 **America.** Map of Central America including the States of Guatemala, Salvador, Honduras, Nicaragua, & Costa-Rica, the Territories of Belise & Mosquito, &c. By John Baily. In case. London, 1853.

7393 **Azov.** Sea of, Stanford's Map of the Sea of Azov, compiled from the Russian, English, & French Documents, 1855. In case. London, ——.

7394 **Baltic Sea.** Gall & Inglis' Map of the Baltic Sea and adjacent Provinces. 1 Sheet folded. Edinburgh, ——.

7395 **Bulgarie.** Carte de la. See Valachie, No. 7431.

7396 **Central America.** Map of, See America, No. 7392.

7397 **Cherbourg.** Plan général du Port et de la Ville de Cherbourg, avec les Fortifications de Terre et de Mer. In case. ——, ——.

7398 **Connecticut.** Map of Connecticut, from the actual Surveys of Warren & Gillet, with the addition of new towns, turnpike roads, &c., by George Gillet, Esqr., 1831. On roller. ——, ——.

7399 **Copenhagen.** Environs of, (Danish maps.) 6 sheets. ——, ——.

7400 **Crimea.** Stanford's Map of the Roads, &c., between Odessa, Nikolaief, Perekop, Simferopol, and Sebastopol. Compiled from Russian Maps in the Possession of the Royal Geographical Society, the Admiralty charts, and other documents, 1855. In case. London, ——.

7401 **Crimea.** The Russian Military Map of the Krima, or Crimea. By Major T. B. Jervis, F. R. S. In case. London, 1854.

7402 **Crimée.** La Crimée a vol d'oiseau. In frame. Paris, ——.

7403 **Danish Maps.**

1. Map of Denmark and the Duchy of Schleswig. 2 sheets.
2. Environs of Copenhagen. 6 sheets.
3. A section of the Country watered by the small River "Skjern-Aa" with a special view to irrigation. 9 sheets.

Fields of the Schleswig-Holstein war in the years 1848, 1849, and 1850.

4. Plan of the Battle of Fredericia fought 6th July, 1849. 1 sheet.
5. Environs of Kolding. (A city in Jutland.) 1 sheet.
6. Environs of Rendsborg. (A fortress in Holstein.) 1 sheet.
7. "Sundevid," a small peninsula on the eastern coast of the Duchy of Schleswig, opposite "Alsen". 1 sheet.
8. The continental Part of the Duchy of Schleswig, with the Island of "Alsen" in 6 sheets. Sheets 2, 5, & 6.
9. The Duchy of Lauenborg. 1 sheet. (2 *copies*.)
10. High-Moen, the eastern & hilly portion of the Island Moen, in the Baltic. 1 sheet.
11. Survey of "Veirhoj" the Weather-hill and environs in Seeland on the scale of the original field notes. 1 sheet.
12. Topographical Atlas of Denmark and Schleswig. Sheets 4, 5, 6, 12, 13, 16, & 21.

7404 **Danubian** Provinces & Greece, &c. Gall & Inglis' Map of the Seat of War in the Danubian Provinces & Greece, the Black Sea and the Caucausus. 1 sheel folded. Edinburgh, ——.

7405 **Danubian Provinces.** Gall & Inglis' Map of the Danubian Provinces. 1 sheet folded. Edinburgh, ——.

7406 **Europe.** Carte Militaire des principaux États de l'Europe, dressée au Dépôt Général de la querre sous la direction de M. le Lieutenant Général Pelet, Directeur du Dépôt et des opérations Militaires. On roller. Paris, 1853.

7407 **European** Kingdoms and Turkey at one view. By Gall & Inglis. 1 sheet folded. Edinburgh, ——.

7408 **Finlande.** Carte autographiée du Golfe de Finlande en 16 feuilles d'aprés la Carte de Russie de Schubert. On muslin & folded. ——, ——.

7409 **Florida.** Military Map of the Peninsula of Florida, South of Tampa Bay, compiled by Lieut. J. C. Ives, Topog'l. Engineers under the General direction of Capt. A. A. Humphreys, Top. Engineers, by order of the Hon. Jefferson Davis, Secretary of War, April, 1856. War Department. With a Memoir. 1 vol. 8vo. (2 *copies.*) New York, 1856.

7410 **Florida.** Map of the State of Florida, compiled in the Bureau of Topographical Engineers from the best authorities, 1846. 1 sheet. ——, ——.

7411 **Fort Laramie** and the Great Salt Lake. Sketch exhibiting the Routes between, January, 1858. 1 sheet. (3 *copies.*) ——, ——.

7412 **Fredericia.** Plan of the Battle of Fredericia, fought 6th July, 1849. (Danish map.) 1 sheet. ——, ——.

7413 **Kolding.** Environs of, (A city in Jutland.) (Danish map.) 1 sheet. ——, ——.

7414 **Lake Erie,** compiled from Surveys made under the direction of the Bureau of Topographical Engineers, War Department, in obedience to acts of Congress requiring the Survey of the Northern and North Western Lakes. 1 sheet. (3 *copies.*) ——, 1849.

7415 **Lauenborg.** The Duchy of, (Danish map.) 1 sheet. (2 *copies.*) ——, ——.

7416 **Lyon.** Nouveau Plan de Lyon dressé en 1854, comprenant les quatre communes qui composent l'agglomération Lyonnaise, &c. In case. Lyon, 1855.

7417 **Map** of the Territory of the United States from the Mississippi to the Pacific Ocean, ordered by the Hon. Jeff'n Davis, Secretary of War, to accompany the Reports of the Explorations for a Railroad Route. 1 large sheet. Washington, 1857.

7418 **Mentz,** or Mayence, or Mainz. Neuester Plan der Stadt Mainz, von A. Glaser, 1852. | Latest Plan of the City of Mentz, by A. Glaser, 1852. In case. Mentz, 1852.

7419 **Nebraska and Dakota.** A Military Map of, by Lieut. G. K. Warren, Top'l. Eng'rs. from the Explorations made by him in 1855–6, while attached to the Staff of Brev. Brig.-Gen. W. S. Harney, and in 1857 under the Direction of the Office Expl[ns.] and Surveys Capt. A. A. Humphreys in charge. Exhibiting also Routes reconnoitred & Surveyed by Lewis & Clark, Long, Allen, Nicollet, Fremont, Franklin, Stansbury, &c., &c. 1 sheet. ——, ——.

7420 **Norwich.** Map of, from actual Survey, by William Lester, Jr. Published by Thomas Robinson, 1833. On roller. ——, ——.

7421 **Orange County,** New York. Map of, from actual Surveys. By J. C. Sidney. On roller. (2 *copies.*) Newburgh, ——.

7422 **Plata** (La). Map of the Basin of La Plata, based upon the Results of the Expedition under the command of Thomas J. Page, U. S. Navy, in the years 1853,–'54,–'55 & '56. And of the adjacent countries, compiled from the best authorities. In case. New York, ——.

7423 **Posen.** Plan von der umgegend von Posen. Von von Schmude. | Plan of the environs of Posen. By von Schmude. In case. ——, ——.

7424 **Rendsborg.** Environs of, (A fortress in Holstein.) (Danish map.) 1 sheet. ——, ——.

7425 **Roumélie.** Carte de la. See Valachie, No. 7431.

7426 **Russia** in Europe. Map indicating the Stations of the Army in, (In the Russian language.) 1 sheet folded. ——, 1838.

7427 **Sevastopol.** The Environs of, with the Batteries and approaches. By James Wyld. 1 sheet folded. London, ——.

7428 **Track-Survey** of the Rivers Salado, Parana, and Colastiné. Surveyed by Commander Ths. J. Page, U. S. S. Water Witch, 1855.
Parana & Paraguay. 15 sheets. ——, ——.
Uruguay. 2 sheets. ——, ——.
Reference Chart to the Track-Survey of the Tributaries of the Rio La Plata. 1 sheet. ——, ——.

7429 **Turkey.** General-Karte von der Europäischen Turkei, bearbeitet und Gezeichnet von Heinrich Kiepert. On muslin. Berlin, 1853.

7430 **United States** Coast Survey. Maps of,
Charleston Harbor. 1 sheet. ——, 1855.
Galveston entrance, (Texas). 1 sheet. ——, 1853.
Gloucester Harbor, (Mass.). 1 sheet. ——, 1855.
Key West Harbor. 1 sheet. ——, 1855.
Mobile Bay, (Alabama). 1 sheet. ——, 1856.
Newburyport Harbor, (Mass.). 1 sheet. ——, 1855.
Salem Harbor, (Mass.). 1 sheet. ——, 1855.
Western Coast of the U. S. 2 sheets. ——, 1854–55.
York River Harbor, (Maine). 1 sheet. ——, 1854.

7431 **Valachie,** Bulgarie et Roumélie. Carte Générale de la Valachie, de la Bulgarie et de la Roumélie. Par J. J. Hellort. [On muslin.] Paris, 1843.

7432 **Venice,** Venezia. Carta Topografica della Laguna di Venezia, e del Territorio conterminante, fino a 37 chilometri di distanza dalla Città con cenni descrittivi del Gran Ponte Sulla Laguna 1847. In case. Venice, 1847.

Subj. 54. VOYAGES AND TRAVELS.

7433 **Atkinson** (Thomas William). Oriental and Western Siberia: a Narrative of seven years' Explorations and Adventures in Siberia, Mongolia, the Kirghis Steppes, Chinese Tartary, and part of Central Asia. With a Map and numerous illustrations. 1 vol. 8vo. New York, 1858.

7434 **Barth** (Henry). Travels and Discoveries in North and Central Africa. Being a Journey of an Expedition undertaken under the Auspices of H. B. M.'s Government in the years 1849–1855. In three volumes. 3 vols. 8vo. New York, 1857–59.

7435 **Bayard Taylor.** The Lands of the Saracen, or Pictures of Palestine, Asia Minor, Sicily, and Spain. 1 vol. 12mo. New York, 1855.

7436 **Bayard Taylor.** Journey to Central Africa; or, Life and Landscapes from Egypt to the Negro Kingdoms of the White Nile. With a Map and Illustrations. 10th edition. 1 vol. 12mo. New York, 1854.

7437 **Bayard Taylor.** Eldorado, or, Adventures in the Path of Empire, a Voyage to California, via Panama, &c. Two volumes complete in one. 6th edition. 1 vol. 12mo. New York, 1854.

7438 **Bayard Taylor.** Visit to India, China, and Japan, in the year 1853. 1 vol. 12mo. New York, 1855.

7439 **Bermuda,** a Colony, a Fortress, and a Prison; or, eighteen months in the Somers' Island. (With Map and illustrations.) By a Field Officer. 1 vol. 8vo. London, 1857.

7440 **Bremer** (Fredrika). The Homes of the New World; impressions of America. Translated by Mary Howitt. 2 vols. 12mo. New York, 1854.

7441 **Burckhardt** (John Lewis). Travels in Arabia, comprehending an account of those Territories in Hedjaz which the Mohammedans regard as Sacred. 2 vols. 8vo. London, 1829.

7442 **Chappell** (Lieut. Edward). Narrative of a Voyage to Hudson's Bay in his Majesty's ship Rosamond, containing some account of the North-Eastern Coast of America, and of the Tribes inhabiting that remote Region. 1 vol. 8vo. London, 1817.

7443 **De Vries** (David Peterson). Voyages from Holland to America, A. D. 1632 to 1644. Translated from the Dutch, by Henry C. Murphy. 1 vol. 4to. New York, 1853.

7444 **English** Women in Russia; impressions of the Society and Manners of the Russians at Home. By a Lady, ten years Resident in that Country. 1 vol. 12mo. London, 1855.

7445 **Ewbank** (Thomas). Life in Brazil; or, a Journal of a Visit to the Land of the Cocoa and the Palm. With an Appendix, containing illustrations of ancient South American Arts, with over one hundred illustrations. 1 vol. 8vo. New York, 1856.

7446 **Ferris** (Benjamin G.). Utah and the Mormons. The History, Government, Doctrines, Customs, and Prospects of the latter-day Saints, from Personal Observation during a six months' Residence at Great Salt Lake City. 1 vol. 12mo. New York, 1854.

7447 **Gibson** (Walter M). The Prison of Weltevreden; and a Glance at the East Indian Archipelago. Illustrated from original Sketches. 1 vol. 8vo. New York, 1856.

7448 **Gregg** (Josiah). Commerce of the Prairies; or the Journal of a Santa Fé Trader, during eight Expeditions across the Great Western Prairies, and a Residence of nearly nine years in Northern Mexico. Illustrated with Maps and Engravings. 2 vols. 12mo. New York, 1844.

7449 **Haxthausen** (Baron von). Transcaucasia. Sketches of Nations and Races between the Black Sea and the Caspian. With Illustrations by Graeb. 1 vol. 8vo. London, 1854.

7450 **Hillard** (George Stillman). Six Months in Italy. 3d edition. 2 vols. 12mo. Boston, 1854.

7451 **Holton** (Isaac F.). New Granada: Twenty Months in the Andes. With Maps and Illustrations. 1 vol. 8vo. New York, 1857.

7452 **Howitt** (William). Land, Labor, and Gold; or, two years in Victoria: with Visits to Sydney and Van Diemen's Land. 2 vols. 12mo. Boston, 1855.

7453 **Huc** (M.). Journey through the Chinese Empire. 2 vols. 12mo. New York, 1855.

7454 **Kane** (Elisha Kent). The U. S. Grinnell Expedition in Search of Sir John Franklin. A Personal Narrative. 1 vol. 8vo. New York, 1854.

7455 **Kane** (Elisha Kent). Arctic Explorations: the Second Grinnell Expedition in Search of Sir Sohn Franklin, 1853, '54, '55. Illustrated by upwards of three hundred Engravings. 2 vols. 8vo. Philadelphia, 1857.

7456 **Layard** (Austin H.). Discoveries in the Ruins of Nineveh and Babylon; with Travels in Armenia, Kurdistan, and the Desert: being the result of a second Expedition undertaken for the Trustees of the British Museum. With Maps, Plans, and Illustrations. 1 vol. 8vo. New York, 1853.

7457 **Le Vert** (Madame Octavia Walton). Souvenirs of Travel. 2 vols. 16mo. New York, 1857.

7458 **Life** in Fejee; or, five years among the Cannibals. By a Lady. 1 vol. 12mo. Boston, 1851.

7459 **Livingstone** (David). Missionary Travels and Researches in South Africa, and a Journey from the Cape of Good Hope to Loanda on the West Coast: thence across the Continent, down the River Zambesi, to the eastern Ocean. With Portrait; Maps by Arrowsmith; and numerous Illustrations. 1 vol. 8vo. New York, 1858.

7460 **Macintosh** (Major-Gen. A. F.). A Military Tour in European Turkey, the Crimea, and on the Eastern Shores of the Black Sea: including Routes across the Balkan into Bulgaria, and Excursions in the Turkish, Russian, and Persian Provinces of the Caucasian Range, with Maps, 2d edition, revised and enlarged. 1 vol. 12mo. London, 1854.

7461 **Mackinnon** (Captain). Atlantic and Transatlantic Sketches, afloat and ashore. 2 vols. 12mo. London, 1852.

7462 **Maximilian** (Prince of Wied). Travels in the Interior of North America. With numerous Engravings on Wood and a large Map. Translated from the German, by H. Evans Lloyd. (Map wanting.) 1 vol. 4to. London, 1843.

7463 **Miller** (Hugh). First Impressions of England and its People. 1 vol. 12mo. Boston, 1856.

7464 **Murray** (Hon. Amelia M.). Letters from the United States, Cuba and Canada. (Two volumes complete in one.) 1 vol. 12mo. New York, 1856.

7465 **Nolte** (Vincent). Fifty years in both Hemispheres, or Reminiscences of the life of a former Merchant. Translated from the German.
1 vol. 12mo. New York, 1854.

7466 **Olmsted** (Frederick Law). Journey in the Seaboard Slave States, with remarks on their Economy. 1 vol. 12mo. New York, 1856.

7467 **Perry** (Commodore M. C.). Narrative of the Expedition of an American Squadron to the China Seas and Japan, performed in the years 1852, 1853, and 1854. Compiled from the Original Notes and Journals of Commodore Perry, and his officers, at the Request and under his supervision, with numerous Illustrations. 1 vol. roy. 8vo. New York, 1856.

7468 **Perry** (Commodore M. C.). The same. See Ex. Doc. House of Rep. 2d sess. 33d Cong. Vol. 12, Part 1st in 4to.

7469 **Perry** (Commodore M. C.). The same. Senate Ex. Doc. 2d sess. 33d Cong. No. 79, vol. 2d in 4to.

7470 **Prime** (Samuel Irenaeus). Travels in Europe and the East: a year in England, Scotland, Ireland, Wales, France, Belgium, Holland, Germany, Austria, Italy, Greece, Turkey, Syria, Palestine, and Egypt.
2 vols. 12mo. New York, 1855.

7471 **Reports** of Explorations and Surveys, to ascertain the most practicable and economical Route for a Railroad from the Mississippi River to the Pacific Ocean. Made under the Direction of the Secretary of War, in 1853-4. Senate Ex. Doc. No. 78. 2d sess. 33d Cong.
10 vols. 4to. in triplicate, except vol. 2d in duplicate. Washington, 1855-59.

7472 **Seymour** (H. D.). Russia on the Black Sea and Sea of Azof: being a Narrative of Travels in the Crimea and bordering Provinces; with notices of the Naval, Military, and Commercial Resources of those Countries. With Map, &c. 3d edition. 1 vol. 8vo. London, 1855.

7473 **Silliman** (Prof. Benjamin). Visit to Europe in 1851. With Illustrations.
2 vols. 12mo. New York, 1854.

7474 **Ternaux-Compans.** Voyages, Relations et Mémoires originaux pour servir à l'Histoire de la découverte de l'Amérique, publiés pour la première fois en Français. Relation du Voyage de Cibola, entrepris en 1840.
1 vol. 8vo. Paris, 1838.

7475 **United States** Exploring Expedition during the years 1838, 1839, 1840, 1841, 1842. Under the command of Charles Wilkes, U. S. N.
5 vols. 4to. ——, ——.

Vol. 7. Ethnography & Philology, by Horatio Hale.
" 8. Zoophytes. With a folio Atlas of 61 Plates, by James D. Dana.
" 10. Geology. With a folio Atlas of 21 Plates, by James D. Dana.
" 12. Mollusca & Shells. With an Atlas of Plates, (Atlas wanting), by A. A. Gould.
" 13. In 2 parts. Crustacea. With a folio Atlas of 96 Plates, (Atlas wanting), by J. D. Dana.

7476 **Vielé** (Mrs.). "Following the Drum:" A Glimpse of Frontier Life.
1 vol. 12mo. New York, 1858.

7477 **Wilkes** (Charles). Exploring Expedition during the years 1838, 1839, 1840, 1841, 1842. See No. 7475.

7478 **Wolff** (Rev. Joseph). Narrative of a Mission to Bokhara, in the years 1843-1845, to ascertain the fate of Colonel Stoddart and Captain Conolly. 3d edition. 1 vol. 8vo. London, 1846.

Subj. 55. UNIVERSAL HISTORY AND CHRONOLOGY.

7479 **Blair's** Chronological Tables, revised and enlarged. Comprehending the Chronology and History of the World from the earliest times to the Russian Treaty of Peace, April, 1856. By J. Willoughby Rosse. 1 vol. 12mo. London, 1856.

7480 **Dew** (Thomas). A Digest of the Laws, Customs, Manners, and Institutions of the ancient and modern Nations. 1 vol. 8vo. New York, 1856.

7481 **Oxford** Chronological Tables of ancient and modern History, compiled from the best authorities. 1 vol. folio. Oxford, 1835–39.

7482 **Ralegh** (Sir Walter). The History of the World in five books. 1 vol. folio. London, 1614.

7483 **Schlegel** (Frederick). Course of Lectures on Modern History; to which are added historical Essays on the beginning of our History, and on Cæsar and Alexander. Translated by Lyndsey Purcell and R. H. Whitelock. 1 vol. 12mo. London, 1849.

7484 **Schlosser** (F. C.). History of the Eighteenth Century and of the Nineteenth till the overthrow of the French Empire, with particular reference to Mental Cultivation and Progress. Translated by D. Davison. 8 vols. 8vo. London, 1843–52.

7485 **Usher** (James). Annals of the World. Deduced from the origin of time, and continued to the beginning of the Emperour Vespasians Reign, and the total Destruction and Abolition of the Temple and Commonwealth of the Jews. Containing the History of the Old and New Testament, with that of the Macchabees, &c. 1 vol. fol. London, 1658.

7486 **Weber** (Dr. George). Outlines of Universal History, from the creation of the world to the present time. Translated from the German by Dr. M. Behr, revised and corrected, with the addition of a History of the United States of America, by Francis Bowen, 3d edition. 1 vol. 8vo. Boston, 1854.

Subj. 56. ANCIENT HISTORY, ANTIQUITIES, AND MYTHOLOGY.

7487 **Arrien.** Expéditions d'Alexandre. See vol. I., No. 7495.

7488 **Bundy** (R.). Catrou & Rouillé's Roman History. See Catrou, No. 7491.

7489 **Cæsar.** Les Commentaires de César. Traduction Nouvelle. Suivie d'un examen de l'analyse Critique que M. Davon a faite de ses Guerres. Par M. de Vaudrecourt. 2 vols. 8vo. Paris, 1787–88.

7490 **Cæsar.** Commentaries. See vol. III., No. 7495.

7491 **Catrou & Rouillé.** The Roman History: with Notes, Historical, Geographical, and Critical; and illustrated with Copper-plates, Maps, and a great number of Authentick Medals. Done into English, from the original French of the Rev. Fathers Catrou and Rouillé. To which is prefixed a new and connected Summary of the Work. R. Bundy. 6 vols. folio. London, 1728–37.

7492 **Denys d'Halycarnasse.** Les Antiquités Romaines. Traduites en Français par Bellanger. Nouvelle édition, augmentée d'une Table des Matières. 6 vols. 8vo. Paris, 1807.

7493 **Grote** (George). History of Greece. 12 vols. 8vo. London, 1849–56.

7494 **Guyon** (l'Abbé.) Histoire des Amazones anciennes et modernes, enrichie de Médailles. 2 vols. 18mo. Paris, 1740.

7495 **Liskenne & Sauvan.** Bibliothéque Historique et Militaire: contenant Thucydide, Xénophon, Arrien, César, Végéce, Onosander, l'Empéreur Léon, Frontin, Polyen, Polybe, &c., &c., et Mémoires de Napoléon. 6 vols. roy. 8vo. Paris, 1835–42.

7496 **Mallet's** Northern Antiquities; or an Historical account of the Manners, Customs, Religion, and Laws, Maritime Expeditions and Discoveries, Language and Literature of the ancient Scandinavians, (Danes, Norwegians, and Icelanders.) With incidental notices respecting our Saxon ancestors. Translated from the French of M. Mallet, by Bishop Percy. New edition, revised throughout, and considerably enlarged, &c., &c., by I. A. Blackwell. 1 vol. 12mo. London, 1847.

7497 **Marchand** (M.). Précis des Guerres de César, par Napoléon. See Napoléon, No. 7498.

7498 **Napoléon.** Précis des Guerres de César. Ecrit par M. Marchand, à l'Ile Saint-Héléne, sous la dictée de l'Empereur; suivi de plusieurs fragmens inédits. 1 vol. 8vo. Paris, 1836.

7499 **Newman** (Francis W.). Regal Rome, an Introduction to Roman History. 1 vol. 8vo. New York, 1852.

7500 **Noel** (Fr.). Abrégé de la Mythologie Universelle: ou Dictionnaire de la Fable. 2 vols. 18mo. Bruxelles, 1828.

7501 **Polybe.** Histoire Générale. Traduction de Dom Thuillier, revue et corrigée. See vol. II., No 7495.

7502 **Thucydides.** Eight Books of the Peloponnesian War, Interpreted with faith and diligence immediately out of the Greek, by Thomas Hobbes. 1 vol. fol. London, 1634.

7503 **Thucydide.** Guerre du Péloponnèse. Traduction de J.-B. Gail. See vol. I., No. 7495.

7504 **Xénophon.** Retraite des Dix Mille. Traduction de la Luzerne. See vol. I., No. 7495.

7505 **Xénopoon.** La Cyropédie. Traduction de J.-B. Gail. See vol. I., No. 7495.

7506 **Young** (Thomas). Account of some recent discoveries in Hieroglyphical Literature and Egyptian Antiquities. Including the Author's Original Alphabet, as extended by Mr. Champollion, with a translation of five unpublished Greek and Egyptian Manuscripts. 1 vol. 8vo. London, 1823.

Subj. 57. MODERN HISTORY OF CONTINENTAL EUROPE.

7507 **Alison** (Archibald). History of Europe from the Fall of Napoleon in 1815' to the accession of Louis Napoleon in 1852. 2 vols. 8vo. New York, 1855.

7508 **Bouvet** (Francis). The Turks in Europe. See Gilson, No. 7618.

7509 **Campbell's** Present State of Europe; explaining the Interests, Connections, Political and Commercial, Views of its several Powers, comprehending also, a clear and concise History of each country, so far as to shew the Nature of their present constitutions. 5th edition. 1 vol. 8vo. London, 1757.

7510 **Conde** (Don José Antonio). Historia de la Dominacion de los Arabes en España, sacada de varios Manuscritos y Memorias Arabigas. 1 vol. 8vo. Paris, 1840.

7511 **Custine** (Marquis de). Russia. Translated from the French. 1 vol. 12mo. New York, 1854.

7512 **Flagg** (Edmund). Venice; The City of the Sea, from the invasion by Napoleon in 1797 to the Capitulation to Radetzky in 1849; with a contemporaneous view of the Peninsula. With a Map and embellishments. 2 vols. 12mo. New York, 1853.

7513 **Frédéric II.**, Roi de Prusse. Histoire de mon Temps. See vol. V., No. 7495.

7514 **Guizot.** Histoire de la Civilisation en France depuis la chute de l'Empire Romain. Nouvelle édition. 4 vols. 12mo. Paris, 1853.

7515 **Guizot.** Histoire de la Civilisation en Europe depuis la chute de l'Empire Romain jusqu' à la Révolution Française. Nouvelle édition. 1 vol. 12mo. Paris, 1855.

7516 **Gurowski** (Count A. de). Russia as it is. 2d edition. 1 vol. 12mo. New York, 1854.

7517 **Hyta** (Ginés Perez de). Guerras civiles de Granada, dos partes en un Tomo. 1 vol. 8vo. Paris, 1847.

7518 **Lafuente** (Don Modesto). Historia general de España, desde los tiempos mas remotos hasta nuestros dias. 21 vols. 8vo. Madrid, 1850–58.

7519 **Motley** (John Lothrop). The Rise of the Dutch Republic. A History. 3 vols. 8vo. New York, 1856.

7520 **Paton** (A. A.). Highlands and Islands of the Adriatic, including Dalmatia, Croatia, and the Southern Provinces of the Austrian Empire. With illustrations. 2 vols. 8vo. London, 1849.

7521 **Prescott** (William H.). History of the Reign of Philip the Second, King of Spain. 3 vols. 8vo. Boston, 1856–58.

7522 **Prescott's** Robertson's History of the Reign of the Emperor Charles the Fifth, by William Robertson, D. D. With an account of the Emperor's life after his abdication, by William H. Prescott. 3 vols. 8vo. Boston, 1857.

7523 **Robertson** (William). The History of the Reign of the Emperor Charles the Fifth, with an account of the Emperor's life after his abdication, by William H. Prescott. 3 vols. 8vo. Boston, 1857.

7524 **Schnitzler** (J. H.). Secret History of the Court and Government of Russia, under Alexander the First, and the Emperor Nicholas. 2 vols. 8vo. London, 1854.

7525 **Tegoborski** (M. L. de). Commentaries on the Productive Forces of Russia. (Vol. 3d wanting). 3 vols. 8vo. London, 1855–56.

Subj. 58. ENGLISH, SCOTCH, AND IRISH HISTORY.

7526 **Chamberlayne** (John). Magnæ Britanniæ Notitia: or, the Present State of Great-Britain, with divers remarks upon the ancient State thereof. In two parts. 1 vol. 8vo. London, 1708.

7527 **Charles.** The Works of King Charles the Martyr: with a collection of declarations; Treatises, and other Papers concerning the differences betwixt his said Majesty and his two Houses of Parliament. 1 vol. fol. London, 1662.

7528 **Chronicles.** Six old English Chronicles, of which two are now first translated from the Monkish Latin originals. Ethelwerd's Chronicle. Asser's life of Alfred. Geoffrey of Monmouth's British History. Gildas Nennius, and Richard of Cirencester. Edited with illustrative notes, by J. A. Giles, D. C. L. 1 vol. 12mo. London, 1848.

7529 **Dickens** (Charles). A Child's History of England. 2 vols. 16mo. New York, 1854.

7530 **Harris** (Walter). History of the Life and Reign of William-Henry. See William III., No. 7542.

7531 **Historical Narrative.** Impartial Historical Narrative of those momentous events which have taken place in this Country during the Period from the year 1816 to 1823. Illustrated with Engravings by the first artists. 1 vol. fol. London, 1823.

7532 **James & Charles.** The Annals of King James and King Charles the first both of happy Memory, containing a faithful History, and impartial account of the great affairs of State, and Transactions of Parliaments in England, from the tenth of King James, 1612, to the eighteenth of King Charles, 1642. Wherein several material passages, relating to the late Civil Wars, omitted in former Histories. 1 vol. fol. London, 1681.

7533 **Keating** (Jeoffry). General History of Ireland. Faithfully translated from the original Irish language, with many curious amendments, &c. By Dermo'd O'Connor. (Two volumes in one). 1 vol. 8vo. Dublin, 1841.

7534 **Lingard** (John). A History of England from the first Invasion by the Romans. 3d edition. 14 vols. 8vo. London, 1825–31.

7535 **Macaulay** (Thomas Babington). History of England from the Accession of James II. 4 vols. 8vo. London & New York, 1849–56.

7536 **Malmesbury** (William of). Chronicle of the Kings of England. From the earliest period to the Reign of King Stephen. With notes and Illustrations. By J. A. Giles. 1 vol. 12mo. London, 1847.

7537 **Nedham** (Marchamont). The Case of the Common-Wealth of England, stated: or, the Equity, Utility, and Necessity, of a submission to the present Government; two parts. 1 8vo. Pamphlet. London, 1650.

7538 **Sammes** (Atlett). Britannia antiqua illustrata: or, the Antiquities of ancient Britain. 1 vol. fol. London, 1676.

7539 **State** of England (The True). Containing the Particular duty, Business, and Salary of every officer, Civil and Military, in all the Public offices of Great Britain. 1 vol. 8vo. London, 1729.

7540 **Sydney** (Sir Henry). Letters and Memorials of State in the Reigns of Queen Mary, Queen Elizabeth, King James, King Charles the first, part of the Reign of King Charles the second, and Oliver's usurpation. 2 vols. fol. London, 1746.

7541 **Townshend** (Heywood). Historical Collections: or, An exact account of the Proceedings of the four last Parliaments of Q. Elizabeth of famous memory, wherein is contained the complete Journals both of the Lords & Commons. 1 vol. fol. London, 1680.

7512 **William III.** The History of the Life and Reign of William-Henry, Prince of Nassau and Orange, Stadtholder of the United Provinces, King of England, Scotland, France, and Ireland are more particularly handled, than in any other History. With an Appendix containing copies of some original papers not hitherto published, &c. By Walter Harris, Esq. 1 vol. fol. Dublin, 1749.

7543 **William** of Malmesbury's Chronicle. See Malmesbury, No. 7536.

Subj. 59. FRENCH HISTORY AND CIVIL MEMOIRS.

7544 **Gourgaud & Montholon.** Mémoires pour servir à l'Histoire de France, sous Napoléon, écrits à Sainte-Hélène, par les généraux qui ont partagé sa Captivité, et Publiés sur les manuscripts entièrement corrigés de la Main de Napoléon. See vol. VI., No. 7495.

7545 **Guizot.** Histoire de la Civilisation en France. See Nos. 4441 & 7514.

7546 **Lamartine** (Alphonse de). The History of the Restoration of Monarchy in France. 4 vols. 12mo. New York, 1851–53.

7547 **Ranke** (Leopold). Civil Wars and Monarchy in France, in the 16th & 17th Centuries: A History of France principally during that Period. Translated by M. A. Garvey. 1 vol. 12mo. New York, 1854.

7548 **Thiers** (A.). Histoire du Consulat et de l'Empire faisant suite à l'histoire de la Révolution Française. (Avec Plans et Cartes.) 16 vols. 8vo. & Atlas fol. Paris, 1849–57.

Subj. 60. ASIATIC AND AFRICAN HISTORY.

7549 **Ferdoosee.** Episodes from the Shah Nameh; or Annals of the Persian Kings: Translated into English Verse, with Notes and Authorities, a Verbal Index, Persian and English, and some account of the contents of the whole Poem. By Stephen Weston. 1 vol. 8vo. London, 1815.

7550 **Mill** (James). The History of British India, second edition, in six volumes. With Notes and Continuation. By Horace Hayman Wilson. 9 vols. 8vo. London, 1820–48.

7551 **Pulszky** (Francis). The Tricolor on the Atlas: or, Algeria and the French Conquest. From the German of Dr. Wagner and other sources. 1 vol. 8vo. New York, 1855.

7552 **Recherches** Philosophiques sur les Egyptiens et les Chinois. Par M. de P.*** Auteur de Recherches sur les Américains. Nouvelle édition. 2 vols. 18mo. Berlin, 1774.

7553 **Tableau** de la Situation des Établissement Français dans l'Algérie en 1839 à 1852. 8 vols. folio. Paris, 1840–53.

7554 **Ubicini** (M. A.). Lettres sur la Turquie, ou tableau statistique, religieux, politique, administratif, militaire, commercial, &c., de l'Empire Ottoman, depuis le Khatti-Cherif de Gulkhané (1839). 2e édition. 1 vol. 12mo. Paris. 1853.

7555 **Vaillant** (le Maréchal). Rapport présenté à l'Empereur sur la Situation de l'Algérie en 1853. 1 vol. 8vo. Paris, 1854.

7556 **Wilson** (Horace Hayman). The History of British India. From 1805 to 1835. Forming a continuation to Mill's History of British India. 3 vols. 8vo. London, 1845–48.

Subj. 61. AMERICAN HISTORY.

7557 **Annals** of San Francisco; containing a Summary of the History of the first Discovery, Settlement, Progress, and present Condition of California, and a complete History of all the Important events connected with its great City: to which are added, Biographical Memoirs of some prominent Citizens. By Frank Soulé, John H. Gihon, and James Nisbet. Illustrated with 150 fine Engravings. 1 vol. large 8vo. New York, 1855.

7558 **Arthur** (T. S.) **& Carpenter** (W. H.). History of Virginia, from its earliest settlement to the present time. 1 vol. 18mo. Philadelphia, 1853.

7559 **Bancroft** (George). History of the United States, from the Discovery of the American Continent. 7 vols. 8vo. Boston, 1838–58.

7560 **Bromwell** (William). History of Immigration to the United States, exhibiting the number, sex, age, occupation, and country of birth, of Passengers arriving in the United States by sea from Foreign Countries, from September 30, 1819, to December 31, 1855: and an Appendix containing the Naturalization and Passenger Laws of the United States, &c., &c. 1 vol. 8vo. New York, 1856.

7561 **Bucaniers** of America; or, a true account of the most remarkable Assaults committed of late years upon the Coasts of the West Indies, by the Bucaniers of Jamaica and Tortuga, both English and French. Wherein are contained more especially the unparalleled Exploits of Sir Henry Morgan, our English Jamaican Hero, who sacked Puerto Velo, burnt Panama, &c. 1 vol. 4to. London, 1684.

7562 **Carpenter** (W. H.) **& Arthur** (T. S.). History of Virginia, from its earliest settlement to the present time. 1 vol. 18mo. Philadelphia, 1853.

7563 **Castillo** (Bernal Diaz del). The Memoirs of, written by himself, containing a true and full account of the discovery and conquest of Mexico and New Spain. Translated from the Original Spanish by John Ingram Lockhart. 2 vols. 8vo. London. 1844.

7564 **Cortes** (Hernando). The Despatches of, addressed to the Emperor Charles V. Written during the Conquest, and containing a Narrative of its events. Now first translated into English from the Original Spanish with an introduction and notes by George Folsom. 1 vol. 8vo. New York, 1843.

7565 **De Peyster** (J. Watts). The Dutch at the North Pole and the Dutch in Maine. A paper read before the New York Historical Society, 3d March, 1857. 1 8vo. Pamphlet. New York, 1857.

7566 **Diaz del Castillo** (Bernal). Conquest of Mexico. See Castillo, No. 7563.

7567 **Dillon** (John B.). History of Indiana, from its earliest Exploration by Europeans, to the close of the Territorial Government in 1816: with an introduction containing historical notes of the discovery and settlement of the Territory of the United States, Northwest of the River Ohio. Vol. 1st in 8vo. Indianapolis, Ia., 1843.

7568 **Documentary** History of the State of New York. Arranged under direction of the Hon. Christopher Morgan, Secretary of State. By E. B. O'Callaghan. 4 vols. 8vo. Albany, 1849–51.

7569 **Documentary.** The same. 4 vols. 4to. (2 *copies.*) Albany, 1850–51.

7570 **Documents** relative to the Colonial History of the State of New York; procured in Holland, England, and France, by John Romeyn Brodhead. 10 vols. 4to. Albany, 1853–57.

7571 **Gibbes** (R. W.). Documentary History of the American Revolution: consisting of Letters and Papers relating to the Contest for Liberty, chiefly in South Carolina, from originals in the possession of the Editor, and other sources, 1764–1782. 2 vols. 8vo. New York, 1855–57.

7572 **Gibbes** (R. W.). Documentary History of the American Revolution, consisting of Letters and Papers relating to the Contest for Liberty, chiefly in South Carolina, in 1781 and 1782, from originals in the possession of the Editor and from other sources. 1 vol. 8vo. Columbia, S. C., 1853.

7573 **Gordon** (Thomas F.). History of Pennsylvania, from its discovery by Europeans to the Declaration of Independence in 1776. 1 vol. 8vo. Philadelphia, 1829.

7574 **Graydon** (Alexander). Memoirs of his Own Time. With Reminiscences of the Men and Events of the Revolution. Edited by John Stockton Littell. 1 vol. 8vo. Philadelphia, 1846.

7575 **Grimshaw** (William). History of the United States from their first settlement as Colonies to the Peace with Mexico in 1848. 1 vol. 12mo. Philadelphia, 1853.

7576 **Historical** and Statistical Information respecting the History, Condition and Prospects of the Indian Tribes of the United States: collected and prepared by Henry K. Schoolcraft. Illustrated by S. Eastman, Capt. U. S. Army. (Parts 1, 2, 3, 4, & 5.) 5 vols. 4to. Philadelphia, 1851–55.

7577 **Hollister** (G. H.). History of Connecticut, from the first settlement of the Colony to the adoption of the Present Constitution. 2 vols. 8vo. New Haven, 1855.

7578 **Lacroix** (Lieut.-Gén. Baron Pamphille de). Mémoires pur servir à l'Histoire de la Revolution de Saint-Domingue. 2e édition. 2 vols. 8vo. Paris, 1820.

7579 **Mackenzie** (Charles). Notes on Haiti, made during a Residence in that Republic. 2 vols. 12mo. London, 1830.

7580 **Mayer** (Brantz). Mexico, Aztec, Spanish and Republican: a Historical, Geographical, Political, Statistical and Social account of that country from the period of the invasion by the Spaniards to the present time: with a view of the ancient Aztec Empire and Civilization; a historical sketch of the late War: and notices of New-Mexico and California. 2 vols. 8vo. Hartford, 1853.

7581 **New England** Historical and Genealogical Register, published quarterly under the Patronage of the New England Historic, Genealogical Society. For the years 1847 to 1855, inclusive. 9 vols. 8vo. Boston, 1847–55.

7582 **Palfrey** (John Gorham). History of New England. Vol. 1st in 8vo. Boston, 1855.

7583 **Park** (Roswell). A Sketch of the History and Topography of West Point and the U. S. Military Academy. 1 vol. 18mo. Philadelphia, 1840.

7584 **Pennsylvania.** Historical Society of,

Vol. 5. The History of an Expedition against Fort Du Quesne in 1755, under Major General Edward Braddock, edited from the original manuscripts, by Winthrop Sargent. In 8vo. Philadelphia, 1855.

Vol. 6. Contributions to American History; or, Memoirs of the Historical Society of Pennsylvania. In 8vo. Philadelphia, 1858.

7585 **Quincy** (Josiah). Municipal History of the Town and City of Boston. From Sept. 17, 1630, to Sept. 17, 1830. 1 vol. 8vo. Boston, 1852.

7586 **Schoolcraft** (Henry R.). History of Indian Tribes. See No. 7576.

7587 **Solis** (Antonio de). Historia de la Conquista de Méjico, poblacion y progresos de la Merica Septentrional, Conocida par el nombre de Nueva España. Nueva edicion aumentada con un resumen historico, desde la rendicion de Méjico hasta el fallecimiento de Hernan Cortés, é ilustrada con notas por Don José de la Revilla. 1 vol. 8vo. Paris, 1858.

7588 **Soulé, Gihon & Nisbet.** Annals of San Francisco. See Annals, No. 7557.

7589 **Squier** (E. G.). Notes on Central America; particularly the States of Honduras and San Salvador: their Geography, Topography, Climate, Population, Resources, Productions, &c., &c., and the proposed Honduras Inter-Oceanic Railway. With Original Maps and Illustrations. 1 vol. 8vo. New York, 1855.

7590 **Valentine** (David T.). History of the City of New York. 1 vol. 8vo. New York, 1853.

7591 **Winthrop** (John). History of New England from 1630 to 1649. From his original manuscripts. With notes to illustrate the Civil and Ecclesiastical Concerns, the Geography, Settlement and Institutions of the Country, and the lives and manners of the principal Planters. By James Savage, new edition. 2 vols. 8vo. Boston, 1853.

7592 **Yoakum** (H.). History of Texas, from its first settlement in 1685 to its annexation to the United States in 1846. 2 vols. 8vo. New York, 1856.

Subj. 62. BIOGRAPHICAL, HISTORICAL, AND CLASSICAL DICTIONARIES.

7593 **Anthon** (Charles). Smith's Dictionary of Greek and Roman Antiquities. See Smith, No. 7596.

7594 **Canseco** (Vicente Dioz). Diccionario Biografico universal de Mujeres célebres ó compendio de la Vida de Todas las Mujeres que han adquirido celebridad en las Naciones Antiguas y Modernas, desde los Tiempos mas remotos hasta nuestros dias. 3 vols. 8vo. Madrid, 1844–45.

7595 **Pilkington** (Matthew). A General Dictionary of Painters; containing Memoirs of the Lives and Works of the most eminent Professors of the Art of Painting, from its Revival by Cimabue, in the year 1250, to the present time. A new edition. 2 vols. 8vo. London, 1829.

7596 **Smith** (William). Dictionary of Greek and Roman Antiquities. Illustrated by numerous Engravings on wood. 3d American edition, carefully revised, and containing numerous additional Articles relative to the Botany, Mineralogy, and Zoology of the Ancients. By Charles Anthon, LL. D. 1 vol. roy. 8vo. New York, 1854.

7597 **Spooner** (Shearjashub). A Biographical and Critical Dictionary of Painters, Engravers, Sculptors, and Architects, from ancient to modern times. 1 vol. roy. 8vo. New York, 1853

Subj. 63. BIOGRAPHY AND PERSONAL MEMOIRS.

7598 **Abbott** (Jacob & John S. C.). Histories; Josephine, Madame Roland, Xerxes the Great, Cyrus the Great, Darius the Great, Alexander the Great, Julius Cæsar, Alfred the Great, William the Conqueror, Queen Elizabeth, Mary Queen of Scots, Charles the First, Charles the Second, Maria Antoinette, Cleopatra Queen of Egypt, Hannibal the Carthaginian, Romulus, Nero, King Philip, Pyrrhus, Hernando Cortez, King Richard the First, Henry the Fourth. 23 vols. 16mo. New York, ——.

7599 **Alexander the Great.** History of, by Jacob Abbott. See Abbott, No. 7598.

7600 **Alfred the Great.** History of, by Jacob Abbott. See Abbott, No. 7598.

7601 **Baldwin** (Jo. G.). Party Leaders; sketches of Thomas Jefferson, Alex'r Hamilton, Andrew Jackson, Henry Clay, John Randolph, including notices of many other distinguished American Statesmen. 1 vol. 12mo. New York, 1855.

7602 **Bedell** (Rev. Gregory T.). Memoir of the, by Stephen H. Tyng. 2d edition, enlarged and improved. 1 vol. 12mo. Philadelphia, 1836.

7603 **Bowditch** (N. J.). Suffolk Surnames. 1 vol. 8vo. Boston, 1857.

7604 **Burke** (John & John Bernard). Encyclopædia of Heraldry, or, General Armory of England, Scotland, and Ireland, comprising a Registry of all armorial bearings from the earliest to the present Time, including the late grants by the College of Arms. 3d edition, with a supplement. 1 vol. roy. 8vo. London, 1851.

7605 **Cæsar** (Julius). History of, by Jacob Abbott. See Abbott, No. 7598.

7606 **Charles,** King, the First. History of, by Jacob Abbott. See Abbott, No. 7598.

7607 **Charles,** King, the Second. History of, by Jacob Abbott. See Abbott, No. 7598.

7608 **Clay** (Hon. Henry). Life of the, See No. 7806.

7609 **Cleopatra,** Queen of Egypt. History of, by Jacob Abbott. See Abbott, No. 7598.

7610 **Cortez** (Hernando). History of, by John S. C. Abbott. See Abbott, No. 7598.

7611 **Cyrus the Great.** History of, by Jacob Abbott. See Abbott, No. 7598.

7612 **Darius the Great.** History of, by Jacob Abbott. See Abbott, No. 7598.

7613 **De Veaux** (James). Memoir of, by Robert W. Gibbes, M. D. 1 vol. 8vo. Columbia, S. C., 1846.

7614 **Elizabeth** (Queen). History of, by Jacob Abbott. See Abbott, No. 7598.

7615 **Ellet** (Elizabeth F.). The Women of the American Revolution. 3 vols. 12mo. New York, 1853–54.

7616 **Frédéric** (le grand Roi de Prusse). Vie de, See Grimoard, No. 7619.

7617 **Gibbes** (R. W.). Memoir of James De Veaux. See De Veaux, No. 7613.

7618 **Gilson** (Adrian). The Czar and the Sultan, or, Nicholas and Abdul Medjid: their Private Lives and Public actions. To which is added, the Turks in Europe: their rise and decadence. By Francis Bouvet.
1 vol. 18mo. New York, 1853.

7619 **Grimoard** (le Comte de). Tableau Historique et Militaire de la Vie et du Régne de Frédéric le grand, Roi de Prusse.
1 vol. 8vo. Londres, 1788.

7620 **Hannibal** the Carthaginian. History of, by Jacob Abbott. See Abbott, No. 7598.

7621 **Hawks** (Rev. Francis L.). Richard the Lion Hearted. See Richard, No. 7649.

7622 **Haydon** (Benjamin Robert). Life of, historical Painter, from his Autobiography and Journals. Edited and compiled by Tom. Taylor.
2 vols. 12mo. New York, 1853.

7623 **Henry,** the Fourth, King of France & Navarre. History of, by John S. C. Abbott. See Abbott, No. 7598.

7624 **Herbert** (Henry William). The Captains of the Old World.
1 vol. 8vo. New York, 1851.

7625 **Irving** (Washington). Life of George Washington. See Washington, No. 7663.

7626 **Josephine** (Empress). Historical and secret Memoirs of the, by M'lle M. A. le Normand, translated from the French, new edition.
2 vols. 12mo. Philadelphia, 1852.

7627 **Josephine** (Empress). History of the, by John S. C. Abbott. See Abbott, No. 7598.

7628 **Lamartine** (Alphonse de). Memoirs of Celebrated Characters.
3 vols. 12mo. New York, 1854.

7629 **Lamb** (General John). Memoir of the Life and Times of, an officer of the Revolution, who commanded the Post at West Point at the time of Arnold's defection, and his correspondence with Washington, Clinton, Patrick Henry, and other distinguished Men of his time. By Isaac Q. Leake. 1 vol. 8vo. Albany, 1850.

7630 **Leake** (Isaac Q.). Memoir of the Life and Times of General John Lamb. See Lamb, No. 7629.

7631 **Livingston** (John). Portraits of eminent Americans now living: with Biographical and Historical Memoirs of their Lives and actions.
4 vols. 8vo. New York, 1853-54.

7632 **Lockhart** (J. G.). Life of Sir Walter Scott. See Scott, No. 7653.

7633 **Lodge** (Edmund). Portraits of illustrious Personages of Great Britain. With Biographical and Historical Memoirs of their Lives and actions.
8 vols. 12mo. London, 1849-50.

7634 **Lossing** (B. J.). Biographical sketches of the Signers of the Declaration of American Independence: the Declaration historically considered and a sketch of the leading events connected with the adoption of the articles of confederation, and the Federal Constitution. Illustrated by 50 Portraits and other Engravings. 1 vol. 12mo. New York, 1854.

7635 **Maria Antoinette.** History of, by John S. C. Abbott. See Abbott, No. 7598.

7636 **Marsh** (Miss). Memorials of Captain Hedley Vicars, Ninety-Seventh Regiment. See Vicars, No. 7662.

7637 **Marsh** (Rev. James). Memoir of his Life. See Marsh, No. 7687.

7638 **Mary** Queen of Scots. History of, by Jacob Abbott. See Abbott, No. 7598.

7639 **Montrose.** The Life and Times of Montrose. With Portraits and Autographs. By Mark Napier. 1 vol. 12mo. Edinburgh, 1840.

7640 **Napier** (Mark). Life and Times of Montrose. See Montrose, No. 7639.

7641 **Nero.** History of, by Jacob Abbott. See Abbott, No. 7598.

7642 **Normand** (M'lle M. A. le). Historical and secret Memoirs of the Empress Josephine. See Josephine, No. 7626.

7643 **Pellico** (Silvio). Mis Prisiones. Memorias de Silvio Pellico, traducidas del Italiano y Precedidas de una Noticia de Autor por D. A. S. B. 1 vol. 18mo. Paris, 1835.

7644 **Philip,** King. History of, by John S. C. Abbott. See Abbott, No. 7598.

7645 **Pickell** (John). A new chapter in the early Life of Washington, in connection with the Narrative History of the Potomac Company. 1 vol. 8vo. New York, 1856.

7646 **Pyrrhus.** History of, by Jacob Abbott. See Abbott, No. 7598.

7647 **Queens** of England & Scotland. See Nos. 7655 to 7657.

7648 **Quintana** (Don Manuel Josef). Vidas de Españoles cèlebres. 1 vol. 8vo. Paris, 1845.

7649 **Richard** the Lion Hearted. Edited by the Rev. Francis L. Hawks. 2d edition. 1 vol. 18mo. New York, 1855.

7650 **Richard** the First, King. History of, by Jacob Abbott. See Abbott, No. 7598.

7651 **Roland** (Madame). History of, by John S. C. Abbott. See Abbott, No. 7598.

7652 **Romulus.** History of, by Jacob Abbott. See Abbott, No. 7598.

7653 **Scott** (Sir Walter). Life of, begun by himself and continued by J. G. Lockhart, Esq. 2d edition with 12 Engravings. 1 vol. 12mo. Edinburgh, 1853.

7654 **Smith** (Reverend Sydney). Memoir of the, by his Daughter Lady Holland. With a selection from his Letters, edited by Mrs. Austin. 2 vols. 12mo. New York, 1855.

7655 **Strickland** (Agnes). Lives of the Queens of England from the Norman Conquest; with anecdotes of their Courts. 12 vols. 8vo. bound in 6. Philadelphia, 1852.

7656 **Strickland** (Agnes). Queens of England: a series of Portraits of Distinguished Female Sovereigns, drawn and engraved by eminent artists; with Biographical and Historical Sketches. New edition. 1 vol. roy. 8vo. New York, 1852.

7657 **Strickland** (Agnes). Lives of the Queens of Scotland and English Princesses connected with the Regal succession of Great Britain. 4 vols. 8vo. New York, 1851–54.

7658 **Sumner** (Increase Gov. of Mass.). Memoir of, by his Son William H. Sumner. Together with a Genealogy of the Sumner Family. 1 vol. 8vo. Boston, 1854.

7659 **Swedenborg** (Emanuel). A Biography. By James John Garth Wilkinson. 1 vol. 16mo. Boston, 1849.

7660 **Taylor** (Tom.). Life of Benjamin Robert Haydon. See Haydon, No. 7622.

7661 **Tyng** (Stephen H.). Memoir of the Rev. Gregory T. Bedell. See Bedell, No. 7602.

7662 **Vicars** (Captain Hedley). Memorials of, by the Author of "the Victory Won". 1 vol. 18mo. New York, 1856.

7663 **Washington** (George). Life of, by Washington Irving. 5 vols. 8vo. New York, 1855–59.

7664 **Washington** (George). Early Life of, by John Pickell. See Pickell, No. 7645.

7665 **William** the Conqueror. History of, by Jacob Abbott. See Abbott, No. 7598.

7666 **Xerxes** the Great. History of, by Jacob Abbott. See Abbott, No. 7598.

Subj. 64. LITERARY HISTORY.

7667 **Bouterwek** (Frederick). History of Spanish Literature. Translated from the original German by Thomasina Ross. With additional Notes by the Translator. 1 vol. 16mo. London, 1847.

7668 **Donaldson** (John William). Theatre of the Greeks, a series of Papers relating to the History and Criticism of the Greek Drama. 4th edition. 1 vol. 8vo. Cambridge, 1836.

7669 **Schlegel** (Augustus William). Course of Lectures on Dramatic Art and Literature, translated by John Black, revised, according to the last German edition, by the Rev. A. J. W. Morrison. 1 vol. 12mo. London, 1846.

7670 **Schlegel** (Frederick). The Æsthetic and Miscellaneous Works. See Schlegel, No. 7882.

7671 **Taylor** (Isaac). Process of Historical Proof; exemplified and explained with observations on the peculiar points of the Christian evidence. 1 vol. 8vo. London, 1828.

7672 **Taylor** (Isaac). History of the Transmission of ancient books to modern times. 1 vol. 8vo. London, 1827.

7673 **Willmott** (Rev. Robert Aris). Pleasures, Objects, and Advantages of Literature. 2d edition, revised. 1 vol. 18mo. London, 1852.

Subj. 65. METAPHYSICAL PHILOSOPHY.

7674 **Ampere** (André-Marie). Essai sur la Philosophie des Sciences, ou exposition analytique d'une classification naturelle de toutes les connaissances humaines. 2 vols. 8vo. (of vol. 1st 2 *copies.*) Paris, 1843–56.

7675 **Brewster** (Sir David). More Worlds than one the creed of the Philosopher and the hope of the Christian. 1 vol. 18mo. New York, 1854.

7676 **Brewster** (Francis E.). The Philosophy of the Human Nature. 1 vol. 12mo. Philadelphia, 1851.

7677 **Comte** (Auguste). Cours de Philosophie Positive. 6 vols. 8vo. Paris, 1830–42.

Tome 1er contenant les Préliminaires généraux et la Philosophie Mathématique.
" 2e " la Philosophie Astronomique et la Philosophie de la Physique.
" 3e " la Philosophie Chimique et la Philosophie Biologique.
" 4e " la partie Dogmatique de la Philosophie Sociale.
" 5e " la partie Historique de la Philosophie Sociale.
" 6e " le complément de la Philosophie Sociale.

7678 **Comte** (Auguste). Philosophy of Mathematics. (A translation of volume first) by W. M. Gillespie. 1 vol. 8vo. New York, 1856.

7679 **Cousin** (Victor). Course of the History of Modern Philosophy. Translated by O. W. Wight. 2 vols. 8vo. New York, 1854.

7680 **Cousin** (Victor). Lectures on the True, the Beautiful, and the Good. Increased by an Appendix on French Art. Translated, with the approbation of M. Cousin, by O. W. Wight. 1 vol. 8vo. New York, 1854.

7681 **Field** (George). Outlines of Analogical Philosophy: being a primary view of the Principles, Relations, and Purposes of Nature, Science, and Art. 2 vols. 8vo. London, 1839.

7682 **Hamilton** (Sir William). Philosophy, arranged and edited by O. W. Wight. 4th edition. 1 vol. 8vo. New York, 1857.

7683 **Hamilton** (Sir William). Discussions on Philosophy and Literature, Education and University Reform. Chiefly from the Edinburgh Review, corrected, vindicated, enlarged, in notes and appendices. With an introductory Essay by Robert Turnbull. 1 vol. 8vo. New York, 1856

7684 **Hitchcock** (Edward). The Plurality of Worlds. With an introduction by Edward Hitchcock. See Plurality, No. 7689.

7685 **Hume** (David). Essays and Treatises on several subjects. New edition. 2 vols. 8vo. London, 1784.

7686 **Hume** (David). Treatise of Human Nature. See Hume, No. 7701.

7687 **Marsh** (Rev. James). The Remains of the Rev. James Marsh, D. D., late President and Professor of Moral and Intellectual Philosophy, in the University of Vermont; with a Memoir of his Life. 2d edition. 1 vol. 8vo. Burlington, 1845.

7688 **Oersted** (Hans Christian). The Soul in Nature, with supplementary contributions. Translated from the German by Leonora and Joanna B. Horner. 1 vol. 16mo. London, 1852.

7689 **Plurality** of Worlds. With an Introduction by Edward Hitchcock. A new edition, to which is added a Supplementary Dialogue, in which the Author's reviewers are reviewed. 1 vol. 12mo. Boston, 1855.

7690 **Powell** (Rev. Baden). The Unity of Worlds and of Nature: three Essays on the spirit of the Inductive Philosophy; the Plurality of Worlds; and the Philosophy of Creation. 2d edition, revised and enlarged. 1 vol. 12mo. London, 1856.

7691 **Powell** (Rev. Baden). Plurality of Worlds. See Plurality, No. 7689.

7692 **Raymundi** (Lullii). Opera ea quae ad inventam ab ipso artem universalem, &c., &c., pertinent. 1 vol. 12mo. Agentinæ, 1592.

7693 **Ritter** (Dr. Heinrich). The History of ancient Philosophy. Translated from the German, by Alexander J. W. Morrison. 4 vols. 8vo. London, 1838–46.

7694 **Schlegel** (Frederick). The Philosophy of Life and Philosophy of Language in a course of Lectures, translated from the German by the Rev. A. J. W. Morrison. 1 vol. 12mo. London, 1847.

Subj. 66. LOGIC AND INTELLECTUAL PHILOSOPHY.

7695 **Aristotle.** The Organon, or Logical Treatises of, with the Introduction of Prophyry. Literally translated with notes, syllogistic examples, analysis, and introduction. By Octavius Freire Owen, M. A. 2 vols. 12mo. London, 1853.

7696 **Aristotle.** Logique. See Saint-Hilaire, No. 7702.

7697 **Bailey** (Samuel). Letters on the Philosophy of the Human Mind. 1st series. 1 vol. 8vo. London, 1855.

7698 **Blakey** (Robert). Historical sketch of Logic, from the earliest times to the present day. 1 vol. 8vo. London, 1851.

7699 **Boyd** (Rev. James R.). Elements of Logic: on the basis of Lectures, by William Barron. With large supplementary additions, chiefly from Watts, Abercrombie, Brown, Whately, Mills, and Thomson. 1 vol. 12mo. New York, 1856.

7700 **Heineccii** (Jo. Gottl.). Elementa Philosophiæ Rationalis et Moralis, ex principiis admodum evidentibus justo ordine adornata. Bræmissa est Historia Philosophica. Editio quinta emendatior. 1 vol. 8vo. Amstelædami, 1757.

7701 **Hume** (David). Treatise of Human Nature: being an attempt to introduce the experimental method of reasoning into Moral Subjects. 2 vols. 8vo. London, 1817.

7702 **Saint-Hilaire** (J. Barthélemy). De la Logique d'Aristote. 2 vols. 8vo. Paris, 1838.

7703 **Taylor** (Isaac). Elements of Thought, 2d edition. 1 vol. 12mo. New York, 1851.

7704 **Thomson** (William). An outline of the necessary Laws of Thought; a Treatise on pure and applied Logic. 3d edition, much enlarged. 1 vol. 12mo. London, 1854.

Subj. 67. MORAL PHILOSOPHY.

7705 **Bruce** (John). Elements of the Science of Ethics, on the Principles of Natural Philosophy. 1 vol. 8vo. London, 1786.

7706 **Charron** (Peter). On Wisdome, three Books written in French. Translated by Samson Lennard. 1 vol. 8vo. London, 1630.

7707 **Charron** (Pierre). De la Sagesse. See No. 5278.

7708 **Duty of Man.** See No. 7717.

7709 **Felltham** (Owen). Resolves, Divine, Moral, and Political, a new edition, revised and amended. With a short account of the Author and his writings. By James Cumming. 1 vol. 12mo. London, 1806.

7710 **Heineccii** (Jo. Gottl.). Moralis. See Heineccii, No. 7700.

7711 **Hickox** (Laurens P.). System of Moral Science. 1 vol. 8vo. Schenectady, 1853.

7712 **Hume** (David). Essays and Treatises on several subjects. New edition. 2 vols. 8vo. London, 1784.

7713 **Smith** (Adam). Theory of Moral Sentiments; or, an Essay towards an Analysis of the Principles by which men naturally judge concerning the conduct and character, first of their neighbours, and afterwards of themselves. To which is added, a dissertation on the origin of languages. New edition, with a Biographical and Critical Memoir of the Author, by Dugald Stewart. 1 vol. 12mo. London, 1853.

7714 **Smith** (Reverend Sydney). Elementary Sketches of Moral Philosophy, delivered at the Royal Institution in the years 1804, 1805, and 1806. 1 vol. 12mo. New York, 1855.

7715 **Taylor** (Isaac). Fanaticism. 1 vol. 12mo. New York, 1834

7716 **Urcullu** (J. B. de). Lecciones de Moral, Virtud y Urbanidad, nueva edicion. 1 vol. 24mo. Paris, 1858.

7717 **Whole Duty of Man,** laid down in a plain and familiar way, for the use of all, but especially the meanest reader. A new edition. 1 vol. 16mo. London, 1821.

Subj. 68. POETRY AND FICTIONS.

7718 **Alfieri** (Vittorio). The Tragedies of, translated from the Italian by Charles Lloyd. 3 vols. 18mo. London, 1815.

7719 **André** (Major J.). The Cow-Chace, an Heroic Poem, in three Cantos. See Cow-Chace, No. 7734.

7720 **Arnold** (W. D. Lieut. 58th Reg. B. N. I.). Oakfield; or, Fellowship in the East. 1 vol. 16mo. Boston, 1855.

7721 **Baskerville** (Alfred). The Poetry of Germany, consisting of selections from upwards of seventy of the most celebrated poets, translated into English Verse, with the original text on the opposite page, 2d edition. 1 vol. 12mo. Philadelphia, 1856.

7722 **Biernatzki.** The Hallig: or, the Sheepfold in the Waters. A tale of humble life on the Coast of Schleswig. Translated from the German by Mrs. George P. Marsh. With a Biographical Sketch of the Author. 1 vol. 12mo. Boston, 1856.

7723 **Boccaccio.** The Decameron, or Ten Days' Entertainment. With 18 Steel Engravings. 1 vol. 12mo. New York, 1855.

7724 **Brace** (Charles Loring). Home-Life in Germany. 1 vol. 12mo. New York, 1853.

7725 **Breton de los Herreros** (Don Manuel). Obras escogidas, edicion autorizada por su autor y selecta por si mismo, Con un Prologo, por Don Juan Eugenio Hartzenbusch. 2 vols. 8vo. Paris, 1853.

7726 **Brown** (Charles Brockden). Novels. 7 vols. 12mo. Boston, 1827.

1. Wieland, with a Memoir of the Author.
2. Arthur Mervyn; or Memoirs of the year 1793. 2 vols.
3. Ormond; or the Secret Witness.
4. Edgar Huntly; or Memoirs of a Sleep Walker.
5. Jane Talbot.
6. Clara Howard.

7727 **Bulfinch** (Thomas). The Age of Fable; or, Stories of Gods and Heroes. 3d edition. 1 vol. 12mo. Boston, 1858.

7728 **Bulfinch** (Thomas). The Age of Chivalry. Part I. King Arthur and his Knights. Part II. The Mabinogeon; or Welsh Popular Tales. 1 vol. 12mo. Boston, 1859.

7729 **Bulwer Lytton** (Sir Edward). The Poetical and Dramatic Works. 5 vols. 12mo. London, 1852–54.

7730 **Cervantes** (Miguel de). Don Quijote de la Mancha. Nueva edicion, corregida y anotada. Por Don Eugenio de Ochoa. 1 vol. 12mo. Nueva-York, 1854.

7731 **Cervantes** (Miguel de). Obras escogidas. Nueva edicion clásica, arreglada, corregida é ilustrada con notas Historicas, Gramaticales y criticas, por D. Agustin Garcia de Arrieta. 10 vols. 32mo. Paris, 1826.

7732 **Clark** (L. Gaylord). Knick-Knacks from an Editor's Table. 1 vol. 12mo. New York, 1852.

7733 **Clarke** (Mrs. Cowden). Complete Concordance of Shakspere: being a verbal index to all the passages in the Dramatic Works of the Poet. New and revised edition. 1 vol. roy. 8vo. Boston, ——.

7734 **Cow-Chace,** in three Cantos, Published on occasion of the Rebel General Wayne's attack of the Refugees Block-House on Hudson's River, on Friday the 21st of July, 1780. The American Times, a satire, in three Parts. In which are delineated the Characters of the Leaders of the American Rebellion. 1 vol. 12mo. New York, 1780.

7735 **Dickens** (Charles). Bleak House. With Illustrations, by H. K. Browne. 2 vols. 12mo. New York, 1853.

7736 **Dickens** (Charles). Hard Times. 1 vol. 8vo. ——, ——.

7737 **Dryden** (John). The Works of, in Verse and Prose. With a life. By Rev. John Mitford. 2 vols. 8vo. New York, 1856.

7738 **Fowle** (William Bentley). The hundred Dialogues, new and original; designed for reading and exhibition in Schools, Academies, and private Circles. 1 vol. 12mo. Boston, 1857.

7739 **Fowle** (William Bentley). Parlor Dramas, or Dramatic scenes, for home Amusement. 1 vol. 12mo. Boston, 1857.

7740 **Gil y Zarate** (D. Antonio). Obras Dramaticas. Edicion precedida de una noticia Biografica, y dada a luz. Por D. Eugenio de Ochoa. 1 vol. 8vo. Paris, 1850.

7741 **Goethe** (J. Wolfgang von). Faust: a Tragedy, translated into English verse. By J. Birch, embellished with 29 Engravings on steel after Moritz Retszch. (In two parts,) 1 vol. roy. 8vo. London, 1839–43.

7742 **Hartzenbusch** (Don J. E.). Obras escogidas. Edicion que contiene las correcciones hechas ultimamente por el Autor. 1 vol. 8vo. Paris, 1850.

7743 **Hawkins** (Thomas). Prometheus: 1 vol. roy. 8vo. London, 1850.

7744 **Herbert** (George). The life and works of, in Prose and Verse. 2 vols. 8vo. London, 1846.

7745 **Hermosilla** (Don Josè Gomez). Juicio critico de los Principales Poetas Españoles de la ultima era. Obra Postuma. 1 vol. 12mo. Paris, 1855.

7746 **Hogg** (James). Winter evening Tales, collected among the Cottagers in the South of Scotland. (2 vols. in one.) 1 vol. 12mo. Hartford, 1852.

7747 **Irving** (Washington). Wolfert's Roost and other Papers, now first collected. 1 vol. 12mo. New York, 1855.

7748 **Kennedy** (John P.). Horse-Shoe Robinson: a tale of the Tory ascendency. Revised edition. 1 vol. 12mo. New York, 1854.

7749 **Kennedy** (John P.) Swallow Barn, or a Sojourn in the Old Dominion. Revised edition. 1 vol. 12mo. New York, 1853.

7750 **Kennedy** (John P.). Rob of the Bowl. A Legend of St. Inigoe's. Revised edition. 1 vol. 12mo. New York, 1856.

7751 **Klopstock's** Messiah. Attempted from the German, to which is prefixed his introduction on Divine Poetry. (2 vols. in one.) 1 vol. 12mo. Dublin, 1764.

7752 **Lady Lee's** Widowhood. 1 vol. 8vo. New York, 1853.

7753 **Le Sage** (A. R.). Historia de Gil Blas de Santillana. Traducida al Castellano por El Padre Isla. 1 vol. 8vo. Paris, 1855.

7754 **Longfellow** (Henry Wadsworth). The Song of Hiawatha. 1 vol. 12mo. Boston, 1855.

7755 **Ochoa** (Don Eugenio de). Apuntes para una Biblioteca de escritores Españoles contemporaneos en Prosa y Verso. 2 vols. 8vo. Paris, 1840.

7756 **Ochoa** (Don Eugenio de). Tresoro del Teatro Español, desde su origen (año de 1356) hasta nuestros dias; arreglado y dividido en cuatro partes. 5 vols. 8vo. Paris, 1838.

7757 **Plautus'** Comedies. Translated into familiar blank verse, by Bennell Thornton. 2 vols. 8vo. London, 1769.

7758 **Porden** (Eleanor Anne). Cœur de Lion; or, the Third Crusade. A Poem, in sixteen books. (2 vols. in one.) 1 vol. 8vo. London, 1822.

7759 **Richter** (Jean Paul Friederich). Flower, Fruit, and Thorn Pieces: or, the Married Life, Death, and Wedding of the advocate of the Poor, translated from the German by Edward Henry Noel. First and Second Series. 2 vols. 12mo. Boston, 1845.

7760 **Simms** (W. Gilmore). Novels; or Works. 15 vols. 12mo. New York, 1854–56.

1. Mellichampe, a Legend of the Santee.
2. Woodcraft, or Hawks about the Dovecote.
3. Southward Ho! a Spell of Sunshine.
4. The Yemasee, a Romance of Carolina.
5. The Partisan, a Romance of the Revolution.
6. Guy Rivers, a Tale of Georgia.
7. Richard Hurdis, a Tale of Alabama.
8. Border Beagles, a Tale of Mississippi.
9. Katharine Walton, or the Rebel of Dorchester.
10. The Scout, or the Black Riders of Congaree.
11. The Forayers, or the Raid of the Dog days.
12. Eutaw, a Sequel to the Forayers.
13. Charlemont, or the Pride of the Village, a Tale of Kentucky.
14. Beauchampe, or the Kentucky Tragedy, a Sequel to Charlemont.
15. Confession, or the Blind Heart, a Domestic Story.

7761 **Smith** (Horace). Gaicties and Gravities. 1 vol. 12mo. New York, 1852.

7762 **Tennyson** (Alfred). Maud, and other Poems. 1 vol. 16mo. Boston, 1855.

7763 **Tesoro** del Teatro Español, desde su origen (año de 1356) hasta nuestros dias; arreglado y dividido en cuatro partes, por Don Eugenio de Ochoa. 5 vols. 8vo. Paris, 1838.

7764 **Thackeray** (William M.). The Paris Sketch Book. 2 vols. 12mo. New York, 1852.

7765 **Thackeray** (William M.). A Shabby Genteel Story, and other Tales. 1 vol. 12mo. New York, 1852.

7766 **Thackeray** (William M.). The Yellowplush Papers. 1 vol. 12mo. New York, 1852.

7767 **Thackeray** (William M.). The Confessions of Fitz-Boodle; and some Passages in the Life of Major Gahagan. 1 vol. 12mo. New York, 1852.

7768 **Thackeray** (William M.). Vanity Fair. A Novel without a Hero. With Illustrations by the Author. 1 vol. 8vo. New York, ——.

7769 **Thackeray** (William M.). Men's Wives.
1 vol. 12mo. New York, 1852.

7770 **Thackeray** (William M.). The Book of Snobs.
1 vol. 12mo. New York, 1852.

7771 **Tkackeray** (William M.). Stubb's Calendar; or the Fatal Boots.
1 vol. 18mo. New York, 1850.

7772 **Thackeray** (William M.). Mr. Brown's Letters to a young man about Town; with Prose and other Papers. 1 vol. 12mo. New York, 1853.

7773 **Thackeray** (William M.). The Luck of Barry Lyndon; a Romance of the last Century. 2 vols. 12mo. New York, 1853.

7774 **Thackeray** (William M.). The History of Pendennis. His Fortunes and Misfortunes, his Friends and his greatest Enemy. With Illustrations by the Author. 2 vols. 8vo. New York, 1850.

7775 **Thackeray** (William M.). The Great Hoggarty Diamond.
1 vol. 8vo. New York, ——.

7776 **Thackeray** (William M.). The History of Henry Esmond, Esq., Colonel in the Service of her Majesty Queen Anne, written by himself.
1 vol. 8vo. New York, 1852.

7777 **Thackeray** (William M.). The Newcomes. Memoirs of the most Respectable Family. (2 vols. in one.) 1 vol. 8vo. New York, 1855.

7778 **Thornbury** (G. W.). Lays and Legends, or Ballads of the New World.
1 vol. 8vo. London, 1851.

Subj. 69. GRAMMAR AND PHILOLOGY.

7779 **Barnes** (William). Philological Grammar, grounded upon English, and formed from a comparison of more than sixty languages.
1 vol. 8vo. London, 1854.

7780 **Brown** (Goold). The Grammar of English Grammars, with an introduction Historical and Critical; the whole methodically arranged and amply illustrated, &c., &c. 4th edition, revised and improved.
1 vol. roy. 8vo. New York, 1858.

7781 **Bullions** (Rev. Peter). The Pinciples of Latin Grammar. 6th edition, revised and improved. 1 vol. 12mo. New York, 1855.

7782 **Bullions** (Rev. Peter). The Principles of Greek Grammar. 29th edition, revised and improved. 1 vol. 12mo. New York, 1855.

7783 **Bythneri** (Victorini). Methodica Institutio Linguæ sanctæ. (Bound with Bythner's Lyra Prophetica, &c.) Londini, 1664.

7784 **Cabrera** (Don Ramon). Diccionario de Etimologias de la Lengua Castellana. Obra Postuma. 2 vols. 8vo. Madrid, 1837.

7785 **Diccionario** de Sinónimos de la Lengua Castellana, por una Sociedad de Literatos. Publicada por Don Pedro Maria de Olive.
1 vol. 4to. Paris, 1853.

7786 **Dictionary** of Latin Quotations. See Riley, No. 7796.

7787 **Eichhoff** (F. G.). Parallèle des Langues de l'Europe et de l'Inde, avec un essai de Transcription générale. 1 vol. 4to. Paris, 1836.

7788 **Fowler** (William C.). English Grammar. The English Language in its Elements and Forms. With a history of its Origin and Development. Designed for use in Colleges and Schools. Revised and enlarged. 1 vol. 8vo. New York, 1858.

7789 **Fowler** (William C.). English Grammar. The English Language in its Elements and Forms. With a History of its Origin and Development. Abridged from the octavo edition. Designed for general use in Schools and Families. 1 vol. 12mo. New York, 1858.

7790 **Latham** (R. G.). A Hand-Book of the English Language. 2d edition. 1 vol. 12mo. London, 1855.

7791 **Lowth's** short introduction to English Grammar. With critical notes. 1 vol. 8vo. London, 1762.

7792 **Ollendorff's** New method of learning to read, write, and speak the French Language: with an appendix containing the Cardinal and Ordinal numbers, and full paradigms of regular and irregular, auxiliary, reflective, and impersonal verbs. By J. L. Jewett. 1 vol. 12mo. New York, 1853.

7793 **Pinney & Barcelo.** The Practical Spanish Teacher; or a new method of learning to read, write, and speak the Spanish Language, in a series of Lessons: with a system of Pronunciation; a synopsis of Grammar; and a table of Spanish verbs. By Norman Pinney and Juan Barceló. 1 vol. 12mo. New York, 1855.

7794 **Reiff** (Charles Philip). English-Russian Grammar, or Principles of the Russian Language for the use of Englishmen. 2d edition, completely remodelled. 1 vol. 8vo. Carlsruhe & Leipzig, 1853.

7795 **Renan** (Ernest). Histoire générale et système comparé des Langues sémitiques, ouvrage couronné par l'Institut. Première partie. Histoire générale des Langues sémitiques. 2e édition, revue et augmentée. 1 vol. 8vo. Paris, 1858.

7796 **Riley** (H. T.). Dictionary of Latin Quotations, Proverbs, Maxims, and Mottos, Classical and Mediæval, including Law terms and phrases. With a selection of Greek Quotations. 1 vol. 12mo. London, 1856.

7797 **Roget** (Peter Mark). Thesaurus of English Words and Phrases, classified and arranged so as to facilitate the expression of ideas and assist in Literary Composition. 6th edition, enlarged and improved. 1 vol. 8vo. London, 1857.

7798 **Sanchez** (D. T. A.). Vocabulario de voces anticuadas, para facilitar la lectura de los autores Españoles anteriores al siglo XV. 1 vol. 24mo. Paris, 1842.

7799 **Trench** (Richard Chenevix). On the Study of Words. From the second London edition, revised and enlarged. 1 vol. 12mo. New York, 1854.

7800 **Wilson** (John). Treatise on English Punctuation; designed for Letter-Writers, Authors, Printers, and correctors of the Press; and for the use of Schools and Academies. With an appendix, containing rules on the use of Capitals, a list of abbreviations, &c., &c. 10th edition. 1 vol. 12mo. Boston, 1856.

Subj. 70. RHETORIC AND CRITICISM.

7801 **Coppée** (Henry). Elements of Rhetoric: designed as a Manual of Instruction. 1 vol. 12mo. Philadelphia, 1859.

7802 **Hermosilla** (D. Josef Gómez). Arte de Hablar en Prosa y Verso. Nueva edicion, aumentada con muchas é importantes notas y observaciones. Por D. Vicente Salvá. 1 vol. 12mo. Paris, 1853.

7803 **Rush** (James). The Philosophy of the Human Voice: embracing its Physiological History: together with a System of Principles, by which Criticism in the Art of Elocution may be rendered intelligible, and instruction, definite and comprehensive. To which is added a brief Analysis of Song and Recitation. 3d edition, enlarged. 1 vol. 8vo. Philadelphia, 1845.

7804 **Russell** (William). The American Elocutionist; comprising lessons in Enunciation, exercises in Elocution, and rudiments of Gesture; with a Selection of new Pieces for practice in reading and declamation, &c. 5th edition. 1 vol. 12mo. Boston, 1853.

Subj. 71. ADDRESSES.

7805 **Bayard** (Samuel J.). Address delivered at West Point before the Graduating Class of Cadets, June 16, 1854. 1 8vo. Pamphlet. Camden, N. J., 1854.

7806 **Clay** (Henry). The Life and Speeches of the Hon. Henry Clay, compiled and edited by Daniel Mallory. 1 vol. 8vo. New York, 1843.

7807 **Columbia** College. Addresses of the newly-appointed Professors of Columbia College, with an introductory Address by William Betts, LL. D. February, 1858. 1 vol. 8vo. (2 *copies.*) New York, 1858.

7808 **De Peyster** (J. Watts). An Address to the officers of the New York State Troops. 1 8vo. Pamphlet. ——, 1858.

7809 **Draper** (Prof. J. W.). An Address to the Alumni of the University of the City of New York at their 21st Anniversary, 28th June, 1853. 1 8vo. Pamphlet. New York, 1853.

7810 **Dudley** Observatory. An Address to the Citizens of Albany, and the Donors and Friends of the Dudley Observatory, on the recent Proceedings of the Trustees; from the Committee of Citizens appointed at a Public Meeting held at Albany on the 13th of July, 1858. 1 8vo. Pamphlet. Albany, 1858.

7811 **Dudley** Observatory and the Scientific Council. Statement of the Trustees. 1 vol. 8vo. Albany, 1858.

7812 **Dudley** Observatory. Defence of Dr. Gould by the Scientific Council of the Dudley Observatory. 1 vol. 8vo. Albany, 1858.

7813 **Gould** (Dr.). Defence by the Scientific Council of the Dudley Observatory. 1 vol. 8vo. Albany, 1858.

7814 **Harris** (Hon. Thomas L.). Obituary Address on the occasion of the Death of the, See No. 7818.

7815 **Henry** (C. S.). An Address before the Association of the Alumni of the University of the City of New York, June 28, 1852. 1 8vo. Pamphlet. New York, 1853.

7816 **Hilliard** (Henry W.). Speeches and Addresses. 1 vol. 8vo. New York, 1855.

7817 **Kewen & Soule.** Oration and Poem before the Society of California Pioneers, at their Celebration of the Anniversary of the Admission of the State of California into the Union. San Francisco, September 9th, 1854. 1 8vo. Pamphlet. San Francisco, 1854.

7818 **Quitman & Harris.** Obituary Addresses on the occasions of the Death of the Hon. John A. Quitman, of Mississippi, and of the Hon. Thomas L. Harris, of Illinois, delivered in the Senate of the United States, on the 5th and 17th of January, 1859. 1 8vo. Pamphlet. Baltimore, 1859.

7819 **Rayner** (Hon. Kenneth). Address delivered before the Graduating Class of the United States Military Academy, West Point, June 17th, 1853. 1 8vo. Pamphlet. New York, 1853.

7820 **Schaff** (Dr. Philip). America. A Sketch of the Political, Social, and Religious character of the United States of North America, in two Lectures. Translated from the German. 1 vol. 12mo. New York, 1855.

7821 **Voice** to America; or, the Model Republic, its Glory or its fall: with a review of the causes of the Decline and Failure of the Republics of South America, Mexico, and of the Old World; applied to the present crisis in the United States. 1 vol. 12mo. New York, 1855.

7822 **Warren** (Gen.). Inauguration of the Statue of General Warren on Bunker Hill, June 17th, 1857. 1 vol. 8vo. Boston, 1858.

7823 **Washington's** Farewell Address to the People of the United States of America. 1 vol. 4to. New York, 1850.

7824 **Williams** (Henry). An Address delivered on laying the Corner Stone of a Monument to Pulaski, in the City of Savannah, October 11, 1853. With an account of the Ceremonies upon that occasion, and at the completion of the Monument, January 8th, 1855. To which is added a summary of the evidence designating the Burial Place of Pulaski, prepared by Col. William P. Bowen. Published by the Commissioners of the Monument fund. 1 8vo. Pamphlet. Savannah, 1855.

7825 **Worth** (General William Jenkins). Reports on the erection of a Monument to the memory of William Jenkins Worth, late Major-General of the United States Army, by the special committees appointed by the Common Council of the City of New York. 1 vol. 8vo. New York, 1857.

Subj. 72. JOURNALS AND TREATISES UPON EDUCATION.

7826 **Barnard** (Prof. F. A. P.). On Collegiate Education and College Government. 1 vol. 8vo. New York, 1855.

7827 **Barnard** (F. A. P.). Improvements Practicable in American Colleges. 1 8vo. Pamphlet. Hartford, 1856.

7828 **Décret** impérial portant réorganisation de l'École de Cavalerie. Compiégne, le 17 Octobre, 1853. (Lithog.). 1 fol. Pamphlet. ——, ——.

7829 **Examination** Papers, both entrance and periodical, of the Ordnance School at Carshalton, and of the Royal Military Academy at Woolwich, accompanied by Diagrams illustrative of the work. Printed by permission from the original documents. 1 vol. 8vo. Woolwich, 1853.

7830 **Herbert** (Edward, Lord of Cherbury). Dialogue between a Tutor and his Pupil. 1 vol. 4to. London, 1768.

7831 **Instructions** with regard to the Education of pupils at the Military Schools. (In the Russian language.) 1 vol. roy. 8vo. St. Petersburg, 1849.

7832 **Jones** (Col. William D.). Records of the Royal Military Academy at Woolwich, 1741 to 1840. 1 vol. fol. Woolwich, 1851.

7833 **Military** Schools. Outline of the Organization and Condition of the Military Schools. (In the Russian language.) 1 vol. roy. 8vo. St. Petersburg, 1851.

7834 **Military** Schools. New Organization of Military Schools—may be regarded as a 10th Supplement to Part I., Book III., Code of Military Laws. (In the Russian language.) 1 No. fol. ——, ——.

7835 **Miller** (Hugh). My Schools and Schoolmasters; or, the Story of my Education. 1 vol. 12mo. Boston, 1855.

7836 **New York** Free Academy. Examination Papers of the New York Free Academy, July, 1857. 1 vol. 8vo. New York, 1857.

7837 **Parker** (Richard Green). Aids to English Composition, prepared for Students of all grades; embracing specimens and examples of School and College exercises and most of the higher departments of English Composition, both in Prose and Verse. 20th edition. 1 vol. 12mo. New York, 1858.

7838 **Programmes** of the Course of Instruction of Cadets at the "Michael" Artillery School. (In the Russian language.) (Lithog.) 10 Nos. fol. ——, ——.

7839 **Programmes** of the Course of Instruction of the Junior Class of Officers at the "Michael" Artillery School. (In the Russian language.) (Lithog.) 4 Nos. fol. ——, ——.

7840 **Programme** of the Course of Descriptive Geometry in the Military Schools. (In the Russian language.) 1 roy. 8vo. Pamphlet. ——, ——.

7841 **Programme** of the Course of Natural Sciences in the Military Schools. (In the Russian language.) 1 roy. 8vo. Pamphlet. ——, ——.

7842 **Programme** of the Course of Foreign languages in the Military Schools. (In the Russian language.) 1 roy. 8vo. Pamphlet. ——, ——.

7843 **Programme** of the Course of Algebra, Analytical Geometry, Differential and Integral Calculus. (In the Russian language.) (Lithog.) 3 sheets fol. ——, ——.

7844 **Programme** of the Course of Lectures on Astronomy and Geodesy in the School of État Major. (In the Russian language.) (Lithog.) 1 No. fol. ——, ——.

7845 **Programme** and Summary of the third special class composed in 1853. (In the Russian language.) (Lithog.) 2 vols. imperial 8vo. ——, ——.

7846 **Programme** of the Final Examination of Officers educated at the School of the État Major. (In the Russian language.) 1 vol. 4to. St. Petersburg, 1853.

7847 **Programme** of the Course of Military Science in the Military Schools. (In the Russian language.) 1 roy. 8vo. Pamphlet. ——, ——.

7848 **Programme** of the Course on Political Science in the Military Schools. (In the Russian language.) 1 roy. 8vo. Pamphlet. ——, ——.

7849 **Programme** of the Course of Mathematics in the Military Schools. (In the Russian language.) 1 roy. 8vo. Pamphlet. ——, ——.

7850 **Programme** of the Course on Religion in the Military Schools. (In the Russian language.) 1 roy. 8vo. Pamphlet. ——, ——.

7851 **Programme** of the examination of officers on entering the School of the État Major. (In the Russian language.) 1 8vo. Pamphlet. (2 *copies.*) St. Petersburg, 1852.

7852 **Programme** of the Course on the Russian language and literature, in the Military Schools. (In the Russian language.) 1 roy. 8vo. Pamphlet. ——, ——.

7853 **Rapport** sur l'enseignement de l'École Polytechnique, adressé à M. le Ministre de la guerre par commission mixte nommée en exécution de la loi du 5 Juin 1850. 1 vol. 4to. Paris, 1850.

7854 **Reglement** pour l'exécution des travaux des Éléves de l'École Impériale d'application de l'artillerie et du Génie. (Lithog.). Decembre 1854. 1 4to. Pamphlet. ——, ——.

7855 **Report** of the Commissioners appointed to consider the best mode of Re-organizing the System for training officers for the scientific corps; together with an account of foreign and other Military Education. With an Appendix. Ordered to be printed 20th March, 1857. 2 vols. fol. (Bound in one). ——, ——.

7856 **Sandhurst** Royal Military College. Report from the select Committee on Sandhurst Royal Military College; together with the Proceedings of the Committe, Minutes of Evidence, Appendix, and Index. 1 vol. fol. ——, 1855.

7857 **Smith** (William). The Student's Vade Mecum. (Bound with Heineccius' Elementa Philosophiæ Rationalis et Moralis.) In 8vo. London, 1770.

7858 **Spearman** (Capt. J. Morton). Notes on Military Education. 1 vol. 8vo. London, 1853.

7859 **Taylor** (Isaac). Home Education. 5th edition. 1 vol. 18mo. London, 1851.

7860 **Woolwich.** Royal Military Academy at, See Nos. 6345, 6353, 6354, 6355, 6356, 6692, 7018, 7829, 7832.

Subj. 73. WORKS ON PAINTING, SCULPTURE, MUSIC, AND ILLUSTRATED WORKS OF ENGRAVINGS.

7861 **Adam.** Une Lettre. Réfutation par Émile Chevé. Mars, 1855. 1 8vo. Pamphlet. Paris, 1855.

7862 **Barry** (James). Lectures on Painting. See No. 7873.

7863 **Burney** (Charles). Present State of Music in France and Italy; or the Journal of a Tour through those countries, undertaken to Collect Materials for a general History of Music. 1 vol. 8vo. London, 1771.

7864 **Chevé** (M. et Mme Émile). Méthode élémentaire de Musique Vocale. Ouvrage repoussé à l'unanimité le 9 Avril, 1850, par la commission du chant de la Ville de Paris. 6e édition. 3e Tirage. 1 vol. roy. 8vo. Paris, 1854.

7865 **Chevé** (Émile). Historique et Procès-Verbal du Concours Musical Ouvert à Paris le 12 Juin, 1853, sous la Présidence de M. Henri Reber. 1 vol. 8vo. Paris, 1853.

7866 **Chevé** (Émile). Réfutation d'une Lettre de M. Adam, Mars, 1855. 1 8vo. Pamphlet. Paris, 1855.

7867 **Dwight** (M. A.). Introduction to the Study of Art. 1 vol. 12mo. New York, 1856.

7868 **Ecole** de dessin, journal des jeunes Artistes et des Amateurs, donnant tous les mois des Modéles élémentaires et nouveaux pour tous les genres de dessin, figure, paysage, fleurs et fruits, &c., &c. 10 vols. 4to. (bound in five.) Paris, 1851–56.

7869 **Fétis** (F. J.). Antoine Stradivari Luthier Célébre connu sous le nom de Stradivarius précédé de Recherches historiques et critiques sur l'origine et les transformations des Instruments à archet et suivi d'analyses théoriques sur l'archet et sur François Tourte auteur de ses derniers perfectionnements. 1 vol. 8vo. Paris, 1856.

7870 **Fitz William** (Edward Francis). Music. See No. 7883.

7871 **Fuseli** (Henry). Lectures on Painting. See No. 7873.

7872 **Harding** (J. D.) The Principles and Practice of art. With Illustrations drawn and engraved by the Author. 1 vol. fol. London, 1845.

7873 **Lectures** on Painting, by the Royal Academicians. Barry, Opie, and Fuseli. Edited with an Introduction and Notes critical and illustrative, by Ralph N. Wornum. 1 vol. 12mo. London, 1848.

7874 **Modern Painters.** By a Graduate of Oxford. 4th edition. 3 vols. 8vo. London, 1848–57.

7875 **Opie** (John). Lectures on Painting. See No. 7873.

7876 **Photographic** and Fine Art Journal. H. H. Snelling, Editor, 1856. Vol. 9, in 4to. New York, 1856.

7877 **Photographs** of the Graduating Classes of the U. S. Military Academy, West Point, New York. For the years 1857 and 1859. 2 vols. 4to. ——, ——.

7878 **Read & Co.** Panoramic Views of the Seat of War, East and North. See No. 6714.

7879 **Reicha** (Antoine). Cours de Composition Musicale, ou Traité complet d'Harmonie pratique de Mélodie de l'emploi des voix et des Instrumens, de haute Composition et du Contrepoint double, de la Fugue et du Canon, &c. (In the French and German languages.) 4 vols. 4to. Vienne, ——.

7880 **Reicha** (Antoine). Art du Compositeur Dramatique, ou Cours Complet de Composition Vocale divisé en six parties. (In the French and German languages.) 1 vol. 4to. Vienne, ——.

7881 **Ruskin** (John). Modern Painters. 3 vols. 8vo. London, 1848–57.

7882 **Schlegel** (Augustus William.) The Æsthetic and Miscellaneous Works. Translated from the German, by E. J. Millington. 1 vol. 12mo. London, 1849.

7883 **Songs** of a Student, the Poetry selected from the Works of Lord Byron, Shelley, Coleridge, Leigh Hunt, Sir Edward Bulwer Lytton, Laman Blanchard, Sidney Godolphin, Mrs. Hemans, &c., &c., the Music composed by Edward Francis Fitzwilliam. 1 vol. roy. 8vo. London, 1850.

7884 **Spooner** (Shearjashub). A Biographical and Critical Dictionary of Painters, Engravers, Sculptors, and Architects, from ancient to modern times. 1 vol. roy. 8vo. New York, 1853.

7885 **Spooner** (Shearjashub). Anecdotes of Painters, Engravers, Sculptors, and Architects, and curiosities of Art. 3 vols. 16mo. New York, 1853.

7886 **Stanford's** Panoramic View of Helsingfors and Svéaborg. See No. 6719.

Subj. 74. GYMNASTICS AND SWIMMING.

7887 **Laisné** (Napoléon). Gymnastique pratique, contenant la Description des Exercices, la Construction et le Prix des Machines, et des chants spéciaux inédits; ouvrage destiné aux Familles, aux Établissements d'éducation, aux Corps Militaires. Avec une Préface par M. Barthélemy Saint-Hilaire. 1 vol. 8vo. Paris, 1850.

Subj. 75. LITERARY AND POLITICAL PERIODICALS, REPORTS AND REGISTERS.

7888 **Annuaire** des deux Mondes. Histoire générale des divers États. 1854–56. 2 vols. roy. 8vo. Paris, 1855–56.

7889 **Blackwood's** Edinburgh Magazine. (Vols. 65 to 80, inclusive.) 16 vols. 8vo. New York, 1849–56.

7890 **Congressional Globe:** containing the Debates, Proceedings, and Laws, of the 1st session of the 32d Congress. 4 vols. 4to. Washington, 1852.

7891 **Dickens** (Charles). Household Words. See No. 7896.

7892 **Exhibition** of the Works of Industry of all Nations, 1851. Reports by the Juries on the subjects in the thirty classes into which the Exhibition was divided. 1 vol. roy. 8vo. London, 1852.

7893 **Exhibibion** of Science & Mechanism in 1853–4. See Goodrich, No. 7894.

7894 **Goodrich** (C. R.). **& others.** Science and Mechanism: illustrated by examples in the New York Exhibition, 1853–4. Including extended descriptions of the most important contributions in the various Departments, with annotations and notes relative to the Progress and present state of applied science and the useful arts. 1 vol. fol. New York, 1854.

7895 **Harper's** New Monthly Magazine. 13 vols. 8vo. New York, 1850–56.

7896 **Household Words.** A weekly Journal. Conducted by Charles Dickens. Vols. 8 to 14, inclusive. 7 vols. 8vo. London & New York, 1854–56.

7897 **Knickerbocker;** or, New York Monthly Magazine. (Vols. 33 to 48, inclusive.) 16 vols. 8vo. New York, 1849–56.

7898 **Littell's** Living Age. Conducted by E. Littell. 36 vols. 8vo. Boston, 1844–53.

7899 **Littell's** Living Age. Conducted by E. Littell. 2d series. 15 vols. 8vo. Boston, 1853–56.

7900 **Merchants' Magazine** and Commercial Review. Conducted by Freeman Hunt. (Vols. 20 to 35, inclusive.) 16 vols. 8vo. New York, 1849–56.

7901 **New York.** 65th, 66, 67, 68, 69, & 71st Annual Reports of the Regents of the University of the State of New York. 6 vols. 8vo. Albany, 1852–58.

7902 **Penny Magazine** of the Society for the Diffusion of useful Knowledge, 1832–1845. 14 vols. roy. 8vo. London, 1832–45.

7903 **Poole** (W^m. Fred.). An Index to Periodical Literature. 1 vol. 8vo. New York, 1853.

7904 **Report** of Hon. James Meachan, of the special Committe of the Board of Regents of the Smithsonian Institution, on the distribution of the income of the Smithsonian Fund, &c. 1 vol. 8vo. Washington, 1854.

7905 **Report** of the special Committee of the Board of Regents of the Smithsonian Institution, on the distribution of the income of the Smithsonian Fund, &c. 1 8vo. Pamphlet. Washington, 1854.

7906 **Report** of the Portsmouth Relief Association to the Contributors of the Fund for the Relief of Portsmouth, Virginia, during the Prevalence of the Yellow Fever in that Town in 1855; the Exhibit of the Treasurer of the Receipts and Disbursements of the Fund, and Statements of other Members of the Association; together with a sketch of the Fever, &c., &c. 1 vol. 8vo. Richmond, 1856.

7907 **Review.** The North American Review and Miscellaneous Journal. (Several Nos. missing.) 83 vols. 8vo. Boston, 1815–56.

7908 **Review.** Edinburgh Review, or Critical Journal. (Several Nos. missing.) 103 vols. 8vo. Edinburgh & New York, 1804–55.

7909 **Review.** Westminister Review. 19 vols. 8vo. London, 1824–33.
Vols. 50 to 55, in 8vo. New York, 1848–51.

7910 **Review.** London Quarterly Review.
Vols. 84 to 99, incl. in 8vo. New York, 1849–56.

7911 **Review.** North British Review.
Vols. 10 to 25, incl. in 8vo. New York, 1849–56.

7912 **Review.** Southern Quarterly Review.
Vols. 8 to 11 incl. in 8vo. Charleston, 1853–55.

7913 **Revue** des Deux Mondes, pour les années, 1830, 1831, 1855 et 1856.
13 vols. 8vo. Paris, 1830–56.

Subj. 76. BIBLIOGRAPHY.

7914 **Appletons'** Library Manual; containing a Catalogue Raisonné of upwards of 12000 of the most important Works in every Department of Knowledge. 1 vol. 8vo. New York, 1847.

7915 **Appleton & Co.'s** New Catalogue of American and English Books. 1 vol. 8vo. New York, 1855.

7916 **Bibliotheca** Scriptorum Classicorum. Herausgegeben von Wilhelm Engelmann. 1 vol. 8vo. Leipzig, 1847.

7917 **Bibliotheca** Historico-Naturalis. Von Wilhelm Engelmann. 1 vol. 8vo. Leipzig, 1846.

7918 **Bibliotheca** Medico-Chirurgica, &c. Von Wilhelm Engelmann. 1 vol. 8vo. Leipzig, 1848.

7919 **Bibliotheca** Historica. 1 vol. 8vo. Leipzig, 1842.

7920 **Bibliotheca** Philologica. 2 vols. 8vo. Leipzig, 1840–42.

7921 **Bibliotheca** Œconomica. 1 vol. 8vo. Leipzig, 1841.

7922 **Bibliotheca** Psychologica. 1 vol. 8vo. Leipzig, 1845.

7923 **Bibliotheca** Magica et Pneumatica. 1 vol. 8vo. Leipzig, 1843.

7924 **Bibliotheca** Orientalis. 1 vol. 8vo. Leipzig, 1846.

7925 **Hector Bossange** Catalogue, avec 1er, 2e et 3e suppléments. 2 vols. 8vo. Paris, 1845–50.

7926 **Library** of Congress. Catalogue of the Additions made to the Library of Congress, since the first day of December, 1851, to November 1st, 1856. 5 vols. 8vo. Washington, 1852–56.

7927 **New York** State. Annual Reports of the Trustees of the New York State Library, for 1854, '55, '56, & '58. 4 vols. 8vo. Albany, 1854–58.

7928 **New York** State Library. Catalogue of the, 1855. (General Library.) 1 vol. 8vo. Albany, 1856.

7929 **New York** State Library. Catalogue of the, 1855. (Law Library.) 1 vol. 8vo. Albany, 1856.

7930 **New York** State Library. Catalogue of, (1856.) Maps, Manuscripts, Engravings, Coins, &c. 1 vol. 8vo. Albany, 1857.

7931 **New York** State Library. Catalogue of the Books on Bibliography, Typography, and Engraving in the, 1 vol. 8vo. Albany, 1858.

7932 **Putnam & Co.'s** Catalogue of Foreign and American Books, in every Department of Literature, Science, and the Arts. 1 vol. 8vo. New York, 1852.

Subj. 77. DICTIONARIES AND ENCYCLOPÆDIAS.

7933 **Diccionario** universal francés-español, y español francés, por Don Ramon Joaquin Dominguez. Segunda edicion considerablemente corregida y aumentada. 2 vols. large 8vo. Madrid, 1853.

7934 **Dictionary** of the Russian, French, German, and English languages. (Part I. Russian Part.) 1 vol. 8vo. St. Petersburg & Carlsruhe, 1853.

7935 **Dominguez** (Don Ramon Joaquin). Diccionario universal francés-español y español francés, segunda edicion considerablemente corregida y aumentada. 2 vols. large 8vo. Madrid, 1853.

7936 **Hedericus** (Benj.). Græcum Lexicon manuale, primum a Benjamine Hederico institutum, cura J. A. Ernesti et T. Morelli auctum : editio nova cui accedit magnus verborum et exemplorum numerus ex schedis P.-H. Larcheri. 1 vol. 4to. Londini, 1816.

7937 **Landais** (Napoléon). Dictionnaire Général et Grammatical des Dictionnaires Français, extrait et complément de tous les Dictionnaires les plus célébres. 2 vols. large 8vo. Paris, 1834.

7938 **Landais** (Napoléon). Dictionnaire Général et Grammatical des Dictionnaires Français, Tome 3e, complément, A—Z. Par MM. D. Chésurolles et L. Barré. 1 vol. imp. 8vo. Paris, 1857.

7939 **Neuman & Baretti.** Seoane's Neuman & Baretti's Pronouncing Dictionary of the Spanish and English languages : composed from the Spanish Dictionaries of the Spanish Academy, Terreros and Salva, and from the English Dictionaries of Webster, Worcester, and Walker : By Mariano Velazquez de la Cadena. 1 vol. roy. 8vo. New York, 1857.

7940 **Parkhurst** (John.) An Hebrew and English Lexicon without Points, in which the Hebrew and Chaldee words of the Old Testament are explained in their leading and derived senses, the Derivative Words are ranged under their respective primitives. And the meanings assigned to each authorized by references to passages of Scripture, and frequently illustrated and confirmed by citations from various Authors, ancient and modern. To this work are prefixed an Hebrew and a Chaldee Grammar. 1 vol. roy. 8vo. London, 1813.

7941 **Penny** (The). Cyclopædia. Published by the Society for the Diffusion of Useful Knowledge. With Supplement. 29 vols. roy. 8vo. London, 1833–46.

7942 **Quackenbos** (G. P.). Spiers & Surenne's French and English Pronouncing Dictionary. 1 vol. roy. 8vo. New York, 1856.

7943 **Salva** (Don Vincente). Nuevo Diccionario de la lengua Castellana que Comprende la última edicion integra, muy rectificada y mejorada, del publicado por la Academia Españole, quinta edicion añadida con un suplemento de mas de 300 páginas, que contiene las voces de ciencias y artes, &c., &c. 1 vol. 4to. Paris, 1857.

7944 **Seoane's** Neuman & Baretti's Dictionary. See No. 7939.

7945 **Spiers & Surenne's** French and English Pronouncing Dictionary. Newly composed from the French Dictionaries of the French Academy, Laveaux, Boiste, Bescherelle, Landais, &c., and from the English Dictionaries of Johnson, Webster, Worcester, Richardson, &c. By G. P. Quackenbos, A. M. 1 vol. roy. 8vo. New York, 1856.

7946 **Velazquez** (Mariano). Seoane's Neuman & Baretti's Pronouncing Dictionary of the Spanish and English languages. 1 vol. roy. 8vo. New York, 1857.

7947 **Walker** (John). A Critical Pronouncing Dictionary and Expositor of the English language; to which is prefixed Principles of English Pronunciation, &c., &c. 1 vol. 8vo. Philadelphia, 1856.

7948 **Worcester** (Joseph E.). Universal and Critical Dictionary of the English Language: to which are added Walker's Key to the pronunciation of Classical and Scripture Proper Names, much enlarged and improved, and a Pronouncing Vocabulary of modern Geographical Names. 1 vol. roy. 8vo. Boston, 1855.

Subj. 78. THEOLOGY AND ECCLESIASTICAL HISTORY.

7949 **Ashdowne** (William). A Scripture Key to the Evangelists, the acts of the Apostles, the Epistle to the Romans, Galatians, Ephesians, Colossians, and Hebrews. In a method hitherto unattempted.
1 vol. 8vo. Canterbury, 1777.

7950 **Atlas of Prophecy:** being the Prophecies of Daniel and St. John; with a simple exposition, and a series of Maps & Charts, &c.
1 vol. 4to. London, 1849.

7951 **Bagster's** Critical New Testament in Greek and English. See No. 7987.

7952 **Bampton** (Rev. John). Eight Sermons. See No. 7972.

7953 **Barrett** (B. F.). Lectures on the New Dispensation, Called the New Jerusalem. 1 vol. 12mo. New York, 1855.

7954 **Barrington** (Shute, Bishop of Durham). Sermons, Charges, and Tracts.
1 vol. 8vo. London, 1811.

7955 **Benham** (Daniel). Reflections on the Genealogy of our Lord and Saviour Jesus Christ, as recorded by St. Matthew and St. Luke.
1 vol. 4to. London, 1836.

7956 **Bible.** The Holy, containing the Old and New Testaments: Translated out of the Original Tongues: and the former translations diligently compared and revised, by his Majesty's special command.
1 vol. imperial 4to. Oxford, 1852.

7957 **Bible.** The Holy, translated from the Latin Vulgate: diligently compared with the Hebrew, Greek, and other Editions, in divers Languages; the Old Testament first published by the English College, at Douay, A D. 1609; and the New Testament first published by the English College, at Rheims, A. D. 1582. With annotations, references, and an historical and chronological Index. From the last London and Dublin editions.
1 vol. roy. 8vo. New York, 1853.

7958 **Bingham** (Joseph). Origines Ecclesiasticæ. The Antiquities of the Christian Church. With two Sermons and two Letters on the Nature and Necessity of absolution. Reprinted from the original edition, 1708–1722. With an enlarged analytical index.
2 vols. roy. 8vo. London, 1856.

7959 **Bledsoe** (Albert Taylor). A Theodicy; or, Vindication of the Divine Glory, as Manifested in the Constitution and Government of the Moral World. 1 vol. 8vo. New York, 1856.

7960 **Bunsen** (Christian Charles Josias). Signs of the Times: Letters to Ernst Moritz Arndt on the Dangers to Religious Liberty in the present State of the World. Translated from the German by Susanna Winkworth.
1 vol. 8vo. London, 1856.

7961 **Burn** (Richard). Ecclesiastical Law. 6th edition, with notes and references, by Simon Fraser, Esq., Barrister at Law. 4 vols. 8vo. London, 1797.

7962 **Bythneri** (Victorini). Lyra Prophetica Davidis Regis; sive analysis critico-Practica Psalmorum. 1 vol. 8vo. Londini, 1664.

7963 **Caunter** (Rev. John Hobart). The Poetry of the Pentateuch. 2 vols. 8vo. London, 1839.

7964 **Conybeare** (Rev. W. J.). **&** **Howson** (Rev. J. S.). The Life and Epistles of St. Paul. 5th edition. 2 vols. 8vo. New York, 1856.

7965 **Cope** (Sir Anthony). Meditations on twenty select Psalms, reprinted from the edition of 1547; with a Biographical preface and notes. 1 vol. 12mo. London, 1848.

7966 **Crisis.** The Great, See No. 7996.

7967 **Cruden** (Alexander). A complete Concordance to the Holy Scriptures of the Old and New Testament, or, a Dictionary and alphabetical index to the Bible. 14th edition. 1 vol. roy. 8vo. London, 1854.

7968 **D'Aubigné** (J. H. Merle). History of the Reformation of the sixteenth Century. Translated by H. White. 5 vols. 12mo. New York, 1848–53.

7969 **Drummond** (George Hay). Sermons preached in the Cathedral Church of St. Peter, York, August 3, 1794, and at the Church of St. Mary, Woolnoth, London, April 22, 1795. 1 vol. 4to. York & London, 1794–95.

7970 **Erasmus'** Paraphrase on the Gospels. 1 vol. imp. 8vo. ——, ——.

7971 **Fysh** (Rev. Frederic). The Divine History of the Church during the twelve hours' sleep of the Apostles Peter and Paul, the Millennium, and the ages of ages; being a Catechism of the Apocalypse, with a plan of the Apocalyptic Drama; and a Chronological Table. 1 vol. 18mo. London, 1845.

7972 **Goddard** (Charles). Eight Sermons preached before the University of Oxford, in the year 1823, at the Lecture founded by the late Rev. John Bampton. With a Preface, and notes, critical and explanatory. 1 vol. 8vo. Oxford, 1824.

7973 **Gray** (Rev. Robert). Key to the Old Testament and Apocrypha: or an account of their several Books, their Contents and Authors, and of the Times in which they were respectively written. 3d edition. 1 vol. 8vo. London, 1797.

7974 **Greek and English Testament.** See No. 7987.

7975 **Hammond** (Henry). Tracts. 1 vol. 8vo. Oxford, 1644.

7976 **Hayden** (William B.). Science and Revelation: or, the bearing of modern scientific developments upon the interpretation of the first eleven chapters of Genesis. 1 vol. 16mo. Boston, 1853.

7977 **Hoogduit.** Gedichten & Figuren. | Poems & Emblems. 1 vol. fol. ——, ——.

7978 **Koran,** commonly called the Alcoran of Mohammed: Translated from the original Arabic. With Explanatory Notes, taken from the most approved Commentators. To which is prefixed a Preliminary Discourse. By George Sale. A new edition. 2 vols. 8vo. London, 1836.

7979 **Lamennais** (F. de). Essai sur l'indifférence en matiére de Religion. 4 vols. 16mo. Paris, 1843.

7980 **Lardner** (Nathaniel). The History of the Heretics of the two first centuries after Christ: containing an account of their Time, Opinions, and Testimony to the Books of the New Testament. To which are prefixed, general Observations concerning Heretics. Published from the Manuscripts of the late Reverend and Learned Nathaniel Lardner, D. D. With large additions, by John Hogg. 1 vol. 4to. London, 1780.

7981 **Lawd** (William). Relation of the conference between William Lawd and Mr. Fisher, the Jesuite. 1 vol. small fol. London, 1639.

7982 **Llorente** (Don Juan Antonio). Historia critica de la Inquisicion de España. Obra original conforme á lo que resulta de los Archivos del real consejo de la suprema, y de los tribunales del santo-oficio de las provincias. 10 vols. 24mo. Madrid, 1822.

7983 **Mather** (Reverend and Learned Cotton). Magnalia Christi Americana; or the Ecclesiastical History of New England from its first Planting, in the year 1620, unto the year of our Lord 1698. With an introduction and occasional notes, by the Rev. Thomas Robbins, and Translations of the Hebrew, Greek, and Latin Quotations, by Lucius F. Robinson. 2 vols. 8vo. Hartford, 1853.

7984 **Mede** (Mr. Joseph). Works. Being discourses on divers Texts of Scripture, and four Treatises formerly printed: but now revised and corrected according to the Authors own Manuscripts. 1 vol. 8vo. London, 1648–52.

7985 **Molesworth** (Rev. J. E. N.). The Domestic Chaplain; or Sermons on Family duties for every Sunday in the year. Vol. 1st in 8vo. London, 1838.

7986 **New Testament** of our Lord and Saviour Jesus Christ, and an exact Concordance to the Holy Bible. 1 vol. 4to. Cambridge, 1666.

7987 **New Testament** in Greek and English, with a Greek-English Lexicon to the New Testament. 1 vol. 18mo. London, ——.

7988 **Oliver** (Peter). Scripture Lexicon; or a Dictionary of above four thousand proper Names of Persons and Places, mentioned in the Old and New Testament: also the Explanation of many words and things in the Bible, a new edition, corrected. 1 vol. 8vo. Oxford, 1818.

7989 **Pearson** (Rev. Thomas). Evangelical alliance Prize Essay on Infidelity; its aspects, causes, and agencies. From the 40th London edition. 1 vol. 18mo. New York, 1854.

7990 **Philadelphia** Lectures on the Evidences of Christianity. See Potter, No. 7992.

7991 **Philosophy** of the Plan of Salvation. A Book for the times. By an American citizen. With an Introductory Essay by Calvin E. Stowe, a new edition, with a supplementary chapter by the author. 1 vol. 12mo. Boston, 1856.

7992 **Potter** (Alonzo). Lectures on the Evidences of Christianity. Delivered in Philadelphia, by Clergymen of the Protestant Episcopal Church, in the Fall and Winter of 1853–4. With an introductory Essay. 1 vol. 8vo. Philadelphia, 1855.

7993 **Powell** (William Samuel). Discourses on various subjects. Published by Thomas Balguy. 1 vol. 8vo. London, 1776.

7994 **Prideaux** (Humphrey). The Old and New Testament connected in the History of the Jews and Neighbouring Nations, from the Declension of the Kingdoms of Israel and Judah to the time of Christ. 8th edition. 3 vols. 8vo. London, 1720.

7995 **Richer** (Edward). The Religion of Good Sense. 1 vol. 18mo. London, 1852.

7996 **Roach** (R.). The Great Crisis: or, the Mystery of the Times and Seasons unfolded. 1 vol. 8vo. London, 1725. } Bound in one.

7997 **Roach** (R.). The Imperial Standard of Messiah Triumphant. 1 vol. 8vo. London, 1727. }

7998 **St. Paul.** The Life and Epistles of, by the Reverends W. J. Conybeare and J. S. Howson. 5th edition. 2 vols. 8vo. New York, 1856.

7999 **Sandys** (Sir Edwin). Europæ speculum, or a view or survey of the State of Religion in the Western parts of the World. Wherein the Romane Religion, and the pregnant policies of the Church of Rome to support the same, are totably displayed: with some other memorable discoveries and commemorations. 1 vol. small 8vo. London, 1632.

8000 **Scott** (John). The Christian Life, from its beginning to its Consummation in Glory; together with the several means and instruments of Christianity conducing thereunto. With directions for private devotion, and Forms of Prayer. 10th edition. 5 vols. 8vo. London, 1739.

8001 **Stanhope** (George). The Truth and Excellence of the Christian Religion asserted against Jews, Infidels, and Hereticks. 1 vol. 8vo. London, 1702.

8002 **Swedenborg** (Emanuel). Angelic Wisdom concerning the Divine love and the Divine Wisdom. Translated from the Latin, from the last London edition. 1 vol. 8vo. (*2 copies.*) New York, 1853.

8003 **Swedenborg** (Emanuel). Angelic Wisdom concerning the Divine Providence. Translated from the Latin, from the last London edition. 1 vol. 8vo. (*2 copies.*) New York, 1853.

8004 **Swedenborg** (Emanuel). Heaven and its wonders the World of Spirits, and Hell: from things heard and seen. Translated by the Rev. Samuel Noble, of London. 1 vol. 8vo. (*2 copies.*) New York, 1855.

8005 **Swedenborg** (Emanuel). The True Christian Religion; containing the Universal Theology of the New Church. Translated from the Latin. 1 vol. 8vo. (*2 copies.*) New York, 1854.

8006 **Swedenborg** (Emanuel). Heavenly arcana which are contained in the Holy Scriptures or Word of the Lord unfolded, beginning with the book Genesis. Together with wonderful things seen in the World of Spirits, and in the Heaven of angels. (Vol. 2d wanting.)
12 vols. 8vo. & index. Boston, 1853.
10 vols. 8vo. New York, 1853–57.

8007 **Swedenborg** (Emanuel). The Doctrines of the New Jerusalem concerning the Lord, the sacred Scriptures, the White Horse, Faith, Life. Also, the Heavenly doctrines. Translated from the Latin. 1 vol. 16mo. Boston, ——.

8008 **Taylor** (Isaac). Saturday Evening. 3d edition. 1 vol. 12mo. Boston, 1833.

8009 **Taylor** (Isaac). Loyola: and Jesuitism in its Rudiments. 1 vol. 12mo. New York, 1851.

8010 **Taylor** (Isaac). Spiritual Despotism. 1 vol. 12mo. New York, 1835.

8011 **Whowell** (T.). An Analogy of the Old and New Testaments systematically classified, whereby the Dispersed Rays of Gospel truth are concentrated into chapters. With the Prophecies of the Messiah's Kingdom. The Alpha and Omega. 1 vol. 4to. London, 1840.

8012 **Wollaston** (William). Religion of Nature delineated. 6th edition. To which is added a preface, containing a general account of the Life, Character, and Writings of the Author. 1 vol. 4to. London, 1738.

Subj. 79. MISCELLANIES.

8013 **Adler** (G. J.). Letters of a Lunatic, or, a brief Exposition of my University Life, during the years 1853–54.
1 8vo. Pamphlet. New York, 1854.

8014 **Almanach de Gotha.** Annuaire Diplomatique et Statistique pour les années 1854 et 1855. 2 vols. 24mo. Gotha, 1853–54.

8015 **American** Almanac and Repository of useful Knowledge for the years 1851, '52, '53, '54, '55, & 1859. 6 vols. 12mo. Boston, 1851–59.

8016 **American** Historical and Literary Curiosities consisting of Fac-Similes of Original Documents relating to the events of the Revolution, &c., &c. With a variety of Reliques, Antiquities, and Modern Autographs. Collected and edited by J. Jay Smith and John F. Watson. 5th edition, with additions. 1 vol. fol. New York, 1852.

8017 **Bancroft** (George). Literary and Historical Miscellanies.
1 vol. 8vo. New York, 1855.

8018 **Blessington** (Countess of). Life and correspondence of, See Madden, No. 8033.

8019 **Burton** (Robert). Anatomy of Melancholy, what it is, with all Kinds, Causes, Symptoms, Prognostics, and several cures of it. A new edition.
1 vol. 8vo. London, 1854.

8020 **Camden Society.** Ecclesiastical Documents: now first Published by the Rev. Joseph Hunter. 1 vol. 8vo. London, 1840

8021 **Camden Society.** Relation; or, rather a true account of the Island of England; translated from the Italian with notes, by Charlotte Augusta Sneyd. 1 vol. 8vo. London, 1847.

8022 **Camden Society.** The Camden Miscellany.
1 vol. 8vo. London, 1847.

8023 **Carlyle** (Thomas). Letters and Speeches of Oliver Cromwell.
See Cromwell, No. 6166.

8024 **Clay** (Henry). The Private Correspondence. Edited by Calvin Colton.
1 vol. 8vo. New York, 1856.

8025 **Essays** from the London Times. 1 vol. 18mo. New York, 1852.

8026 **Essays** from the London Times. Second series.
1 vol. 18mo. New York, 1852.

8027 **Fuller Ossoli** (Margaret). Woman in the Nineteenth Century, and kindred Papers relating to the Sphere, Condition, and Duties of Woman. Edited by her Brother Arthur B. Fuller. With an introduction by H. Greeley. 3d edition. 1 vol. 12mo. Boston, 1855.

8028 **Goethe's** Sammtliche Werke. | Complete Works.
6 vols. 8vo. Stuttgart, 1854–55.

8029 **Hume** (David). Private Correspondence with several distinguished Persons, between the years 1761 and 1776. Now first Published from the Originals. 1 vol. 4to. London, 1820.

8030 **Knowler** (William). The Earl of Strafforde's Letters and Dispatches, with an Essay towards his Life, by Sir George Radcliffe. From the originals in the Possession of his Great Grandson the Right Honourable Thomas Earl of Malton, Knight of the Bath. 2 vols. fol. Dublin, 1740.

8031 **Lamb** (Charles). The Works of, a new edition. 1 vol. roy. 8vo. London, 1852.

8032 **Lewis** (Elisha J.). The American Sportsman: containing Hints to Sportsmen, notes on the Shooting, and the Habits of the Game, Birds, and Wild Fowl of America. With numerous illustrations. 1 vol. 8vo. Philadelphia, 1855.

8033 **Madden** (R. R.). The Literary Life and Correspondence of the Countess of Blessington. 2 vols. 12mo. New York, 1855.

8034 **Martinez de la Rosa** (D. Francisco). Obras Completas. 5 vols. 8vo. Paris, 1845.

Vol. 1[ero].—Las Poesías varias, completas; Zaragoza Poema, etc.—Poética española, con anotaciones.—Apéndices históricos sobre la poesía didactica, la tragedia, y la comedia española.

Vol. 2do.—Obras dramaticas: Lo que puede un empleo, la Viuda de Padilla, la Niña en casa, los Zelos infundados, Morayma, Edipo, Aben Humeya, en español y en francés, la Conjuracion de Venecia, la Boda y el Duelo, el Español en Venecia.

Vol. 3°.—Hernan Perez del Pulgar, Bosquejo histórico, con las hazañas del gran Capitan. Doña Isabel de Solis, Reina de Granada, novela histórica

Vol. 4° y 5°.—Espirítu del Siglo.

8035 **New Bond of Love** (The). 1 vol. 12mo. New York, 1853.

8036 **Schroeder** (John Frederick). Maxims of Washington, Political, Social, Moral, and Religious. 1 vol. 12mo. New York, 1855.

8037 **Smith** (J. Jay) **& Watson** (John F.). American Historical and Literary Curiosities. 5th edition, with additions. 1 vol. fol. New York, 1852.

8038 **Sparks** (Jared). Letter to Lord Mahon, being an answer to his Letter addressed to the Editor of Washington's Writings. 1 vol. 8vo. Boston, 1852.

8039 **Sparks** (Jared). Remarks on a reprint of the original Letters from Washington to Joseph Reed, during the American Revolution, referred to in the Pamphlets of Lord Mahon and Mr. Sparks. 1 vol. 8vo. Boston, 1853.

8040 **Sparks** (Jared). Correspondence of the American Revolution, being Letters of eminent Men to George Washington, from the time of his taking Command of the Army to the end of his Presidency. Edited from the original Manuscripts. 4 vols. 8vo. Boston, 1853.

8041 **Strafforde** (Earl of). Letters and Dispatches. See Knowler, No. 8030.

8042 **Walpole** (Horace). Letters; including numerous Letters now first published from the original Manuscripts. 4 vols. 8vo. Philadelphia, 1842.

8043 **Walpole** (Horace). Letters to Sir Horace Mann, concluding series. 2 vols. 8vo. Philadelphia, 1844.

8044 **Washington** (George). Correspondence of the American Revolution; being Letters of eminent Men to George Washington, from the time of his taking Command of the Army to the end of his Presidency. Edited from the original Manuscripts, by Jared Sparks.
4 vols. 8vo. Boston, 1853.

8045 **Washington** (George). Maxims. See Schroeder, No. 8036.

8046 **Wentworth** (Thomas, Earl of Strafforde). See Strafforde, No. 8041.

8047 **Willis** (N. Parker). Hurry-Graphs: or, sketches of Scenery, Celebrities, and Society, taken from life. 2d edition. 1 vol. 12mo. New York, 1851.

8048 **Willis** (N. Parker). Life, here and there: or sketches of Society and adventure at far-apart times and Places. 1 vol. 12mo. New York, 1853.

8049 **Willis** (N. Parker). Summer Cruise in the Mediterranean, on Board an American Frigate. 1 vol. 12mo. New York, 1853.

8050 **Willis** (N. Parker). Famous Persons and Places.
1 vol. 12mo. New York, 1854.

8051 **Willis** (N. Parker). Pencilling by the Way: written during some years of Residence and Travel in Europe. 1 vol. 12mo. New York, 1854.

8052 **Willis** (N. Parker). Health Trip to the Tropics.
1 vol. 12mo. New York, 1854.

8053 **Willis** (N. Parker). Rural Letters and other records of Thought at Leisure. 1 vol. 12mo. New York, 1853.

8054 **Willis** (N. Parker). Out-Doors at Idlewild.
1 vol. 12mo. New York, 1855.

8055 **Willis** (N. Parker). People I have met; or Pictures of Society and People of mark drawn under a thin veil of fiction.
1 vol. 12mo. New York, 1853.

8056 **Willis** (N. Parker). Fun-Jottings; or, Laughs I have taken a Pen to.
1 vol. 12mo. New York, 1853.

ALPHABETICAL INDEX.

Abbott (Jacob & John S. C.). Histories, 7598.
Abbott (John S. C.). History of Napoleon Bonaparte, 6765.
Abhandlung über die Kriegs-Minen, 6316.
Abrichtungs-Reglement für die Cavallerie, 6555.
Abrichtungs-Reglement für die Linien-Infanterie, 6583.
Abrichtungs-Reglement für die Linien und Grenz-Infanterie, 6586.
Abrichtungs-Reglement für die Pionniere, 6588.
Abrichtungs-Reglement für die Jäger, 6590.
Abrichtungs-Reglement für die Genie Truppen, 6592.
Académie des Sciences. Comptes rendus des Séances de l', 7162.
Adam. Une Lettre, 7861.
Adams, Backie, & Barton. Manual of Natural History, 7259.
Adams (John). Life and Works of, 6966.
Adler (G. J.). Letters of a Lunatic, 8013.
Administration et Comptabilité de Cavalerie et d'Artillerie, 6637.
Administration et Comptabilité de sous-officiers, &c., d'Infanterie, 6638.
Agassiz (L.). Lake Superior, 7260.
—— Natural History of the United States, 7261.
Ahrenberg (le Prince Ernest d'), 6258.
Aide-Mémoire à l'usage des officiers d'Artillerie, 6342, 6343.
Airy (G. B.). Lecture on the Pendulum-Experiments, 7086.
Aksenovime (Lieut.). Skirmish Drill, 6460.
Aldéguier (Flavien d'). Des Principes de la Cavalerie, 6525.
Alexander the Great. History of, 7599.
Alfieri (V.). Tragedies, 7718.
Alfred the Great. History of, 7600.
Algarotti. Letters Military and Political, 6461.
Alison (Archibald). History of Europe, 7507.
Allen (Z.). Philosophy of the Mechanics of Nature, 7233.
Allin (E. S.). Rules for the Management of the Rifle Musket, 6344.
Almanach de Gotha, 8014.
Alvord (B.). Tangencies of Circles and of Spheres, 7035.
America. Map of Central America, 7392.
American Almanac, 8015.
American Archives, 6967.
American Engineering, 6862, 6863.
American Historical and Literary Curiosities, 8016.
American Philosophical Society, 7163.
Amherst (Maj.-Gen. Jeffrey). Expedition, 6725.
Amiot (A.). Leçons de Géométrie descriptive, 7036.
Ampére (André-Marie). Philosophie des Sciences, 7674.
André (Major J.). The Cow-Chace, an Heroic Poem, 7719.
Andréossy. Opérations des Pontonniers, 6259.
Andrew. Treatise on Agricultural Engineering, 6864.
Angelo's Bayonet Exercise, 6598.
Anleitung für Infanterie, 6568.
Annales des Ponts et Chaussées, 6920, 6921.
Annales (Nouvelles) de la Construction, 6922.
Annales (Nouvelles) de Mathématiques, 7014.
Annales de l'Observatoire de Paris, 7126.
Annales de Chimie et de Physique, 7199, 7200.
Annals of Congress, 6968.
Annals and Magazine of Natural History, 7262 to 7264.
Annals of San Francisco, 7557.
Annibal. Campaigns, 6785.
—— History of, 7620.
Annuaire Militaire Historique, Topographique, &c., 6810.
Annuaire des Armées de terre et de mer, 6811.
Annuaire de la Société Météorologique de France, 7284.
Annuaire des Deux Mondes, 7888.
Annual of Scientific Discovery, 7.64.
Ansted (David T.). Geology and Mineralogy, 7304.
Anthon (C.). Smith's Dictionary of Antiquities, 7593.
Appletons' Cyclopædia of Drawing, 6865.
Appletons' Library Manual, 7914.
Appleton & Co.'s New Catalogue, 7915.
Arago (François). Œuvres, 7165.
Archambault (P. J.). Précis de Physique, 7101.
Ardant (P.). Charpentes à grande portée, 6866.
Arentschildt (Lt.-Col. von). Instructions for officers of Cavalry, 6526.
Aristotle's Organon, or Logical Treatises, 7695.
—— Logique, 7696.
Armengaud & Amouroux. Industrial design, 6867.
Arms in use, 6345.
Army Acts, 6663.
Army Regulations, 6664.
Army Registers, 6812.
Arnold (W. D.). Oakfield, 7720.
Arnoul (H.). Siéges mémorables des Français, 6726.
Arrien. Expéditions d'Alexandre, 7487.
Arthur & Carpenter. History of Virginia, 7558.
Articles de guerre pour l'armée Prussienne, 6665.
Artillerie Nouvelle (1850), 6346.
Artillery drill-evolutions of the line for Foot Batteries, 6347.
Artillery. Notes on, 6348.
Artillery Signals, 6349.
Ashdowne (W.). Scripture Key to the Evangelists, 7949.
Astronomical Journal, 7127.
Astronomical Society of London. Memoirs of the, 7128.

Astronomical Society of London. Monthly notices, 7129.
Astronomical observations, 7148.
Astronomische Nachrichten, 7130, 7131.
Atkinson (T. W.). Oriental and Western Siberia, 7433.
Atlas of Prophecies of Daniel and St. John, 7950
Audé. Nouvelle expériences sur la poussée des terres, 6260.
Audot (L. E.). L'art de Chauffer, 6960.
Auzoux. Leçons d'anatomie et de Physiologie, 7334.
Azov. Map of the Sea of, 7393.

Babinet & Housel. Calculs pratiques, 7057.
Babinet. Études et Lectures sur sciences d'observation, 7102, 7166.
Bagster's Greek and English Testament, 7951.
Bailey (F.). Account of the Rev. John Flamsteed, 7132.
Bailey (S.). Philosophy of the Human Mind, 7697.
Baker (T.). Elements of Mechanism, 6868.
Baker (Capt. V.). British Cavalry, 6527.
Bakewell (F. C.). Manual of Electricity, 7235.
Baldwin (J. G.). Party Leaders, 7601.
Baltic Sea. Map of the, 7394.
Bampton (Rev. J.). Sermons, 7952.
Bancroft (George). History of the United States, 7559.
—— Literary and Historical Miscellanies, 8017.
Bardin. Dictionnaire de l'armée, 6806.
—— La pratique des levers, 6869.
—— Géométrie descriptive, 7037.
Barnard (F. A. P.). On Collegiate Education, 7826.
—— Improvements practicable in American Colleges, 7827.
Barnard (J. G.). Dangers and Defences of New York, 6261.
—— On the Gyroscope, 7087.
Barnes (W.). Philosophical Grammar, 7779.
Barrack accommodation, 6821.
Barracks. Pläne von Casernen, 6822.
Barracks, 6823.
Barre Duparcq. L'art militaire antique, 6462.
—— Commentaires sur Clausewitz, 6463.
—— Eléments d'art et d'historie militaires, 6464.
—— Histoire de l'Infanterie, 6564.
—— Biographie et maximes de Saxe, 6766.
—— Les plus grand homme de guerre, 6767.
—— Biographie et maximes de Montluc, 6768.
—— Capitaines anciens et modernes, 6769.
Barreswil & Davanne. Chimie photographique, 7201.
Barrett (B. F.). New Jerusalem, 7953.
Barrington Shute Bishop of Durham. Sermons, &c., 7954.
Barry (J.). Lectures on Painting, 7862.
Barth (H.). Discoveries in North and Central Africa, 7434.
Bartlett (W. H. C.) Analytical Mechanics, 7088.
—— Spherical Astronomy, 7133.
—— Photographs of solar eclipse, 7149.
Baskerville (A.). Poetry of Germany, 7721.
Bâtiments militaires, 6824 to 6830.
Battle of Tchernaya or Traktir. Map of the, 6727.
Baucher (F.). Œuvres complétes, 6602.
Baumann (B.). Sicherheitsdienst im marsche, 6465.
Baumeister (W.). Kenntnisz des æuszern des Pferdes, 6603.
Bayard (S. J.). Address, 7805.
Bayard Taylor. Lands of the Saracen, 7435.
—— Journey to Central Africa, 7436.
—— Eldorado, 7437.
—— Visit to India, China, and Japan, 7438.
Beamish (N. L.). On the uses of Cavalry in War, 6528.
Becker (M.). Allgemeine Baukunde des Ingenieurs, 6831.
—— Der Straszen und Eisenbahnbau, 6923.
Becquerel. Traité d'Électricité, 7236.
Bedell (Rev. G. T.). Memoir of, 7602.
Beer (Dr. A.). Einleitung in die höhere optik, 7112.
Belanger. Notes sur le cours d'hydraulique, 6896.
Bélidor. La science des Ingénieurs, 6262, 6263.
Bellavéne. Cours élémentaire de fortification, 6264.
Belloc (A.). Catechisme de l'opérateur photographie, 7202.
Benham (D.). Reflections on the Genealogy of Christ, 7955.
Benton (Thomas H.). Thirty Years' View, 6969.
Bergery (C. L.). Cours des machines, 6870.
Bermuda, a Colony, a Fortress, and a Prison, 7439.
Bernadotte (J.-B.-J.). Memoirs and Campaigns, 6770.
Bernard & Huette. Manual of Operative Surgery, 7335.
Bertrand. Campagnes d'Egypte et de Syrie, 6728.
Bertrand (J.). Traité d'Algébre, 7030.
Bible. The Holy, 7956, 7957.
Bibliotheca, 7916 to 7924.
Biddulph (Maj.). Topographical sketch before Sevastopol, 6265.
Biernatzki. The Hallig, or, the Sheepfold in the Water, 7722.
Billet (F.). Traité d'optique physique, 7113.
Bingham (J.). Antiquities of the Christian Church, 7958.
Biot (J. B.). Traité élémentaire d'astronomie, 7134.
Birago. Military Bridges, 6266.
—— Ponts de Chevalets, 6267.
Bird (G.). On urinary deposits, 7336.
Bismark. On the uses of Cavalry in War, 6529.
Blackie (W. G.). Imperial Gazetteer, 7354.
Blackwood's Magazine, 7889.
Blair's Chronological Tables, 7479.
Blakey (R.). Historical Sketch of Logic, 7698.
Bledsoe (A. T.). Liberty and Slavery, 6970.
—— Theodicy, 7959.
Blessington (Countess of). Life and Correspondence, 8018.
Blesson (Louis). Art de la fortification permanente, 6268.
Blue Book for 1855, 6813.
Boccaccio Decameron, 7723.
Boileau. Machines à Vapeur, 6871.
—— Instruction sur l'exécution des levers d'usines, 6872.
Boitard & Ansart-Deusy. Navigation pratique, 7123.
Bonaparte (L. N.). Études sur l'artillerie, 6350.
—— Artillerie de Campagne, 6351.
Bonnet (O.). Mécaniqe élémentaire, 7089.
Booth & Morfit. Chemical Arts, 7203.
Bormann (Maj.-Gen.). The Shrapnel Shell in England and in Belgium, 6352.
Born. Notices sur les Ponts Militaires, 6269.
Boudin (J.-Ch.-M.). De la Ventilation et du Chauffage, 6961.

Bouët-Willaumez (Comte E.). Batailles de terre et de mer, 6729.
Bouley & Reynal. Nouveau Dictionnaire de Médecine Vétérinaires, 6604.
Bourdon. Trigonométrie, 7050.
—— Application de l'algébre à la géométrie, 7053.
Bourne (J.). On the Screw Propeller, 6873.
—— On the Steam Engine, 6874.
Boutault. Cours de Mines, 6270.
Bouterwek (F.). History of the Spanish Literature, 7667.
Bouvet (F.). The Turks in Europe, 7508.
Bowditch (N.). New American practical Navigator, 7124.
Bowditch (N. I.). Suffolk Surnames, 7603.
Bowman (J. E.). Practical Chemistry, 7204.
Boxer (Capt. E. M.). Treatise on Artillery, 6353.
—— On Congreve Rockets, 6354.
—— Diagrams of heavy Ordnance, 6355.
—— Diagrams of Guns, 6356.
Boyd (Rev. J. R.). Elements of Logic, 7699.
Brace (Chas. L.). Home Life in Germany, 7724.
Brack (F. de). Avant-Postes de Cavalerie légère, 6530.
Brackenbury & Simpson. Campaign in the Crimea, 6730.
Braddock (E.). Expedition against Fort Du Quesne, 6731.
Brandon (R. & J. A.). Gothick Architecture, 6832.
Bremer (F.). Homes of the New World, 7440.
Bremiker (C.). Tabula Logarithmorum, 7084.
Bresse. Flexion et la Résistance des Piéces Courbes, 6955.
Bresson (C.). Traité de Mécanique, 7090.
Breton de los Herreros. Obras escogidas, 7725.
Brettes (Martin de). Des artifices éclairants, 6357.
—— Études sur les appareils électro-magnétiques, 6358.
Brewster (Sir D.). More Worlds than one, 7675.
Brewster (F. E.). Philosophy of Human Nature, 7676.
Brightly (F. C.). Digest of the Laws of the United States, 6999.
Brinley. Finite differences. See Mathematical Tracts, 7023.
—— Variable quantities, &c. See Mathematical Tracts, 7023.
Briot (Ch.). Cours de Cosmographie, 7135.
British Army List, 6814, 6815.
British Association Catalogue of Stars, 7156.
British Association, 7167.
Bromwell (W.). History of Immigration, 7500.
Brooks (S. H.). Modern Architecture, 6833.
Brougham (H. Lord). Political Philosophy, 6971.
Brown (C. B.). Novels, 7726.
Brown (G.). Grammar of English Grammars, 7780.
Bruce (J.). Elements of the Science of Ethics, 7705.
Bucaniers of America, 7561.
Buchanan. Examples of Tools, 6875.
Budge (J.). Practical Miner's Guide, 7294.
Bulfinch (T.). The Age of Fable, 7727.
—— The Age of Chivalry, 7728.
Bulgarie. Carte de la, 7395.
Bullions (Rev. P.). Latin Grammar, 7781.
—— Greek Grammar, 7782.
Bullock (J.). American Cottage Builder, 6834.
Bulwer Lytton. Poetical and Dramatic Works, 7729.
Bundy (R.). Roman History, 7488.
Bunsen (C. C. J.). Signs of the Times, 7960.
Bunsen (R.). Gasometry, 7205.
Bunsen & Schischkoff. Combustion de la Poudre, 6359.
Burckhardt (J. L.). Travels in Arabia, 7441.
Burke (J. & J. B.). General Armory, 7604.
Burn (Lt.-Col.). Questions and answers on Artillery 6360.
—— Naval and Military Technical Dictionary, 6807.
Burn (R.). Ecclesiastical Law, 7961.
Burnell (G. R.). Hydraulic Engineering, 6807.
Burney (C.). Present State of Music, 7863.
Burton (R.). Anatomy of Melancholy, 8019.
Busch & Hoffmann. Kriegsfeuerwerkerei, 6361.
Buschbeck (F.). Preussisches Feld-Taschenbuch, 6466.
Byrne (B. M.). On Cholera, 7337.
Byrne (Oliv.). Practical Model Calculator, 6924.
—— Pocket-Book for Rail Road and Civil Engineers, 6925.
Bythneri (V.). Institutio Linguæ Sanctæ, 7783.
—— Lyra Prophetica Davidis Regis, 7962.

Cabrera (R.). Diccionario de Etimologias de la Lengua Castellana, 7784.
Cæsar. Commentaires, 7489, 7490.
—— History of, 7605.
Calhoun (J. C.). Works, 6972.
Callan (J. F.). Military Laws of the United States, 6666.
Cambridge Philosophical Society, 7168.
Camden Society. Works of the, 8020 to 8022.
Campagne sur le Mein et la Rednitz, 6732.
Campbell's Present State of Europe, 7509.
Canseco (V. D.). Diccionario de Mujeres Célebres, 7594.
Carbine, Pistol, and Lance Exercise, 6532.
Carbine Exercise, 6531.
Cardini (F.). Dictionnaire d'hippiatrique et d'équitation, 6605.
Carlyle (T.). Letters and Speeches of Cromwell, 8023.
Carmichael (R.). Calculus of Operations, 7058.
Carnot. Défense des Places, 6271.
Carpenter (W. B.). The Microscope, 7114.
—— Principles of Human Physiology, 7338.
Carpenter & Arthur. History of Virginia, 7562.
Carrillo (D. M.). Prontuario de Arquitectura, 6835.
Carrington (R. C.). Catalogue of 3735 Circumpolar Stars, 7157.
Carte Topographique de la France, 7355, 7356.
Casernes, 6836.
Casse (A. du). Campagne de 1812, 6733.
Castillo. Conquest of Mexico, 7563.
Cathcart. War in Russia and Germany, 6704.
Catrou & Rouillé. Roman History, 7491.
Caunter (Rev. J. H.). Poetry of the Pentateuch, 7963.
Cavalli (J.). Équipages de Ponts Militaires, 6272.
—— Mémoire sur les Canons Chargeant par la Culasse, 6362.
Cavalry Tactics. Kommando-Tabelle, 6533.
Cavalry Tactics, 6534.
Cavalry Instructions, formations and movements, 6535.
Cavalry Signals, 6536.
Census of the United States, 7357.
Census of the State of New York, 7358.
Central America. Map of, 7396.

Cervantes (M. de). Don Quijote, 7730.
—— Obras escogidas, 7731.
Cessac (Comte de). Des connaissances nécessaires, 6467.
—— Guide de l'Officier, 6468.
Chamberlayne (J.). Present State of Great Britain, 7526.
Chambers' Introduction to the Sciences, 7169.
Chapman (E. J.). Practical Mineralogy, 7295.
Chappel (Lt. E.). Voyage to Hudson's Bay, 7442.
Charles, King. Works of, 7527.
—— The Annals of, 7532.
—— The First. History of, 7606.
Charles, King, the Second. History of, 7607.
Charles John Prince Royal of Sweden. Memoirs, 6771.
Charpentier (F. E. A.). Matériel de l'Artillerie, 6363.
Charron (P.). On Wisdome, 7706.
—— De la Sagesse, 7707.
Chasles. Géométrie supérieure, 7054.
Chasseloup de Laubat. System of Fortification, 6273.
Cherbourg. Plan général du Port et de la Ville de, 7397.
Chesney. Russo-Turkish Campaigns, 6734.
Chevé. Méthode élémentarie de Musique Vocale, 7864.
—— Concours Musical ouvert à Paris, 7865.
—— Réfutation d'une lettre de M. Adam, 7866.
Chronicles. Six old English, 7528.
Cibrario. Lettre sur l'Artillerie, 6364.
Ciriacy. Histoire de l'art militaire chez les Anciens, 6786.
Claims between the United States and Great Britain, 6973.
Clark (E.). Britannia and Conway Tubular Bridges, 6898.
Clark (L. G.). Knick-Knacks, 7732.
Clarke (Mrs.). Concordance to Shakspere, 7733.
Clausewitz (le Gén. Charles de). De la Guerre, 6469.
—— Commentaires sur le traité de la Guerre, 6470.
Clay (Henry). Life and Speeches, 7806.
—— Private Correspondence, 8024.
Cleaveland & Bachus. Village and Farm Cottages, 6837.
Clegg (S.). Manufacture of Coal-Gas, 7206.
Cleopatra, Queen. History of, 7609.
Clough (A. B.) Contractor's Manual and Builder's Price Book, 6926.
Coast Survey. Reports of the, 7359.
Coast Survey Maps, 7480.
Cole (G.). Contractor's Book, 6876.
Collection of Cavalry and Horse Artillery Signals, 6537.
Collection of Warrants and Regulations, 6667.
Colton (G. W.). Atlas of the World, 7360.
Columbia College. Addresses, 7807.
Compte Rendu sur le Recrutement, 6639.
Compte général du matériel de la guerre, 6640.
Comptes généraux presentés par le Ministre de la guerre, 6641.
Comte (Aug.). Philosophy of Mathematics, 7015, 7678.
—— Cours de Philosophie, 7677.
Comyns (Sir J.). Digest of the Laws of England, 7000.
Conde (J. A.). Dominacion de los Arabes en España, 7510.
Congressional Directory, 6816.
Congressional Globe, 7890.
Connecticut. Map of, 7398.
Constitution, Rules and Orders for the House and Senate, 7001.
Conybeare & Howson. Life and Epistles of St. Paul, 7964.
Cooper (J. F.). History of the Navy of the United States, 6705.
Cope (Sir A.). Meditations on the Psalms, 7965.
Copenhagen. Environs of, 7399.
Coppée (H.). Elements of Rhetoric, 7801.
Corréard (J.). Recueil des bouches à feu, 6365.
—— Guide maritime et Stratégique dans la mer Noire, 7361.
Corréard jeune (J.). Annuaire des Armées, 6817.
Cortes (Hernando). Despatches, 7564.
—— History of, 7610.
Cotelle. Cours de droit administratif, 7002.
Cours de fortification permanente, 6274.
Cours d'Artillerie, 6366.
Courtenay (E. H.). Calculus, 7059.
Cousin (V.). History of Modern Philosophy, 7679.
—— Lectures on the True, the Beautiful and Good, 7680.
Cow-Chace, in three Cantos, 7734.
Craufurd. Standing Orders, 6668.
Creasy. The fifteen decisive battles, 6735.
Crimea. Stanford's Map of the, 7400.
Crimea. The Russian Military Map of the, 7401.
Crimée. Carte de la, 7402.
Crisis. The Great, 7966.
Cruden. Concordance to the Holy Scriptures, 7967.
Curnieu (le B^on de). Leçons de Science hippique générale, 6606.
Curtis (G. T.). History of the Constitution of the United States, 7003.
Custine (Marquis de). Russia, 7511.
Cuvier (G.). Le Règne Animal, 7265.
Cyrus the Great. History of, 7611.

Daguin (P. A.). Traité de Physique, 7103.
Dahlgren (J. A.). Shells and Shell-Guns, 6367.
—— Boat Armament, 6368.
D'Aldéguier. See Aldéguier, 6525.
Dalyell (J. G.). The Powers of the Creator displayed in the Creation, 7266.
Damitz. Campagne de 1815, 6736.
Dana (J. D.). On Zoophytes, 7267.
—— On Crustacea, 7268.
—— System of Mineralogy, 7296.
—— Geology, 7305.
Danish Maps, 7403.
Danubian Provinces, &c. Maps of the, 7404, 7405.
Darcy (H.). Les Fontaines publiques de Dijon, 6899.
Darius the Great. History of, 7612.
D'Aubigné (J. H. M.). History of the Reformation, 7968.
D'Aubuisson de Voisins. Treatise on hydraulics, 6900.
Davies & Peck. Mathematical Dictionary, 7016.
Deanes' Manual of Fire-Arms, 6369.
Decker (E.). Art de Combattre de l'Artillerie, 6370.
—— Rassemblement et Campement, 6471.
Décret impérial portant Réorganisation de l'école de Cavalerie, 7828.
Delaistre (L.). Cours de dessin linéaire, 7038.
De la Rive (A.). Treatise on Electricity, 7237.

Delaunay (M. Ch.). Traité de mécanique rationnelle, 7091.
—— Cours d'Astronomie, 7136.
Delobel (L.). Revue de Technologie militaire, 6371.
Delwart (L. V.). Traité de médecine Vétérinaire, 6607.
De Massas. Fabrication de bouches à feu, 6372.
Dempsey (G. D.). Engineering Examples, details of Buildings, 6838.
—— Machinery of the Nineteenth Century, 6877.
Denaix. Essais de Géographie méthodique, 7362.
Denys d'Halycarnasse. Antiquités Romaines, 7492.
De Peyster (J. W.). On the Subject of the organization of the National Guards, &c., 6642.
—— Battle of the Sound or Baltic, 6737.
—— Life of General Leonard Torstenson, 6772.
—— The Dutch at the North Pole, and in Maine, 7565.
—— Address to the Officers of the N. Y. State Troops, 7808.
De Veaux (J.). Memoir of, 7613.
De Vries (D. P.). Voyages, 7443.
Dow (T.). Digest of ancient and modern History, 7480.
Diaz del Castillo (Bernal). Conquest of Mexico, 7566.
Diccionario de Sinonimos de la Lengua Castellana, 7785.
Diccionario francés-español y español-francés, 7933.
Dickens (Charles). Child's History of England, 7529.
—— Bleak House, 7735.
—— Hard Times, 7736.
—— Household Words, 7891.
Dictionary of Latin Quotations, 7786.
Dictionary of the Russian, French, German, and English languages, 7934.
Dictionnaire de l'administration Française, 7004.
Didion. Tables de Construction de bouches à feu, 6373.
—— Calcul des Probabilitiés, 6374.
Dillon (J. B.). History of Indiana, 7567.
Diplomatic correspondence of the United States, 6974.
Documents relatifs à l'emploi de l'Électricité, 6275.
Documents relatifs aux Campagnes, 6738.
Documents relative to the Colonial History of New York, 7570.
Documentary History of New York, 7568, 7569.
Dominguez (R. J.). Diccionario francés-español y español-francés, 7935.
Donaldson (J. W.). Theatre of the Greeks, 7668.
D'Orbigny (A.). Prodrome de Paléontologie, 7306.
Douglas (H.). Treatise on Naval Gunnery, 6375.
—— On Naval Warfare with Steam, 6479.
Downing (A. J.). Rural Essays, 6839.
—— Cottage Residences, 6840.
Draper (J. W.). Address, 7809.
Dress of the Officers of the Army, 6473.
Drummond (G. H.). Sermons, 7969.
Dryden (J.). Works, 7737.
Dubois (E. P.). Cours d'Astronomie, 7137.
Dudley Observatory. An address, &c., 7810 to 7812.
Dufrenoy. Cours de Minéralogie, 7297.
Dufrenoy & Bayle. Explication des planches de fossiles, 7307.
Duhamel. Cours d'analyse, 7061.
—— Éléments de Calcul Infinitésimal, 7062.
—— Cours de Mécanique, 7092.
Dunglison (R.). Human Physiology, 7339.
Dunlop (J.). Digest of the Laws of the United States, 7005.
Dupain de Montesson. Vocabulaire de guerre, 6808.
Du Pont's Artesian Well, 6901.
Durand (F. A.). Nouvelle théorie physique, 7104.
Dusaert (E.). Essai sur les obusiers, 6376.
Duty of Man, 7708.
Duvignau (V. J.). Problémes de Mathématique &c., 7017.
Dwight (M. A.). Study of Art, 7867.
Dwyer (F.). Feld-Taschenbuch, 6474.
Dziobek (E.). Taschenbuch für den Preussischen Ingenieur, 6277.

Eclaireur (The). A Military Journal, 6797.
Ecole de Sapes, 6278.
Ecole Polytechnique, Cours d'art militaire, 6475.
Ecole de Ponts et chaussées, 7170 to 7176.
Ecole de dessin, 7868.
Edinburgh Astronomical observations, 7150.
Edinburgh Transactions, 7177.
Eichhoff (F. G.). Parallèle des langues, 7787.
Elementary Course of Mathematics, 7018.
Elizabeth, Queen. History of, 7614.
Ellet (E. F.). Women of the Revolution, 7615.
Emerson (W.). Method of Increments, 7063.
Emy (A. R.). Nouveau Système d'arcs, 6878.
Endres (E.). Manuel du Conducteur des Ponts et chaussées, 6927.
Engel (F.). Axonometrical Projections, 7039.
Engineer and Machinist's Assistant, 1595.
English Woman in Russia, 7444.
Enrile (Don J. M.). Vocabulario Militar, 6809.
Erasmus. Paraphrase on the Gospels, 7970.
Erichsen (J.). Science and art of Surgery, 7340.
Erlam (J. S.). Outlines of Military Fortification, 6279.
Ernest d'Arenberg (le Prince). L'art de la fortification, 6280.
Essai de Tactique, 6476.
Essai sur la Tactique des Grecs, 6787.
Essai sur les Milices Romaines, 6788.
Essays from the London Times, 8025, 8026.
Etudes sur l'art de la guerre, 6477.
Etudes politiques et militaires, 6478.
Europe. Carte militaire de l', 7406.
European Kingdoms and Turkey at one View, 7407.
Ewbank (T.). Life in Brazil, 7445.
Examen du Systéme d'artillerie de Campagne, 6377.
Examination Papers, 7829.
Exercices des bouches à feu, 6378.
Exercir-Reglement für die Cavallerie, 6556, 6558.
Exercir-Reglement für die Infanterie, 6582.
Exercir-Reglement für die Linien Infanterie, 6584.
Exercir-Reglement für die Linien und Grenz-Infanterie, 6585.
Exercir-Reglement für die Pionniere, 6589.
Exercir-Reglement für die Jäger, 6591.
Exercir-Reglement für die Genie-Truppen, 6593.
Exhibition 1851, Reports by the Juries, 7892.
Exhibition of Science and Mechanism, 7893.
Expedition against Ticonderoga and Crown Point, 6739.
Expériences de Bapaume, 6281.
Expériences d'artillerie exécutées à Gavre, 6379.

Fairbairn (W.). Useful Information for Engineers, 6879.
—— On Cast and Wrought Iron, 6956.
Fantaisies Militaires, 6479.
Faraday (M.). Experimental Researches in Electricity, 7238.

Favé. Des nouvelles carabines, 6380.
—— Nouveau Systéme d'artillerie de Campagne, 6381.
Felltham (O.). Resolves, 7709.
Ferdoosee. Episodes from the Shah Nameh, 7549.
Fergusson (J.). On a new system of Fortification, 6282.
Fergusson (W.). Notes and Recollections, 7341.
Ferris (B. G.). Utah and the Mormons, 7446.
Fesca (F. A.). Handbuch der Befestigungskunst, 6283.
Fétis (F. J.). Antoine Stradivarius, 7869.
Feuquière. Extraits, 6480.
Fevre (E.). Cours de tir et de mécanisme des armes à feu portatives, 6382.
Field Battery Exercise, 6383.
Field (G.). Outlines of analogical Philosophy, 7681.
Fielding (N.). Lessons on Fortification, 6284.
Filmer (Sir R.). Free-holders grand inquest, 6975.
Findlay (A. G.). Classical Atlas, 7363.
Finlande. Carte autographiée du Golfe de, 7408.
Fitz Clarence (F.). On the Three Arms, 6384.
Fitz William (E. F.). Music, 7870.
Flagg (E.). Venice; the City of the Sea, 7512.
Flagg (J. F. B.). Ether and Chloroform, 7342.
Flamsteed (Rev. John). Account of, 7138.
Florida. Military Map of, 7409.
Florida. Map of, 7410.
Folard. Extraits, 6481.
Fonblanque (E. B. de). Administration and Organization of the British Army, 6643.
Fonscolombe. Résumé historique de progrés de l'art Militaire, 6482.
Fonton (F.). La Russia dans l'asie-mineure, 6740.
Forrest (R.). Hand Book of Military Engineering, 6285.
Förster (S. Von). Felddienst der leichten Infanterie, 6565.
Fortification. General Principles of, 6286.
Fort Laramie and the Great Salt Lake Routes, 7411.
Fowle (W. B.). Hundred Dialogues, 7738.
—— Parlor Dramas, 7739.
Fowler (W. C.). English Grammar, 7788, 7789.
Fownes (G.). Elementary Chemistry, 7207.
France. Maritime Parts of, 7364.
France. Carte Topographique de la, 7365.
Francis (J. B.). Hydraulic Experiments, 6902.
Francoeur (L. B.). Géodésie, 7074.
Frédéric II., Roi de Prusse. Instruction militaire pour ses Généraux, 6483.
—— Histoire de mon temps, 7513.
—— Vie de, 7616.
Fredericia. Plan of the Battle of, 7412.
French Field Service, 6566.
Fresenius (Dr. C. R.). Qualitative Chemical Analysis, 7208.
Fromont-Coste (A. L. A.). Notice Nécrologique sur, 6778.
Frontin (S. Jul.). Stratagêmes, 6789.
Fuller (Ossoli Marg.). Woman in the 19th Century, 8027.
Fuseli (H.). Lectures on Painting, 7871.
Fysh (Rev. F.). Divine History of the Church, 7971.

Gall & Inglis' Map of the Baltic Sea and adjacent Countries, 7394.
—— Map of the Seats of War in the East, 7404.
—— Map of the Danubian Provinces, 7405.
—— Map of the European Kingdoms and Turkey, 7407.
Garcia (Don J. H.). Fortification permanente, 6287.
Gardner (C. K.). Dictionary of the United States Army, 6818.
Garrel (Al.). Ordonnance du Roi sur le service intérieure des Troupes à cheval, 6669.
Gauss (Ch. F.). Méthode des moindres carrés, 7064.
Gazetteer of the United States, 7366.
Gazetteers of the World, 7367.
General Instructions for the Sapper and Pioneer Battalions, 6288, 6484.
General Regulations New York State Militia, 6670.
Geological Map of Europe, 7308.
Geological Surveys, 7309 to 7313.
Ghega (Ch. de). Atlas pittoresque du chemin de fer du Semmering, 6929.
—— Ubersicht der Hauptfortschritte des Eisenbahnwesens, 6930.
Gibbes (R. W.). History of the American Revolution, 7571, 7572.
—— Memoir of James De Veaux, 7617.
Gibson (W. M.). Prison of Weltevreden, East Indian Archipelago, 7447.
Gil y Zarata (Don A.). Obras Dramaticas, 7740.
Gillespie (W. M.). Land-Surveying, 7075.
Gilson (A.). The Czar and the Sultan, 7618.
Girault (Ch.). Géométrie appliquée à la Transformation du mouvement dans les Machines, 6880.
Giustiniani (H. de). Opérations Militaires en Crimée, 6485.
Gleig (Capt.). The Crimean Enterprise, 6486.
Gmelin (L.). Hand Book of Chemistry, 7209.
Goddard's Bampton Lecture, 7972.
Goethe. Theory of Colors, 7115.
—— Faust: a Tragedy, 7741.
—— Sammtliche Werke, 8028.
Gomard (A. J.—J. P.). Théorie de l'escrime, 6599.
Gompertz. Imaginary quantities. See Mathematical Tracts, 7023.
Goodrich (C. R.). Science and Mechanism, 7894.
Gordon (T. F.). History of Pennsylvania, 7573.
Gosse (P. H.). Tenby: A Sea-side Holiday, 7269.
—— Life in its lower, intermediate, and higher forms, 7270.
Gould (A. A.). On Mollusca and Shells, 7271.
Gould (Dr.). Defence, 7813.
Goulier. Lever de fortification à la planchette, 6289.
—— Lever de reconnaissance militaire, 6290.
—— Lever à la boussole nivelante, 7076.
—— Cours de Topographie, 7368.
Gourgaud & Montholon. Mémoires de Napoléon, 7544.
Gournerie (J. de la). Traité de Perspective linéaire, 7040
Grafe (C.). Reitzeug und die Geschirre der Preussischen Artillerie, 6385.
Graham (Lt. Col. J. D.). Report, Mexican boundary, 7369.
Graham (Lt. Col. J. J.). History of the Art of War, 6487.
Graham (T.). Elements of Chemistry, 7210.
Grassi (C.). Chauffage et Ventilation, 6962.
Gray and Adams. Elements of Geology, 7314.
Gray (Rev. R.). Key to the Old Testament, 7973.
Graydon (A.). Memoirs of his own Time, 7574.
Greek and English Testament, 7974.
Greener (W.). Gunnery in 1858, 6386.

Greenwell (G. C.). Treatise on mine Engineering, 7298, 7315.
Greenwich Catalogue of Stars, 7158, 7159.
Gregg. Commerce of the Prairies, 6997, 7448.
Gregory (D. F.). Differential and Integral Calculus, 7065.
Gregory (W.). Hand Book of Chemistry, 7211.
Griffith & Henfrey. Micrographic Dictionary, 7116.
Grimoard. Vie de Frédéric le grand, 7619.
Grimshaw (W.). History of the United States, 7575.
Grivel (M. R.). La Marine dans l'attaque des fortifications, 6291.
—— Attaque et Bombardement Maritimes, 6292.
Gross (S. D.). Treatise on Foreign Bodies, 7343.
Grote (G.). History of Greece, 7493.
Grove (W. R.). Correlation of Physical Forces, 7239.
—— Corrélation des Forces Physiques, 7240.
Guerin (A.). École du Cavalier, 6539.
Guibert. Politique et science militaire en Europe, 6488.
Guide (le). Des sous-officiers de l'Infanterie, 6567.
Guide.—Anleitung für Infanterie, 6568.
Guillot (L.). Legislation et administration militaire, 6671.
Guizot. Histoire de la Civilisation, 7514, 7515.
—— Histoire de la Civilisation en France, 7545.
Gummere (J.). Treatise on Astronomy, 7139.
Gurowski (Count A. de). Russia as it is, 7516.
Günther (Dr. F. A.). Der homöopathische Thierarzt, 6608.
Guthrie (G. J.). On urinary and Sexual Organs, 7344.
Guy. Leçons de mécanique Industrielle, 7093.
Guyon. Histoire des Amazones, 7494.
Guzman (Seb.). Lecciones de Artilleria, 6387.
Gwilt (J.). Encyclopædia of Architecture, 6841.

Haddon (J.). Differential Calculus, 7066.
Hamilton (Alex.). Works, 6976.
Hamilton (Sir W.). Philosophy, 7682.
—— Discussions on Philosophy, 7683.
Hamilton (Sir W. R.). Lectures on Quaternions, 7067.
Hammond (H.). Tracts, 7975.
Hand Book for Engineers and Sappers, 6293.
Hand Book.—Handbuch des Ingenieur-Dienstes, 6294.
Hand Book for Field Service, 6489.
Hand Book for Engineers and Architects, 6931.
Hand Book.—Handbuch für Cavallerie offiziere, 6540.
Hannibal. Campaigns, 6785.
—— History of, 7620.
Hannover (A.). On the Microscope, 7117.
Hardee. Rifle and light Infantry Tactics, 6569.
Harding. Principles and Practice of art, 7872.
Hardwich (T. F.). Manual of Photographic Chemistry, 7212.
Harper's Gazetteer of the World, 7370.
—— New Monthly Magazine, 7895.
Harrington (G. F.). Systematic Philosophy, 7105.
Harris (T. L.). Obituary address on the occasion of the death of, 7814.
Harris (W.). History of William III., 7530.
Hartzenbusch (Don J. E.). Obras escogidas, 7742.
Harvey. Sea-Side Book, 7272.
Haskoll (W. D.). Railway Construction, 6932.
—— Practice of Engineering Field Work, 6933.
Hassall (A. H.). Microscopic Examination of Water, 7118.
—— British Freshwater Algæ, 7273.
Hauser (G. F. V.). Abhandlung über die Befestigungskunst, 6296.
Hawkins (T.). Great Sea-Dragons, 7316.
—— Prometheus, 7743.
Hawks (R. F. L.). Richard the Lion Hearted, 7621.
Haxthausen (Baron Von). Transcaucasia, 7449.
Haycock (W.). Principles and Practice of Veterinary Medicine, 6609.
Haydon (B. R.). Life of, 7622.
Haydon (W. B.). Science and Revelation, 7976.
Headland (F. W.). Action of Medicines, 7345.
Headley (J. T.). Second War with England, 6706.
Heather (J. F.). Descriptive Geometry, 7041.
Hector Bossange's Catalogue, 7925.
Hedericus (B.). Græcum Lexicon, 7986.
Heineccii (J. R.). Opera, 6964.
—— Elementa Philosophiæ Rationalis et Moralis, 7700.
Henry the Fourth. History of, 7623.
Henry (C. S.). Address, 7815.
Herbert (G.). Works, in Prose and Verse, 7744.
Herbert (H. W.). Captains of the Old World, 7624.
Herbert (Lord). Dialogue between a Tutor and his Pupil, 7830.
Hermosilla (Don J. G.). Principales Poetas Españoles, 7745.
—— Arte de Hablar, 7802.
Herschel (J. F. W.) Essays, 7178.
Herstatt (C.). Anweisung zum Satteln und Packen, 6541.
—— Reit Instruction für die leichte Kavallerie, 6542.
—— Eskadrons-Exerziren der Kavallerie, 6543.
—— Kavallerie-Katechismus, 6544.
—— Exerzieren mit dem Pistol und Karabiner, 6545.
Hertwig (Dr. C. H.). Praktische arzneimittellehre, 6610.
—— Taschenbuch der Pferdekunde, 6611.
Hertwig (Dr. H. C.). Praktisches Handbuch der chirurgie, 6612.
Heth (Capt. H.). System of Target Practice, 6389.
Hetzel (A. R.). Military Laws, 6672.
Hewitt (A. S.). On the Production of Iron, 7371.
Hewitt (J.). Ancient armour and Weapons in Europe, 6791.
Hickox (L. P.). System of Moral Science, 7711.
Hill (Rev. T.). Solar Eclipse, 7151.
Hillard (G. S.). Six Months in Italy, 7450.
Hilliard (H. W.). Speeches and addresses, 7816.
Hirn (G.-A.). Recherches sur l'équivalent mécanique de la chaleur, 7241.
Hirtenfold (J.). Allgemeines Militärisches Handbuch, 6645.
Historical Narrative, 7531.
History, Condition, and Prospects of the Indian Tribes, 7576.
Hitchcock (E.). Plurality of Worlds, 7684.
Hoburg (K.). Geschichte der Festungswerke Danzigs, 6297.
Hoffmann (W.). Waffenlehre, 6390.
Hofzinser (F. X.). Ueber den innern Dienst der Cavallerie, 6546.
Hogg (J.). Winter evening Tales, 7746.
Hollister (G. H.). History of Connecticut, 7577.
Holton (I. F.). New Granada, 7451.
Holtzapffel. Turning and Mechanical Manipulation, 6881.
Hoogduit. Gedichten und Figuren, 7977.

Horner. Solving Equations. See Mathematical Tracts, 7023.
Hough (W.). Precedents in Military Law, 6673.
Household Words, 7896.
Houzeau. Physique du Globe, 7106.
Howitt (W.). Land, Labor, and Gold, 7452.
Hoyt (E.). Practical Instructions for Officers, 6490.
Huc (M.). Journey through the Chinese Empire, 7453.
Humboldt (A. de). Mélanges de Géologie et de Physique Générale, 7317.
—— Volcans des Cordilleres, 7318.
Hume (D.). Essays, 7685, 7712.
—— Treatise of Human Nature, 7701.
—— Private Correspondence, 8029.
Hunersdorf (L.). Anleitung zu Pferde abzurichten, 6618.
Hunt (R.). Manufactures in Metal, 7179.
—— Manual of Photography, 7213.
Hurd (J. C.). Topics of Jurisprudence, 7006.
Hurtrel d'Arboval. Dictionnaire de médecine Vétérinaires, 6614.
Hyta (G. P. de). Guerras civiles de Granada, 7517.

Indiana. Documents of the General Assembly, 6977.
Infantry Manual, 6570.
Infantry Drill, 6571.
Infantry Sword Exercise, 6600.
Ingersoll (Ch. J.). History of the Second War, 6707.
Instruction sur le dessin de fortification, 6298.
Instruction of Musketry, 6391.
Instruction for Foot Artillery, 6392.
Instruction sur le tir, 6393.
Instruction provisoire sur le tir, 6394.
Instruction militaire du Roi de Prusse pour ses Généraux, 6491.
Instruction secrette, dérobée à Frédéric II., 6492.
Instruction for the Carbine, Pistol, and Lance Exercise, 6547.
Instruction for the Sword, Carbine, Pistol, and Lance Exercise, 6548.
Instruction for the conduct of Infantry, 6572.
Instruction for Markers, 6573.
Instruction for the Sword and Lance, 6601.
Instruction sur le mode d'éxécution des dessins, 6842.
Instruction sur le projet de bâtiment militaire, 6843.
Instruction sur le lever de bâtiment, 6844.
Instruction für die bei der Landesvermessung, 7077.
Instructions with regard to the education, 7831.
Irish Academy. Transactions of the, 7180.
Irving (Washingtion). Life of George Washington, 7625.
—— Wolfert's Roost, 7747.
Izarn (J.). Lithologie Atmosphérique, 7242.

Jackson (Lt. Col. Basil). Military Surveying, 7078.
Jackson (C. T.). Geology of Rhode Island, Maine, etc., 7319 to 7321.
Jackson (Col. J. R.). On Military Geography, 7372.
Jacobi (G. A.). Artillerie Autrichienne, 6395.
James & Charles. Annals of, 7532.
Jariez (J.). Cours de Mécanique Industrielle, 6882, 7094.
Jeffers (W. N.). Naval Gunnery, 6396.
Jefferson (Thomas). Writings, 6978.
Jervis. Our Engines of War, 6897.
Jervis. Manual of Field Operations, 6493.
Johnson (M. J.). Astronomical Observations, 7152.
Johnston (Alex. K.). School Atlas of Physical Geography, 7373.
Johnston (G.). Introduction to Conchology, 7274.
Johnston (J. F. W.). Chemistry of Common Life, 7214.
—— Agricultural Chemistry and Geology, 7215.
Joly de Maizeroi. Théorie de la guerre, 6494.
Jomini (Baron de). Précis de l'art de la guerre, 6495.
—— Summary of the Art of War, 6496.
—— Campaign of Waterloo, 6741, 6774.
Jones (Rev. G.). On the Zodiacal Light, 7119.
Jones (W. D.). Military Academy at Woolwich, 7832.
Jopling (J.). Isometrical Perspective, 7042.
Josephine (Empress). Secret Memoirs of the, 7626.
—— History of the, 7627.
Jourjon (C. L.). Fortification passagère, 6299.
Journal des Sciences Militaires, 6798 to 6800.
Journal des Armes Spéciales, 6801, 6802.
Journal of Engineering, 6803, 6934.
Journal de Mathématiques, 7019, 7020.
Journal de l'École Polytechnique, 7181.
Jullien (P. M.). Problémes de mécanique rationnelle, 7095.

Kalkstein (R. V.). Die Preuszische Armee, 6646.
Kameke (H. F.). Die Einrichtung des Perkussions-Gewehrs, 6398.
—— Die Preussische Artillerie, 6399.
—— Die Preussische Feld-Artillerie, 6400.
Kamptz. Progrés du fusil d'Infanterie, 6401.
Kane (E. K.). U. S. Grinnell Expedition, 7454.
—— Arctic Explorations, 7455.
Kane (R.). Elements of Chemistry, 7216.
Keating (J.). History of Ireland, 7538.
Keith (Thomas). On the Globes, 7140.
Kellermann (Duc deValmy). Campagne de 1800, 6742.
Kennedy (J. P.). Horse-Shoe Robinson, 7748.
—— Swallow Barn, 7749.
—— Rob of the Bowl, 7750.
Kent (James). Commentaries on American Law, 7007.
Kewen and Soule. Oration and Poem, 7817.
Kimber (T.). Field Works, 6300.
King (C.). Memoir of the Croton Aqueduct, 6903.
Klapka (Gen. G.). War in the East, 6708.
Klopstock's Messiah, 7751.
Knickerbocker; or, New York Monthly Magazine, 7897.
Knowler (W.). Strafforde's Letters and Dispatches, 8030.
Koch. Ternay's Traité de Tactique, 6497.
—— Mémoires de Massena, 6709.
Kolding. Environs of, 7418.
Koran of Mohammed, 7978.
Köszegh (C. M. de). Versuche über den Seitendruck der Erde, 6935.
Kühne. Militairisches Zeichnen und Aufnehmen, 7079.

La Barre Duparcq. See Barre Duparcq.
Labretonniere. Notice Nécrologique sur Froment-Coste, 6775.
Lacroix. La Revolution de Saint-Domingue, 7578.
Lacuée (Comte de Cessac). 6498.
Lady Lee's Widowhood, 7752.

Lafay. Aide-Mémoire d'Artillerie Navale, 6402.
Lafuente. Historia General de España, 7518.
Lagrange (J.-L.). Mécanique Analytique, 7096.
Laisné (Napoléon). Gymnastique pratique, 7887.
Lake Erie, 7414.
Lallemand (M.). On Spermatorrhœa, 7346.
Lamartine (A. de). Restoration of Monarchy in France, 7546.
—— Memoirs of Celebrated Characters, 7628.
Lamb (Charles). Works, 8031.
Lamb (Gen. J.). Life and Times of, 7629.
Lamé (G.). Leçons sur l'élasticité des Corps Solides, 7107.
Lamennais. Essai sur l'indifférence, 7979.
Landais (Napoléon). Dictionnaire général, 7937, 7938.
Landmann (I.). Principles of Fortification, 6301.
Lardner (N.). History of the Heretics, 7980.
Latham (J. H.). Construction of Wrought Iron Bridges, 6904.
Latham (R. G.). Hand Book of the English Language, 7790.
Lauenborg. The Duchy of, 7415.
Laurent. Calcul différentiel, 7068.
Lavallée (Théo.). Military Topography of Europe, 7374.
—— Géographie Pysique et Militaire, 7375.
Lavelaine de Maubeuge. Les évolutions de ligne, 6574.
Law (Henry). Civil Engineering, 6936.
Lawd and Fisher. Conference, 7981.
Lawrence (W.). On the Eye, 7347.
Lawson. Tangencies. See Mathematical Tracts, 7023.
Layard (A. H.). Ruins of Nineveh and Babylon, 7456.
Leake (J. Q.). Life and Times of General Lamb, 7630.
Lebas (L.). Aide-Mémoire d'art Militaire, 6302, 6499.
Leblanc & Trousseau. Anatomie Chirurgicale, 6615.
Lecreulx. Formation des Rivières, etc., 6905.
Lectures on Fortification, 6303.
Lectures on Painting, 7873.
Lee (T. J.). Tables and Formulæ, 7080.
Legendre (A. M.). Elements of Geometry and Trigonometry, 7033.
Lehon (H.). Périodicité des grands Déluges, 7322.
Le Noble. Administration Militaire, 6647.
Léon (l'Empereur). Institutions Militaires, 6792.
Leroy (C. F. A.). Traité de Stéréotomie, 7049.
Le Sage (A. R.). Histoire de Gil Blas, 7753.
Lettres sur les Mathématiques, 7021.
Le Vasseur. Commentaires de Napoléon, 6500.
Le Verrier (U.-J.). Annales de l'observatoire de Paris, 7141.
Le Vert (Madame O. W.). Souvenirs of Travel, 7457.
Lewis (E. J.). American Sportsman, 8032.
Library of Congress. Catalogue of the, 7926.
Lieber (O. M.). Woehler's Analytical Chemist's Assistant, 7217.
Liebig & Kopp. Annual report of the progress of Chemistry, 7218.
Liège. Forerie &c. de Liège, 6403.
Life in Feejee, 7458.
Lingard (J.). History of England, 7534.
Lionnet. Éléments d'arithmétique, 7026.
—— Complément des éléments d'arithmétique, 7027.
Liskenne & Sauvan. Bibliothéque Militaire, 7495.
Littell's Living Age, 7898, 7899.
Livingston (D.). Travels in South Africa, 7459.
Livingston (J.). Portraits of eminent Americans, 7631.
Llorente (J. A.). Inquisicion de España, 7982.
Lloyd (Gén.). Mémoires militaires et politiques, 6501.
Lockhart (J. G.). Life of Sir Walter Scott, 7632.
Lodge (E.). Portraits of Illustrious Personages, 7633.
London Philosophical Transactions, 7182.
Longfellow (H. W.). Song of Hiawatha, 7754.
Loomis (E.). Analytical Geometry and Calculus, 7055.
—— Natural Philosophy, 7108.
—— Practical Astronomy, 7142.
Lord de Ros. Young officers' Companion, 6502.
Lossing (B. J.). Signers of the declaration of Independence, 7634.
Lovett (R.). Electrical Philosopher, 7243.
Lowe. Captivity of Napoleon at St. Helena, 6776.
Löwig (Dr. C.). Organic and Physiological Chemistry, 7219.
Lowth's Introduction to English Grammar, 7791.
Lullii Raymundi. See Raymundi, 7692.
Lyon. Nouveau Plan de, 7416.

Macaulay (J. S.). Treatise on Field Fortification, 6304.
—— Description of Chasseloup de Laubat's System of Fortification, 6305.
Macaulay (T. B.). History of England, 7535.
Macdougall (Lt.-Col. P. L.). Theory of War, 6503.
—— Campaigns of Hannibal, 6793.
Macintosh. Military Tour in European Turkey, 7460.
Mackenzie (Charles). Notes on Haiti, 7579.
Mackinnon. Atlantic and Transatlantic Sketches, 7461.
Madden (R. R.). Countess of Blessington, 8033.
Magnetical and Meteorological Observations, 7244, 7245.
Mahan (D. H.). Industrial Drawing, 6883.
Mallet (R.). On the Construction of Artillery, 6404.
Mallet's Northern Antiquities, 7496.
Malmesbury (W.). Chronicle of the Kings of England, 7536.
Mangeot (H.). Des armes rayées, 6405.
Mannheim (A.). Transformation des propriétés métriques des figures, 7056.
Manövrir-Reglement für die Cavallerie, 6557.
Manövrir-Reglement für die Infanterie, 6587.
Manual of Natural History, 7275.
Manual of Geographical Science, 7376.
Manuel de Maréchalerie, 6616.
Manuel d'administration et de Comptabilité, 6648, 6674.
Manuel des pensions de l'armée de terre, 6675.
Manuel Réglementaire, 6676.
Manufactures in Metal, 7183.
Map of the Territory of the United States, 7417.
Marchand. Napoléon's Précis des guerres de César, 7497.
Marguery. Théorie pour apprendre à battre aux tambours, 6575.
Maria Antoinette. History of, 7635.
Marieni (J.). Trigonometrische Vermessungen, 7081.
Marion. Opérations de l'artillerie, 6406.
—— Recueil des bouches à feu, 6407.
Marlborough. Letters and Dispatches, 6677.
Marsh (Miss). Life of Captain Vicars, 7636.
Marsh (Rev. J.). Life and Remains, 7687.
Martinez de la Rosa. Obras Completas, 8034.
Mary Queen of Scots. History of, 7638.
Massas. Fabrication des bouches à feu, 6408.

Massena. Mémoires, 6710.
Mathematical Monthly, 7022.
Mathematical Tracts, 7023.
Mather. Magnalia Christi Americana, 7983.
Matteucci (C.). Cours spécial sur l'induction, 7246.
Matthews (W.). Mode of supplying London with water, 6906.
Maurice. Études de fortification permanente, 6306, 6307.
—— Études sur les places de Mayence et d'Ulm, 6308.
—— Mémoires sur la fortification, 6309.
—— De la défense nationale en Angleterre, 6310.
—— Mémorial de l'Ingénieur militaire, 6311.
—— Ponts de Chevalets, 6312.
Maury (D. H.). Skirmish drill for mounted troops, 6549.
Maury (M. F.). Explanation and Sailing Directions, 7125.
—— Storm and Rains in North and South Atlantic, 7247.
—— Physical Geography of the Sea, 7377, 7378.
Maximilian. Travels in North America, 7462.
Maxwell (W. H.). Victories of Wellington, 6711.
Mayer (B.). Mexico, Aztec, Spanish, and Republican, 7580.
McClellan (G. B.). Report on the armies in Europe, 6649.
McRee (Maj. G. J.). Memoir of, 6777.
Mede (Jos.). Works, 7984.
Mélanges mathématiques et astronomiques, 7024.
Mémoires sur la guerre entre la France et l'Espagne, 6712.
Mémoires de l'Academie Royale des sciences, 7184.
Memoirs of the Astronomical Society of London, 7143.
Memorial de Ingenieros, 6813.
Mémorial de l'officier du Génie, 6314.
Mémorial de l'Artillerie, 6409.
Mémorial des officiers d'Infanterie et de Cavalerie, 6576.
Mentz. Festung, 6315.
Mentz. Neuester Plan der Stadt, 7418.
Merchants' Magazine, 7900.
Meteorological Register, 7248.
Meteorological observations, 7249.
Mexican History of the War in Mexico, 6713.
Michon. Stabilité des Constructions, 6937.
—— Instruction sur la résistance des matériaux, 6957, to 6959.
Migout & Bergery. Cours de Machines, 6884.
Miles (W.). Treatise on Horse-shoeing, 6617.
Military Academy, 1291, 6697.
Military Regulations Concerning Infantry Service, 6577, 6678.
Military Schools. Organization and Condition of, 7833, 7834.
Mill (James). History of British India, 7550.
Miller (H.). Old Red Sandstone, 7323.
—— First Impressions of England and its People, 7463.
—— My Schools and Schoolmasters, 7835.
Miller (W. A.). Elements of Chemistry, 7220.
Milner (I.). Communication of Motion, etc. See Mathematical Tracts, 7023.
Minard (M.). Navigation des Rivières, 6907.
Mines; Abhandlung über die Kriegs-Minen, 6316.
Mitchell (J.). Manual of Practical Assaying, 7221.
Mitchell (S. A.). New Universal Atlas, 7879.
Modern Painters, 7874.
Molesworth (Rev. I. E. N.). Domestic Chaplain, 7985.
Mone (F.) Treatise on American Engineering, 6885.
Moniteur des Architectes, 6845.
Montecuculli. Extraits, 6504.
Montrose. Life and Times of, 7639.
Moore (N. F.). Ancient Mineralogy, 7299.
Moorsom (Capt. W.). Organization and Manœuvres of Steam Fleets, 6505.
Morfit (C.). Noad's Chemical Analysis, 7222.
Moricière. Rapport sur les travaux de la session de 1850, 7380.
Morton (J. C.). Cyclopedia of Agriculture, 7289.
Moseley (H.). Engineering and Architecture, 6886, 6887.
Motley (J. L.). Rise of the Dutch Republic, 7519.
Muirhead. Mechanical Inventions of Watt, 6888.
Murchison (R. I.). Siluria, 7325.
Murchison, Nicol, & Johnson. Geological Map of Europe, 7324.
Murray (A. M.). Letters from the United States, Cuba, and Canada, 7464.
Murray (J.). On the Stability of Retaining Walls, 6938.
Musketry. Instruction of, 6410.
Mussot (P.). Commentaires historiques sur l'Équitation et la Cavalerie, 6618.

Nádosy (Alex. Von). Equitations-Studien, 6619.
Napier (Gen.). Comments upon a Memorandum of Wellington, 6650.
Napier (James). Electro-metallurgy, 7223, 7250.
Napier (Mark). Life and Times of Montrose, 7640.
Napoléon. Commentaires, 6506.
—— Campagnes d'Egypt et de Syrie, 6743.
—— History of, by Abbott, 6778.
—— Précis des guerres de César, 7498.
Natural History of New York, 7276.
Natural History. Annual Reports of, 7277.
Naumann (Dr. C. F.). Lehrbuch der Geognosie, 7326.
Nautical Almanac, 7160.
Navez. Application de l'Électricité à la mesure de la Vitesse des Projectiles, 6411.
—— Expériences de Balistique, 6412.
Navy Registers, 6819.
Nebraska & Dakota. Military Map of, 7419.
Nedham (M.). Common-wealth of England, 7537.
Nero. History of, 7641.
Neuchéze. Traité de fortification passagére, 6318.
Neuman and Baretti. Dictionary of the Spanish and English Languages, 7939.
Neville (J) Hydraulic Tables and Formulæ, 6908.
New Bond of Love, 8035.
New England Historical and Geneological Register, 7581.
Newman (F. W.). Regal Rome, 7499.
New Testament and Concordance, 7986.
New Testament in Greek and English, 7987.
New York. On the Harbor of, 6909, 6910.
New York. Documents of the Senate of, 6979.
New York. Journal of the Senate of, 6980.
New York. Documents of the Assembly of, 6981.
New York. Journal of the Assembly of, 6982.
New York. Reports of the various Officers of the State of, 6983.
New York State. Code of Criminal Procedure of, 7008.

New York State. Code of Procedure of, 7009.
New York. Laws of the State of, 7010.
New York. Meteorological observations, 7251.
New York. Natural History of, 7276, 7277.
New York Free Academy. Examination papers, 7836.
New York. Annual Reports, 7901.
New York State Library. Annual Reports of the, 7927.
New York State Library. Catalogue of the, 7928 to 7931.
Niel (Gén.). Siége de Sebastopol, 6819, 6744.
Noad (H. M.). Chemical analysis, 7224.
—— Manual of Electricity, 7252.
Noel (F.). Dictionnaire de la Fable, 7500.
Noizet. Cours de fortification permanente, 6320.
—— Principes de fortification, 6321.
Nolan (L. E.). Cavalry; its History and Tactics, 6551.
Nolte (V.). 50 years in both Hemispheres, 7465.
Normand. Memoirs of the Empress Josephine, 7642.
Normandy (A.). Dictionaries to the Chemical Atlas, 7225.
Norris (E.). Prichard's Natural History of Man, 7278.
Norwich. Map of, 7420.
Notice historique sur les Ponts militaires, 6322.
Nott & Gliddon. Types of Mankind, 7279.
Nuttall (T.). North American Sylva, 7290.

Observations sur les applications du fer aux constructions de l'artillerie, 6413.
Ochoa. Apuntes para una Biblioteca de escritores Españoles, 7755.
—— Tresoro del Teatro Español, 7756.
Oersted (H. C.). The Soul in Nature, 7688.
Oeynhausen (B. Von). Leitfaden zur abrichtung von Reiter und Pferd, 6620.
Oliver (P.). Scripture Lexicon, 7988.
Olivier (Théo.). Géométrie descriptive, 7044.
Ollendorff's New method of learning French, 7792.
Olmsted (D.). Aurora Borealis, 7120.
Olmsted (F. L.). Journey in the Seaboard Slave States, 7466.
Onosander. Le Général en chef, 6794.
Opie (John). Lectures on Painting, 7875.
Opinions of Attorneys General of the U. S., 7011.
Orange County. Map of, 7421.
Ordnance Regulations, 6679.
Ordonnance provisoire pour la Cavalerie, 6552.
Ordonnance du Roi sur le Service intérieur des troupes à cheval, 6553, 6681.
Ordonnance sur l'exercice et les manœuvres de l'Infanterie, 6578.
Ordonnance sur le service des armées en Campagne, 6680.
Organisation de l'artillerie en France, 6414.
Owen (C.). History of Serpents, 7280.
Owen (D. D.). Geology of Wisconsin, Iowa, &c., 7327.
Owen (R.). Odontography, 7281.
Oxford Chronological Tables, 7481.
Oxley (T.). The Celestial Planispheres, 7144.

Page (C. E.). Théorie du Pointage, 6415.
Paixhans (H. J.). Constitution militaire, 6682.
Palfrey (J. G.). History of New England, 7582.
Palmer (H. R.). On the improvements of the Rivers, 6911.
Panot (L.). Armes à feu portatives, 6416.
Papillon (M. le Dr.). De la Ventilation, 6963.
Paramelle. L'art de decouvrir les sources, 6912.
Park (R.). History of West Point, 7583.
Parker (R. G.). Aids to English Composition, 7837.
Parkhurst (J.). Hebrew and English Lexicon, 7940.
Parmentier. Fortification Polygonale, 6323.
Parnell (Sir H.). On Roads, 6939.
Paskévitch (Maréchal). Campagnes en 1828 et 1829, 6745.
—— L'attaque et la prise de Varsovie, 6746.
Paton (A. A.). Highlands and Islands of the Adriatic, 7520.
Pearson (Rev. T.). On Infidelity, 7989.
Peirce (B.). Treatise on Curves, Functions, &c., 7069.
—— Physical and Celestial Mechanics, 7097.
Pellico (S.). Mis Prisiones, 7643.
Pembroke. Methode of breaking Horses, 6621.
Pennsylvania. Historical Society of, 7584.
Penny Cyclopædia, 7941.
Penny Magazine, 7902.
Percivall (W.). Lectures on the Veterinary art, 6622.
—— Lectures on the Form and action of the Horse, 6623.
—— Anatomy of the Horse, 6624.
Perdonnet (A.). Traité des chemins de fer, 6940.
Perdonnet & Polonceau. Portefeuille des chemins de fer, 6941.
Pereira (J.). On Polarized light, 7121.
—— Materia Medica and Therapeutics, 7348.
Perkins (G. R.), Geometry, 7034.
—— Plane Trigonometry, 7051.
Perry (Com. M. C.). Expedition to Japan, 7467 to 7469.
Peshel (C. F.). Elements of Physics, 7109.
Petite notice de faire manger les chevaux sans les débrider, 6625.
Philadelphia Lectures on the Evidences of Christianity, 7990.
Philip, King. History of, 7644.
Philippart (J.). Memoirs and Campaigns of Charles John, 6779.
Phillips (J. A.). Manual of Metallurgy, 7226.
Phillips (Sir R.). Phenomena of the Universe, 7110.
Philosophical Transactions, 7185.
Philosophy of the Plan of Salvation, 7991.
Photographic and fine art Journal, 7876.
Photographs of the Graduating Classes of the U. S. Military Academy, 7877.
Pickell (J.). Early life of Washington, 7645.
Pilkington (M.). Dictionary of Painters, 7595.
Pinney & Barcolo. Practical Spanish Teacher, 7793.
Piobert (G.). Mémoires sur les Poudres de guerre, 6417.
—— Propriétés et effets de la poudre, 6418.
Plata (La). Map of the Basin of, 7422.
Platoon Exercise, 6579.
Plautus' Comedies, 7757.
Plotho. Capitulation de Danzig, 6747.
—— Bataille de Leipzig, 6748.
Plurality of Worlds, 7689.
Poisson. Théorie mathématique de la Chaleur, 7253.
Polybe. Histoire générale, 7501.
Polyen. Ruses de guerre, 6795.
Poncelet. L'équilibre des Voûtes, 6942.
Pontécoulant (G. de). Théorie du systéme du Monde, 7098.
Poole (W. F.). Index to Periodical Literature, 7903.
Porden (E. A.). Cœur de Lion, 7758.

Posen. Plan von der umgegend von, 7423.
Potter (A.). Lectures on the Evidences of Christianity, 7992.
Powell (Rev. B.). Unity of Worlds and of Nature, 7690.
—— Plurality of Worlds, 7691.
Powell (W. S.). Discourses, 7993.
Practical Draughtsman's Book of industrial design, 6889.
Practical Engineering. Papers on, 6943.
Préjugés Militaires, 6507.
Prendergast (H.). Law relating to officers in the Army, 6683.
Prescott (W. H.). History of Philip the Second, 7521.
—— Robertson's History of Charles V., 7522.
Preval. Mémoires sur l'avancement Militaire, 6651.
Price (B.). Treatise on Infinitesimal Calculus, 7070.
Price (L.). Photographic Manipulation, 7227.
Prichard (J. C.). Natural History of Man, 7282.
—— Ethnographical Maps to the Natural History of Man. 7283.
Prideaux (H.). Connection of the Old and New Testament, 7994.
Prime (S. I.). Travels in Europe and the East. 7470.
Proceedings of the American Philosophical Society, 7186.
Proceedings of the American Association, 7187.
Proceedings of the National Institute, Washington, 7188.
Programme pour l'enseignement de la fortification permanente, 6324.
Programme du journal d'attaque, 6325.
Programme du Cours de fortification permanente, 6326.
Programme du Simulacre de Siége, 6327.
Programme du Cours de sciences Physiques et chimiques, 6419.
Programme du Cours des sciences appliquées aux arts militaires, 6420.
Programme du Cours d'artillerie, 6421.
Programme du Cours d'art militaires, 6508.
Programme du Cours d'hippiatrique, 6626.
Programme du Cours de Mécanique Appliquée, 6890.
Programme du Cours de Constructions, 6944.
Programme du Cours de Géodésie et de Gnomonique, 7082.
Programme du Cours de Topographie, 7381.
Programme of the Course of Instruction of Cadets, 7838.
Programme of the Course of Instruction of Officers, 7839.
Programme of the Course of Descriptive Geometry, 7840.
Programme of the Course of Natural Sciences, 7841.
Programme of the Course of Foreign Languages, 7842.
Programme of the Course of Algebra, 7843.
Programme of the Course of Lectures on Astronomy and Geodesy, 7844.
Programme and Summary of the Third Special Class, 7845.
Programme of the Final Examination of Officers, 7846.
Programme of the Course of Military Science, 7847.
Programme of the Course on Political Science, 7848.
Programme of the Course of Mathematics, 7849.
Programme of the Course on Religion, 7850.
Programme of the Examination of Officers, 7851.
Programme of the Course on the Russian Language and Literature, 7852.
Projet d'instruction sur le tir, 6422.
Public Buildings of the United States, 6846.
Public Works in Ireland, 6945,
Public Works, both British and American, 6913.
Puffendorf. Law of Nature and Nations, 6965.
Pugin (A. W.). Ancient Timber Houses, 6847.
Puissant (L.). Sur la Projection de Cassini, 7083.
Pulszky (F.). Tricolor on the Atlas, 7551.
Putnam & Co.'s Catalogue, 7932.
Puységur Extraits, 6509.
Pyrrhus. History of, 7646.

Quackenbos (G. P.). Spiers & Surenne's Pronouncing Dictionary, 7942.
Queen's Regulations and Orders, 6684, 6685.
Queens of England and Scotland, 7647.
Quekett's Treatise on the Use of the Microscope, 7122.
Quillet (P. N.). Législation des Troupes, 6686, 6687.
Quin (E.). Atlas of Universal History, 7382.
Quincy (J.). Municipal History of Boston, 7585.
Quintana (M. J.). Vidas de Españoles Célebres, 7648.
Quitman & Harris. Obituary Addresses on, 7818.

Rabusson (A.). Défense général du Royaume, 6328.
Radcliffe Observatory, Oxford, 7153.
Ralegh (Sir W.). History of the World, 7482.
Ranke (L.). Civil Wars and Monarchy in France, 7547.
Rankine (W. J. M.). Applied Mechanics, 6891.
Rapports pour l'Établissement des principes du tir, 6423.
Rapport sur l'enseignement de l'École Polytechnique, 7853.
Rapport sur le travaux de la session de 1850, 7383.
Rarey (J. S.). Art of Taming Horses, 6627.
Raymundi (Lullii). Opera, 7692.
Rayner (Hon. K.). Address, 7819.
Read & Co. Views of the War, East and North, 6714.
Recherches Philosophiques sur les Egyptiens, 7552.
Recueil des bouches à feu, 6424.
Recueil d'hygiène et de médecine Vétérinaires Militaires, 6628.
Redhill Catalogue of 3735 Circumpolar Stars, 7161.
Reech (F.). Dynamiques de la Chaleur, 7254.
Register of Officers Civil, Military, etc., of the United States, 6820.
Reglamento de nueva Constitucion en el Colegio Militar, 6688.
Réglement sur les Exercices et les Évolutions de l'Artillerie Belge, 6425.
Réglement concernant l'exercice et les manœuvres de l'Infanterie, 6580, 6581.
Réglement provisoire sur le service de l'Infanterie, 6689.
Réglement provisoire sur le service des troupes à cheval, 6690.
Réglement pour l'exécution des travaux, 7854.
Regnault (M. V.). Relation des Expériences, 6892.
—— Elements of Chemistry, 7228.
—— Treatise on Crystallography, 7300.
Regulations for the Instruction, etc., of the Cavalry, 6554.
Regulations.—Abrichtungs-Reglement für die Cavallerie, 6555.

Regulations.—Exercir-Reglement für die Cavallerie, 6556
Regulations.—Manövrir-Reglement für die Cavallerie, 6557.
Regulations.—Exercir-Reglement für die Kavallerie, 6558.
Regulations.—Exercir-Reglement für die Infanterie, 6582.
Regulations.—Abrichtungs-Reglement für die Linien-Infanterie, 6583.
Regulations.—Exercir-Reglement für die Linien-Infanterie, 6584.
Regulations.—Exercir-Reglement für die Linien und Grenz-Infanterie, 6585.
Regulations.—Abrichtungs-Reglement für die Linien und Grenz-Infanterie, 6586.
Regulations.—Manövrir-Reglement für die Infanterie, 6587.
Regulations.—Abrichtungs-Reglement für die Pionniere, 6588.
Regulations.—Exercir-Reglement für die Pionniere, 6589.
Regulations.—Abrichtungs-Reglement für die Jäger, 6590.
Regulations.—Exerzir-Reglement für die Jäger, 6591.
Regulations.—Abrichtungs-Reglement für die Genie-Truppen, 6592.
Regulations.—Exercir-Reglement für die Genie-Truppen, 6593.
Regulations for Infantry Tactics, 6594.
Regulations for Admission into Military Academy at Woolwich, 6692.
Regulations for Admission into the Ordnance School, 6693.
Regulations for the Army of the United States, 6694.
Regulations for the Ordnance Department, 6695.
Regulations of the United States Military Academy, 6696, 6697.
Reicha (A.). Cours de Composition Musicale, 7879.
—— Art du Compositeur Dramatique, 7880.
Reiff (C. P.). English-Russian Grammar, 7794.
Reigert (J. F.). On the Cause of Cholera, 7349.
Renan (E.). Histoire des langues Sémitiques, 7795.
Rendsborg. Environs of, 7424.
Rennell (J.). Memoir of Maps of Hindoostan, 7384.
Rennie (J.). Theory, Formations, and Construction of Harbors, 6914.
Réponse à l'article sur l'État-Major-Général, 6652.
Reports of Experiments with Small Arms, 6426.
Report on Barrack Accommodation, 6848.
Report of the Committee on the Machinery of the United States, 6893.
Report (9th). On Roads and Bridges, 6946.
Reports of the British Association, 7189.
Reports of Explorations and Surveys for a Railroad to the Pacific Ocean, 7471.
Report of the Portsmouth relief association, 7906.
Report on Military Education, 7855.
Reports on the distribution and income of the Smithsonian Fund, 7904, 7905.
Restorff (C. Von). Die Theorie des Schieszens, 6427.
Resvoy (Col.). Notes on Artillery, 6428.
Réveil. L'Empereur Napoléon, 6780.
Review. North American, 7907.
Review. Edinburgh, 7908.
Review. Westminster, 7909.
Review. London Quarterly, 7910.
Review. North British, 7911.
Review. Southern Quarterly, 7912.
Revue Générale de l'architecture et de travaux Publics, 6849.
Revue de Deux Mondes, 7913.
Reynal. Nouveau Dictionnaire de Médecine Vétérinaires, 6629.
Reynaud (E.). Resolution de Questions, 7071.
Reynaud (L.). Traité d'Architecture, 6850.
Richard the Lion Hearted, 7649.
Richard the First, King. History of, 7650.
Richardot. De l'organisation de l'artillerie, 6429.
—— Appareils contre la Foudre, 7255.
Richer (Ed.). Religion of Good Sense, 7995.
Richter (J. P. F.). Flower, Fruit, and Thorn Pieces, 7759.
Ricordo Pittorico Militare della Spedizione Sarde in Oriente, 6749.
Ricraft (J.). Survey of England's Champions, 6781.
Rifle Musket, 6430.
Rifled Ordnance, 6431.
Riley (H. T.). Dictionary of Latin Quotations, 7796.
Ringgold (Commander C.). Defence, 6698.
Ritter (E.). Méthode des moindres Carrés, 7072.
Ritter (H.). History of ancient Philosophy, 7693.
Rive. See De la Rive, 7237.
Roach (R.). The Great Crisis, 7996.
—— The Imperial standard of Messiah Triumphant, 7997.
Robbins (Lieut.). Cavalry Catechism, 6559.
Robert (Ch.). Législation et administration militaires, 6699, 6700.
Robert & Arnoul. Siéges mémorables des Français, 6750.
Robertson (W.). History of Charles V., 7523.
Robinet aîné. Cours de lavis, 6851.
Roche (A.). Traitè de Balistique, 6432.
Rodet (H. J. A.). Botanique agricole et médicale, 7291.
Rogers (H. D.). Geology of Pennsylvania, 7328.
Roget (P. M.). Thesaurus of English Words, 7797.
Roguet. De l'approvisionnement des armées, 6654.
Rohan (Duc de). Campagne dans la Valteline, 6751.
Rokitansky (Carl). Manual of Pathological Anatomy, 7350.
Roland (Madame). History of, 7651.
Röll (Dr. M.F.). Lehrbuch der Arzneimittellehre, 6630.
Romulus. History of, 7652.
Ronalds & Richardson. Chemical Technology, 7229.
Rondelet (J.). Traité de l'art de bâtir, 6947.
Roth (M.). Cure of many Chronic Diseases, 7351.
Rouméllie. Carte de la, 7425.
Roy (W.). Military Antiquities, 6796.
Royal Engineers. Professional Papers of the Corps of, 6948.
Rul (Louis). Le Bauchérisme, 6631.
Rush (J.). Philosophy of the Human Voice, 7803.
Ruskin (J.). Lectures on Architecture and Painting, 6852.
—— Stones of Venice, 6949.
—— Modern Painters, 7881.
Russell (W.). American Elocutionist, 7804.
Russell (W. H.). British Expedition to the Crimea, 6752.

Russia in Europe. Map indicating the Stations of the Army, 7426.
Russian War, 6715.
Rüstow (C.). Kriegshandfeuerwaffen, 6433.
Rüstow (W.). Allgemeine Taktik, 6510.
—— Die Feldherrnkunst, 6511.

Safford (J. M.). Geological Reconnoissance of Tennessee, 7329.
Saint-Ange. Abrégé du Cours d'hippologie, 6632.
Saint-Hilaire (J. B.) De la logique d'Aristote, 7702.
Saint Paul. Life and Epistles of, 7998.
Saint-Robert (P. de). Des effets de la Rotation de la terre sur le mouvement des Projectiles, 6434.
Salvá. Nuevo Diccionario de la lengua Castellana, 7943.
Sammes (A.). Antiquities of ancient Britain, 7538.
Sanchez (D. T. A.). Vocabulario de Voces anticuadas, 7798.
Sandhurst Royal Military College, 7856.
Sandys (Sir E.). Europæ Speculum, 7999.
San-Miguel. Capitaines anciens et modernes, 6782.
Sar (P. C.). Cours d'études militaires, 6435.
Sargent (W.). History of Braddock's Expedition, 6758.
Sarrion. Manuel de Géographie, 7385.
Sax (Maréchal de). Extraits, 6512.
Say (T.). Conchology of the United States, 7284.
Schabus (J.). Bestimmung der Krystallgestalten, 7301.
Schaff (Dr. P.). America, Political and Religious, 7820.
Schauenburg (le baron de). Emploi de la Cavalerie, 6560.
Scheutz (G. & E.). Specimens of Tables, 7085.
Schimmel (F.). Die percussionirten Schusz-Waffen, 6436.
—— Compendium des kleinen Krieges, 6513.
Schlegel (A. W.). Lectures on Dramatic art and Literature, 7669.
Schlegel (F.). Philosophy of Life, &c., 7694.
—— Aesthetic and Miscellaneous Works, 7882.
—— Lectures on modern History, 7483.
Schleiden (M. J.), The Plant, 7292.
Schlosser (F. C.). History of the 18th Century, 7484.
Schmid & Schleiden. Ueber die Natur der Kieselhölzer, 7330.
Schnitzler (J. H.). Secret History of Russia, 7524.
Schœdler (F.). Book of Nature, 7190.
Schön (J.). Das gezogene Infanterie-Gewehr, 6437.
—— Geschichte der Handfeuerwaffen, 6438.
Schoolcraft (H. R.). History of Indian Tribes, 7586.
Schooler (S.). Descriptive Geometry, 7046.
Schramke (T.). New York Croton Aqueduct, 6915.
Schrœder (J. F.). Maxims of Washington, 8036.
Schweinitz. Die Expedition gegen die Alands-Inseln, 6754.
Schwink (G.) Fortification Polygonale, 6329.
Scoffern (J.). Projectile Weapons of War, 6439.
Scotland. Plans of Cities of, 7386.
Scott (J.). Christian Life, 8000.
Scott (Sir Walter). Life of, 7652.
Scott (General Winfield). Supplement to the Infantry Tactics, 6595.
Ségur (P. P.). Lettre sur la Campagne, 6755.
Seider (E. F.). Die Dressur difficiler Pferde, 6633.
—— Leitfaden zur Bearbeitung des Pferdes, 6634.
Seifert (J.). Bildliche darstellung des Pferdes, 6635.
Selwyn (W.). Law of Nisi Prius, 7012.
Semmering Railway, 6950.
Seoane's Neuman & Baretti's Dictionary, 7944.
Serret (J. A.). Cours d'Algébre Supérieure, 7031.
—— Traité de Trigonométrie, 7052.
Sevastopol. Photographs of the Forts of, 6330.
Sevastopol. The Environs of, 7427.
Seward (W. H.). Works, 6984.
Sewell (J.) On Steam and Locomotion, 6894.
Seymour (H. D.). Russia on the Black Sea and Sea of Azof, 7472.
Shaw (G.). Manual of Electro-Metallurgy, 7280, 7257.
Shepard (C. U.). Geological Survey of Connecticut, 7331.
Shirley (A.). On the Transport of Cavalry and Artillery, 6655.
Sidney (A.). Discourses on Government, 6985.
Siège de Rome en 1849, 6756.
Siege of Bomarsund in 1854, 6757.
Siegmann (W.). Die Elementartaktik der Reiterei, 6561.
Silliman (B.). First Principles of Physics, 7111.
—— Visit to Europe, 7473.
Silveyra. Cours de Lavis, 6853.
Simcoe's Military Journal, 6716.
Simmons (T. F.). On the Effect of Heavy Ordnance, 6440.
—— Courts Martial, 6701.
Simms (W. G.). Novels, or Works, 7760.
Simons (Capt. F. C.). Leading Principles of Gunnery, 6441.
Sind's Pferdearzt, 6636.
Sketching. Collection of Models for, 7387.
Skirmish Drill for Mounted Troops, 6562.
Sloan (S.). The Model Architect, 6854.
Small Arms. Experiments with, 6442.
Smee (A.). Elements of Electro-Metallurgy, 7231.
Smith (Adam). Moral Sentiments, 7713.
Smith (H.). Gaieties and Gravieties, 7761.
Smith (R. B.). Italian Irrigation, 6916.
Smith (R. S.). Topographical Drawing, 7388.
Smith (Rev. S.). Memoir of the, 7654.
—— Moral Philosophy, 7714.
—— See Sydney Smith, 6246.
Smith (W.). Dictionary of Antiquities, 7596.
—— Student's Vade Mecum, 7857.
Smith & Watson. American Curiosities, 8037.
Smithsonian Institution. Alvord's Tangencies of Circles, 7035.
—— Olmsted's Aurora Borealis, 7120.
—— Occultations, 7145.
—— Contributions to Knowledge, 7191.
—— Reports, 7904, 7905.
—— Notices of Public Libraries in the United States, 5799.
Smola (C. & J. F.). Taschenbuch für Artillerie-Officiere, 6443.
Smyth (P.). On Raising Water, 6917.
—— Report, 7154.
Solis (A. de). Conquista de Méjico, 7587.
Songs of a Student, 7883.
Sonnet (H.). Problémes d'Arithmétique et d'Algébre, 7028.
Sopwith (T.). On Isometrical Drawing, 7047.
Soulé, Gihon, & Nisbet. Annals of San Francisco, 7588.
Soult (Marèchal). Mémoires du, 6717.

Sowerby (H.). Popular Mineralogy, 7302.
Sparks (J.). Letter to Lord Mahon, 8038.
—— Remarks on Washington's Letters, 8039.
—— Letters of Eminent Men to Washington, 8040.
Spearman (Capt. J. M.). British Gunner, 6444.
—— Notes on Military Education, 7858.
Specification for the Erection of a Fort, 6331.
Spectateur Militaire, 6804, 6805.
Spiers & Surenne's French and English Pronouncing Dictionary, 7945.
Spooner (J.). Dictionary of Painters, Engravers, etc., 7597, 7884.
—— Anecdotes of Painters, etc., 7885.
Sprague (J. T.). History of the Florida War, 6718.
Squier (E. G.). Notes on Central America, 7589.
Stanford's Map of the Battle of Tchernaya, 6758.
—— Panoramic View of Helsingfors and Sveaborg, 6719.
—— Map of the Sea of Azof, 7393.
—— Map of the Country between Odessa and Sebastopol, 7400.
Stanhope (G.). Christian Religion, 8001.
State of England, 7539.
Steinle (U.). Die Spitzgeschosse, 6445.
Stier (G.). Grundlage der Baukunst, 6951.
Stobo (Major R.). Memoirs of, 6783.
Strafforde (Earl of). Letters and Dispatches, 8041.
Straight (H.). Treatise on Fortification and Artillery, 6332.
Streffleur (V.). Sämmtlicher Waffengattungen, 6446.
—— Die Dienst-Vorschriften, 6514.
—— Die Organisation im Frieden, 6656.
—— Militär-Justizwesen, 6657.
—— Die Organisation und der Geschäftsbetrieb, 6658.
Streubel (W.). Die 12pfündige Granatkanone, 6447.
Strickland (A.). Lives of the Queens of England, 7655, 7656.
—— Lives of the Queens of Scotland, 7657.
Stuart (C. B.). Naval and Mail Steamers of the United States, 6855.
Stuart & Revett. Antiquities of Athens, 6856.
Sumner (I.). Memoir of, 7658.
Swainson (W.). Treatise on Animals, 7285.
Swedenborg (E.). A Biography, 7659.
—— Divine love and wisdom, 8002.
—— Divine Providence, 8003.
—— Heaven and Hell, 8004.
—— True Christian Religion, 8005.
—— Heavenly arcana, 8006.
—— Doctrines of the New Jerusalem, 8007.
Sydney (A.). See Sidney, 6985.
Sydney (Sir H.). Letters and Memorials of State, 7540.

Tableau de la guerre de la Revolution de France, 6720.
Tableau de la Situation des Établissement Français dans l'Algérie, 7553.
Taitbout de Marigny (E.). Atlas de la Mer Noire, 7389.
Taubert. On the use of Field Artillery, 6448.
Taylor (Isaac). Historical Proof, 7671.
—— On ancient Books, 7672.
—— Elements of Thought, 7703.
—— Fanaticism, 7715.
—— Home Education, 7859.
—— Saturday Evening, 8008.
Taylor (Isaac). Loyola and Jesuitism, 8009.
—— Spiritual Despotism, 8010.
Taylor (J. Bayard). Views A-Foot, 4144.
—— Lands of the Saracen, 7435.
—— Journey to Central Africa, 7436.
—— Eldorado, 7437.
—— Visit to India, China, and Japan, 7438.
Taylor (Tom.). Life of Haydon, 7660.
Tchernaya or Traktir. Battle of, 6759.
Tegoborski Commentaries on the Productive forces of Russia, 7525.
Telegraph. Book of the, 7258.
Téliakoffsky (A.). Manuel de fortification permanente, 6333.
—— Elementary Treatise on permanent fortification, 6334.
—— Elementary Treatise on Field Fortification, 6335.
Tennyson (A.). Maud and other Poems, 7762.
Ternaux-Compans. Relation du Voyage de Cibola, 7474.
Ternay (Marquis de). Traité de Tactique, 6515.
Tesoro del Teatro Español, 7763.
Tevis. Du Service des avant-postes, 6516.
Thackeray (T. J.) Soldier's Manual of Rifle Firing, 6449.
—— Military Organization of France, 6659.
Thackeray (W. M.). Paris Sketch Book, 7764.
—— Shabby Genteel Story, 7765.
—— Yellowplush Papers, 7766.
—— Confessions of Fitz-Boodle, 7767.
—— Vanity Fair, 7768.
—— Men's Wives, 7769.
—— The Book of Snobs, 7770.
—— Fatal Boots, 7771.
—— Mr. Brown's Letters, 7772.
—— Luck of Barry Lyndon, 7773.
—— History of Pendennis, 7774.
—— Great Hoggarty Diamond, 7775.
—— History of Henry Esmond, 7776.
—— The Newcomes, 7777.
Thiébault (P.). Journal du Siége et du Blocus de Gênes, 6760, 6761.
Thierry (Capitaine). Sur le chevalet Belge, 6336.
Thierry. Méthode Graphique et Géométrique, 7048.
Thiers (A.). Histoire du Consulat et de l'Empire, 7548.
Thiroux. Réflexions sur les bouches à feu, 6450.
—— Essai sur les Projectiles allongés, 6451.
—— Essai sur le mouvement des Projectiles, 6452.
—— Mémoire sur le tir à Mitraille, 6453.
Thompson (H.) Stricture of the Urethra, 7352.
Thomson (H.B.). Military forces of Great Britain, 6660.
Thomson (W.). Outline of the Laws of Thought, 7704.
Thornbury (G. W.). Lays and Legends, 7778.
Thucydides. Peloponnesian War, 7502.
—— Guerre du Péloponnése, 7503.
Tidal Harbours, 6918.
Timmerhans (C.). Expériences faits à Liége, 6454.
Todhunter (I.). Differential and Integral Calculus, 7078.
Tolhausen & Gardissal. Technological Dictionary, 7192.
Tondeur (A.). Questionnaires et Exercices Préparatoires, 7025.
Torstenson (General L.). Life of, 6784.
Tower (F. B.). Croton Aqueduct, 6919.
Townshend (H.). Historical Collections, 7541.
Track-Survey of the Rivers Salado, Parana, &c., 7428.

Traité sur la Constitution des troupes légéres, 6702.
Transactions. Philosophical Transactions of the Royal Society of London, 7193.
Transactions of the Royal Society of Edinburgh, 7194.
Transactions of the Cambridge Philosophical Society, 7195.
Transactions of the Royal Irish Academy, 7196.
Transactions of the American Philosophical Society, 7197.
Treadwell (D.). On Cannon of Great Caliber, 6455.
Trench (R. Ch . On the Study of Words, 7799.
Tripon (M. J. B.) Études des Projections d'ombres et de Lavis, 7049.
Tucker (J) On Civil Government, 6986.
Tuileries, 6857.
Tuomey (M.). Geology of South Carolina, 7332.
Turenne (Vicomte de). Mémoires, 6762.
Turkey Map of, 7429.
Tyng (S. H.). Memoir of Bedell, 7661.

Ubicini (M. A.). Lettres sur la Turquie, 7554.
Unger (L. A). Exploits et Vicissitudes de la Cavalerie, 6563.
United States Capitol Extensions, 6858.
United States. American Archives, 6987.
United States. Executive Documents of the House of Representatives of the, 6988.
United States. Miscellaneous Documents of the House of Representatives of the, 6989.
United States. Reports of Committees of the House of Representatives of the. 6990.
United States. Reports from the Court of Claims, 6991.
United States. Journals of the House of Representatives of the, 6992.
United States. Executive Documents of the Senate of the, 6993.
United States. Miscellaneous Documents of the Senate of the, 6994.
United States. Reports of the Committees of the Senate of the, 6995.
United States Journals of the Senate of the, 6996.
United States of America. Statutes at Large and Treaties of, 7013.
United States Coast Survey Maps, 7430.
United States Exploring Expedition, 7475.
Urcullu (J. B. de). Lecciones de Moral, 7716.
Ure (A.). Dictionary of Arts, 7198.
Usher (J.). Annals of the World, 7485.
Usoffskime (Capt.). Treatise on Military Topography. 7390.

Vaillant. Rapport sur la Situation de l'Algérie, 7555.
Valachie. Bulgarie, Roumélie. Carte de la. 7431.
Valentine (D. T.). History of the City of New York, 7590.
Valmy (Duc de). See Kellermann, 6742.
Van Sommer (J.) Tables, 6998.
Vauchelle. Cours d'Administration Militaire, 6661.
Vaudoncourt (le Général de). Campagnes d'Italie, 6764.
Vaux (C.). Villas and Cottages, 6859.
Végéce Traité de l'art militaire, 6517.
—— Institutions Militares, 6518.
Velazquez's Seoane's Neuman & Baretti's Spanish Pronouncing Dictionary, 7946.
Venice. Carta Topografica della Laguna di, 7432.
Verdú (Don G.). Nouvelle Mines de guerre, 6337.
Vessell (General). Artillery, 6456.
Vestiges of Creation, 7286.
Vicars (Capt. H). Memorials of, 7662.
Vieille (J). Théorie générale des approximations numériques, 7029.
Vielé (Mrs.). Following the Drum, 7476.
Vienna. Arsenal at Vienna, 6860.
Views.—Ansichten auf der Eisenbahn über den Semmering, 6952.
Vignau (A du) Ueber die Artillerie-Wesen, 6457.
Vigneron (H.). Précis critique de la guerre d'orient, 6721.
Virlet. Tables de Coustruction des bouches à feu, 6458.
—— Instruction Sommaire sur le Projet de bouche à feu, 6459.
Vogt (C.). Lehrbuch der Geologie und Petrefactenkunde, 7333.
Voice to America, 7821.
Vose (G. L.). Hand Book of Railroad Construction, 6953.
Vues, Tunnels, Viaducts, etc. du Semmering, 6954.

Wailes (B L. C.). On Agriculture and Geology of Mississippi, 7293.
Walker (J). Pronouncing Dictionary of the English Language, 7947.
Walpole (Horace). Letters, 8042, 8043.
Walton (W.). Mechanical Problems, 7099.
War Office Regulations, 6703.
War in the East On the Conduct of the, 6722.
War in the East and North. Views, etc., 6723, 6724.
Ward (J. H.). Manual of Naval Tactics, 6519.
Warren (Gen). Inauguration of the Statue of, 7822.
Washington (G). Life of, 7663.
—— Early Life of, 7664.
—— Farewell Address, 7823.
—— Correspondence of the Revolution, 8044.
—— Maxims, 8045.
Washington Astronomical Observations, 7155.
Wasserthal (K). Pionier-Dienst im Felde, 6338.
Watt (J). Mechanical Inventions, 6895.
Weber (Dr. G.) Outlines of Universal History, 7486.
Weiss (F.). Lehrbuch der Baukunst, 6861.
Wellington's Wisdom; or Maxims, 6520.
Wells (E.). Young Gentlemen's Astronomy, 7146.
Wentworth (Thomas, Earl of Strafforde). 8046.
Whitney (J. D). Metallic Wealth of the United States, 7303.
Whole Duty of Man. 7717.
Whowell (T.). Analogy of the Old and New Testaments, 8011.
Wilkes (Charles). Exploring Expedition, 7477.
William of Malmesbury's Chronicle, 7543.
William the Conqueror. History of, 7665.
William III. Life and Reign of, 7542.
Williams (H.). Address, 7824.
Williams (Rev. S. F.) Mechanics and Hydrostatics, 7100.
Willis (N. P). Hurry-Graphs, 8047.
—— Life Here and There, 8048.
—— Summer Cruise in the Mediterranean, 8049.
—— Famous Persons and Places, 8050.
—— Pencillings by the Way, 8051.

Willis (N. P.). Health Trip to the Tropics, 8052.
—— Rural Letters, 8053.
—— Out-Doors at Idlewild, 8054.
—— People I Have Met, 8055.
—— Fun-Jottings, 8056.
Willmott. Pleasures of Literature, 7673.
Wilson (Commissary). Orderly Book, 6739.
Wilson (E.). On Diseases of the Skin, 7353.
Wilson (H. H.). History of British India, 7556.
Wilson (J.). Treatise on Punctuation, 7800.
Winthrop (J.). History of New England, 7591.
Wittich. Zur Taktik, 6521.
—— Militairisches Vade Mecum, 6522.
—— Rathgeber beim Ausmarsch, 6523.
Witzleben (A. Von). Heerwesen und Infanteriedienst, 6597, 6662.
Woehler (F.). Analytical Chemist's Assistant, 7232.
Wolff (R. J.). Narrative of a Mission to Bokhara, 7478.
Wollaston (W.). Religion of Nature, 8012.
Wood (J. G.). Natural History, 7287.
Woodley (W.). Divine System of the Universe, 7147.
Woodward (S. P.). Manual of the Mollusca, 7288.
Woolwich. Royal Military Academy at, 7860.
Worcester (J. E.). Dictionary of the English Language, 7948.
Worth (Gen. W. J.). Monument to the Memory of, 7825.
Wurmb (J. Von). Lehrbuch der Kriegs-Baukunst, 6389.

Xénophon. La Cyropédie et Retraite des Dix Milles 7504, 7505.
Xerxes the Great. History of, 7666.

Yoakum (H.). History of Texas, 7592.
Young (T.). Hieroglyphical Literature, 7506.
Younghusband. Hand Book for Field Service, 6524.

Zaccone (J.). Résumé de Fortification, 6340.
Zastrow (A. de). Histoire de la Fortification Permanente, 6341.
Zornlin (R. M.). Physical Geography, 7391.

www.ingramcontent.com/pod-product-compliance
Lightning Source LLC
LaVergne TN
LVHW021402110826
845150LV00007B/1755
* 9 7 8 1 4 2 5 5 1 2 5 3 8 *

PRICE, 25 CENTS.

GLANMORE;

OR, THE

BANDITS OF SARATOGA

A ROMANCE OF THE REVOLUTION.

BY PARK CLINTON.

CINCINNATI:
PUBLISHED BY U. P. JAMES,
NO. 167 WALNUT STREET

Abednego, the Money-Lender: a Romance; by Mrs. Gore. 8vo, paper cover. **Price 25 cents.**

"Antonio and old Shylock, both stand forth." —*Shakspeare.*

Adventures of Caleb Williams; or, Things as They Are. By William Godwin. 8vo, paper cover. **Price 50 cents.**

"It is a book which takes rank among the classics of English literature. It is one of the most vigorous, masterly, and philosophic fictions in the language, or in any other."—*Daily Globe.*

"For fifty years it has been considered an extraordinary work, and amid all the changes of taste and circumstances which have been in the literary world since its publication, has kept a position as a classic."

"If the power of William Godwin can be relished now, there is still some hope of a manly literature."—*Cincinnati Daily Gazette.*

"The story is intensely interesting, and the characters admirably delineated; * * * its execution bears the mark of the highest order of intellect."—*Logan Gazette.*

Alonzo and Melissa; or, The Unfeeling Father. An American tale. By Daniel Jackson, Jr. 8vo. **Price 25 cents.**

Adventures of Mr. and Mrs. Sandboys. By Henry Mayhew. 8vo, paper cover. **Price 50 cents.**

Blue Laws of Connecticut. The Code of 1650. Being a Compilation of the Earliest Laws and Orders of the General Court of Connecticut. Also, The Constitution, or Civil Compact entered into and adopted by the towns of Windsor, Hartford, and Wethersfield, in 1638-9. To which are added some extracts from the Laws and Judicial Proceedings of New Haven Colony, commonly called Blue Laws. Paper cover. **Price 50 cents.**

A curious record of the early days of our country.

Caudle, Mrs., Curtain Lectures, by Punch, (Douglas Jerrold.) Paper cover. **Price 25 cents.**

"Rich Humor and Fun in this book."

Christopher Tadpole, The Struggles and Adventures of, by Albert Smith. 8vo, paper cover. **Price 75 cents.**

Charlotte Temple, a tale of Truth, by Mrs. Rowson. Paper cover. **Price 20 cents.**

More copies of this highly interesting and celebrated work have probably been printed, and worn out in reading, than any other book of the class in the English language, and the demand and interest continue unabated.

Clay, Henry, his Principal Speeches, and Sketch of his life. Compiled from the latest and best authorities. 8vo, paper cover. **Price 25 cents.**

Count Monte Leone; or, The Spy in Society: a legend of the Carbonari of France and Italy; translated from the French of H. de St. Georges. 8vo, paper cover. **Price 50 cents.**

Collegians, The, a novel, by Gerald Griffin, Esq., the author of "Tales of the Five Senses," etc. 8vo, paper cover. **Price 50 cents.**

"We regard it quite an era in a reading life to peruse *The Collegians.*"—*Wm. Howitt.*

Doniphan's Expedition, containing an account of the Conquest of New Mexico; Gen. Kearney's Overland Expedition to California; Doniphan's Campaign against the Navajos; his Unparalleled March upon Chihuahua and Durango; and the operations of General Price at Santa Fe; with a sketch of the life of Colonel Doniphan; by John T. Hughes, of the 1st Regiment of Missouri Cavalry. Illustrated with plans of battle-fields and fine engravings. 8vo, paper cover. **Price 50 cents.**

Ellena, a Romance, by Mrs. Radcliffe, author of "Romance of the Forest," "Mysteries of Udolpho," etc. Octavo, paper cover. **Price 50 cents.**

This is a thrilling work by a well-known and talented authoress.

Empress of the Isles; or, The Lake Bravo: a Romance of the Canadian Struggle in 1837. By Charley Clemline. 8vo, paper cover. **Price 25 cents.**

Eveline Mandeville, by Alvin Addison, author of "The Rival Hunters." 8vo, paper cover. **Price 25 cents.**

Grace Willoughby, a Tale of the Wars of King James. By W. H. Maxwell, Esq., author of "Brian O'Linn," etc., etc. 8vo, paper cover. **Price 50 cents.**

Glanmore; or, The Bandits of Saratoga: a Romance of the Revolution. By Park Clinton. 8vo, paper cover. **Price 25 cents.**

Heroic Women of France, comprising examples of the Noble Conduct of Women during the French Revolution. From the French of M. Du Broca. Paper cover. **Price 25 cents.**

Ike McCandliss, and other Stories; or, Incidents in the Life of a Soldier. Illustrated. By George C. Furber, author of "Twelve Months' Volunteer." 8vo, paper cover. **Price 25 cents.**

A truly entertaining and mirth-provoking book.

Jeremiah Saddlebag's Journey to the Gold Diggings. Illustrated with **113** engravings. 8vo, paper cover. **Price 25 cents.**

James Wellard, companion of John A. Murel. Illustrated. 8vo, paper cover. **Price 25 cents.**